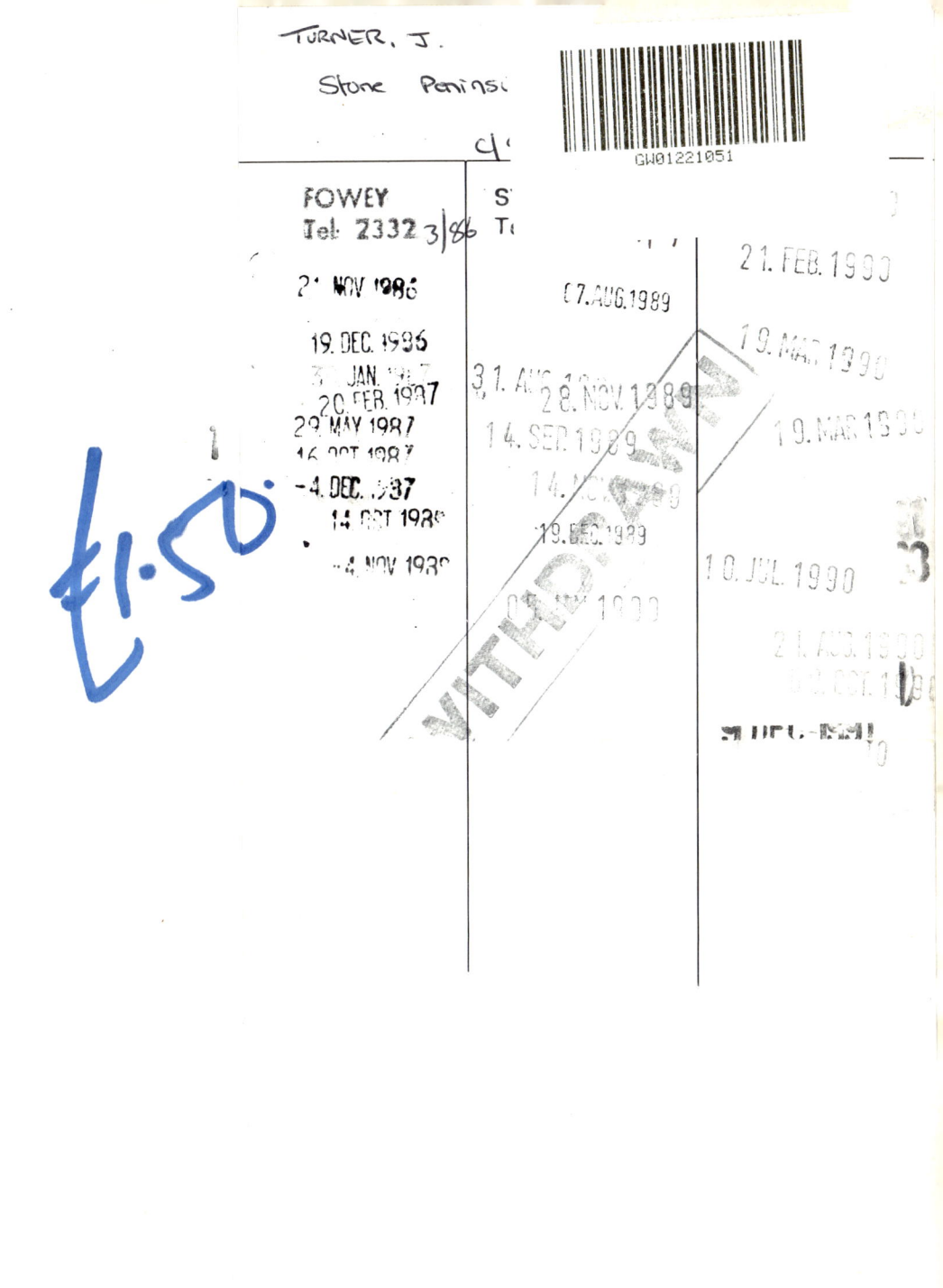

TURNER, J.
Stone Peninsu

FOWEY
Tel 2332 3/86

£1.50

21 NOV 1986
19. DEC. 1986
3 JAN. 1987
20. FEB. 1987
29 MAY 1987
16 OCT 1987
-4. DEC. 1987
14 OCT 1988
-4 NOV 1988

07. AUG. 1989
31. AUG. 1989
28. NOV. 1989
14. SEP. 1989
14. NOV. 1989
19. DEC. 1989

WITHDRAWN

21. FEB. 1990
19. MAR. 1990
19. MAR. 1990
10. JUL. 1990
21. AUG. 1990

THE STONE PENINSULA

By the same author:

Novels
Staircase to the Sea
Murder at Landred Hall
A Death by the Sea
The Strange Little Snakes
The Frontiers of Death
The Crystal Wave
The Dark Index
The Glass Interval
The Deeper Malady
Condell
The Nettle Shade
The Blue Mirror
The Slate Landscape
The Crimson Moth
The Long Avenues
Anna Chevron
Requiem for Two Sisters
The Stone Landscape

History
The Dolphin's Skin
The Shrouds of Glory

Poetry
Pastoral
The Alien Wood
The Hollow Vale
The Interior Diagram
The Accident and other Poems

General
Rivers of East Anglia
Love Letters: An Anthology
Stella C
Ghosts of the South West

Autobiography
Seven Gardens for Catherine
Sometimes into England

The Stone Peninsula

Scenes from the Cornish Landscape

JAMES TURNER

WILLIAM KIMBER · LONDON

First published in 1975 by
WILLIAM KIMBER & CO. LIMITED
Godolphin House, 22a Queen Anne's Gate,
London, SW1 9AE

© James Turner, 1975
ISBN 07183 0413 6

This book is copyright. No part of it may be reproduced in any form without permission in writing from the publishers except by a reviewer wishing to quote brief passages in connection with a review written for inclusion in a newspaper magazine or radio broadcast.

*Typeset by
Specialised Offset Services Ltd., Liverpool
and printed in Great Britain by
The Pitman Press, Bath*

Contents

		page
	Acknowledgements	6
1	The White Pyramids	9
2	The Cathedrals	19
3	The Stone Peninsula	31
4	Burial Grounds and Ghosts	43
5	Pools and Inventors	58
6	A 30	75
7	Bodmin Moor	89
8	Temples	103
9	A Taste for Ruins	111
10	Deserted Railways	121
11	Land of the Virgins	136
12	Slate	152
13	Some Clergy	164
14	Baron Munchausen and the Great Dolcoath Mine	175
15	Night walkers	188
	Epilogue	204
	Index	206

Acknowledgements

The Author's thanks are due to the following;

To the Rev. Gerald L. Matthews for permission to quote from his booklet, 'The Church of St Michael, Brentor.'

To Messrs Weidenfeld & Nicolson Ltd, for permission to quote from Sir Sacheverell Sitwell's book, 'Monks, Nuns and Monasteries'.

To Miss Evelyn Hardy, Robert Gittings and the O.U.P. for permission to quote from their edition of *Some Recollections* by Emma Hardy.

To Messrs Jonathan Cape Ltd, and Mr F.R. Fletcher, for permission to quote from 'Kilvert's Diary' edited by William Plomer.

To the Editor of the Country Gentleman's Magazine, for permission to use parts of essays which have appeared in his magazine.

To the Editor of 'My Cornwall' for permission to use parts of an essay on Bodmin Moor which first appeared in that book.

To Mr William Parsons, of St Teath, Cornwall, for his help with the history of that village.

To the Editor of 'The Cornish Review', for permission to quote from Frank Baker's essay on Father Wason.

To Ray Bishop, Richard Hawken, Wolf Schroeder, Charles Woolf, Delaviews Ltd, for their photographs.

List of Illustrations

	Facing page
The Chapel of St. Clether beside the River Inny	32
Truro Cathedral	33
The Wreck of the *Hemsley II*, off the North Cornwall coast	64
The Weir over the River Camel, at Dunmere	65
Rocks at Penally Point, Boscastle	96
The Water Wheel and Pool at Hingham Mill, near Wadebridge	97
Caradon old railway track and Sharptor	128
Golytha Falls, Draynes Common	128
The Cheesewring	129
Roche Rock, showing the ruins of the old Chapel	160
The Hurlers	161
Mazes in Rocky Valley, cut in the rock face by neolithic man	161
The Slate Quarries at Delabole	176
A Slate Splitter at Delabole	177

1. The White Pyramids

The sun was bursting off the tops of the white pyramids of china clay waste near St Austell. The sky was full of light over this unique and beautiful moonscape. The light was held over the land like a mirror, recently polished, taking the reflection of a sea which stretched away three thousand miles to America. In the wind the whole range of white hills shivered with this light, silver, blue and gold, magenta when a cloud passed over the sea. The wind never let up. It blew continuously, rattling the line of ancient fir trees, like a camel train bent and aged, leading into the heart of the china clay mines this side of Goss Moor.

This wind had a personality of its own, seeming to rise up from the nearby shores below the great cliffs at Bedruthan and come bowling over the common land intent on harassing everything. At evening it would suddenly retreat from the wings of gulls and cormorant as if sucked back into the caves from which it had originally issued. It had no solemnity this wind; it was young and frivolous. The only things which stood against it were the timeless rocks of the coast and the granite farms and cottages of the interior.

Between the branches of the winter trees could be seen the tall silver tail of a plane on St Mawgan airfield. A moment ago it had come in from the sea and landed. The sunlight spiralled up from the plane and winked off the distant clay hills. It fired the whole range and was gone. High airfield light-towers split the wind, causing it to funnel down narrow lanes and into dessicated farm houses in the hamlet of Colan. It ruffled the waters of the reservoirs in the fields above the hamlet and raced on until it banged its head against the white mountains and was destroyed.

From White Moor these pyramids are planted heavily on the earth, stalagmites of the vast open air cave of the peninsula. As you approach and go into them along the clay roads their full beauty emerges in the older hills and the deep pools below the earth's surface. Here the mining is going on, the clay washed from the mine face by powerful hoses. So much of this mining relies on water.

Very few people, other than workers, enter this curious landscape and become absorbed in it. Yet, from the heart of this white land, the most extraordinary prospects appear which are frightening in their originality, shriven in purity, immoveably colourless, languid with a special kind of lustre.

Deep down from the road through the hills is the blue water lapping the edge of the white cliffs of waste quartz sand. They rise up like sheer mountains, these icons of clay. Their effect is magical for this is a faery land of no promise; this man-made beauty is yet mysterious. The older cliffs are covered in vegetation and surmounted by ruined tin mining buildings, many of them like castles, which were submerged when William Cookworthy, in 1745, first dug his spade into the land and discovered the minerals which went to make English porcelain. The presence here of the older mining buildings takes you back into old Cornish history. The tall chimneys and decaying, ivy-covered, buildings are perched on the edges of the white cliffs above the water, like castles of Chillon, ready to fall into it, etched by the white pyramids beyond. Unique in their beauty by virtue of the water below.

The white clay road winds into a landscape of other valleys and seams of vegetation. What grows on these hills cannot be called woods for it clings very low to the surface, undernourished, and is no more than a carpet of bramble and thorn which glows in autumn with the red of its dying leaves. The blackberries and sloes are white with clay dust, the air is filled with it. In the distance Cornwall is spread out, a plain of small fields, to the woodlands in the middle distance, to the many tiny streams flowing into the great rivers of the Camel and Fowey, to deserted farmsteads beyond hedges of stone and slate and, at last, to the range of hills to the north on Bodmin Moor. This corner of Cornwall lies beneath a white shroud of dust. You enter it like men going to the moon.

Yet without the clay mines this superb beauty could never have been, and those who complain about the waste dumps as unsightly can never have been into them and discovered the unbelievable majesty and purity of some of these landscapes. These diamond-shaped hills dominate Cornwall, clustered in their powder desert about St Austell and on Bodmin Moor.

The waste which does not go into making these 'mountains' runs off into streams, turning the water white like cream. Along the neglected Luxulyan valley, near St Blazey, the stream comes down over white waterfalls of massive granite boulders below the granite viaduct which Joseph Treffry built in 1839 for a mineral railway, over one hundred feet above the road. Who now knows this deserted gorge which leads to the small swamps on the marsh south of the village where bog-cotton flourishes and an occasional sea-bird is seen? The valleys and villages below Luxulyan, at the feet of the china clay hills, are full of white dust, the cottages of St Stephen, Bugle, Roche, St Dennis and Nanpean blown through with it. Yet the beauty of these hills remain, savage, overpowering and sometimes monstrous.

They have vast properties of light, growing and changing. The new spoil heaps increase every time a trolley travels upwards and deposits its load of waste. The old pyramids, hanging with bushes of thorny sloe, already half white themselves in the dust-laden air, are going back into ancient landscape. They are the shovelfuls of early Victorian industry and have succumbed to the potent prayers of the non-conformists whose chapels are thick on the ground.

The deep pools in which the clay is purified, are black and blue, bruises in the white skin of clay, mirroring the tall cliffs whose gleaming summits are, at times, reaching out to the clouds and fit into each other, water and mountain, subtle natural jig-saw puzzles. The sea, so near and of an intense blue, spits colour into the clouds, too. The colour falls, a gentle cloak down the sides of the white hills, a vast blue shadow spreading from tip to tip, hairnets of spider's webs.

Such places, for all their beauty, are desolate. Only the light saves you in this valley of dry bones where men have died in white shrouds and in nature. No bird will lift your heart. There is no song but the endless churning of the winding gear from the mine bottom to the tip-head. Your flesh is torn from your hands and face, the back of your throat is powder-dry, your eyes peeling to observe the clay wilderness. Until sunset comes and softens the glare, crimsoning the hills like the tips of red pencils and, finally, to deep red, blood falling down the slopes of the last light. You should go barefoot, your toes in the wet clay, into this unspoken idiom of clay and the doomed fields which men once ploughed and reaped.

The buzzard hovers over the gorse of Goss Moor, turning its eyes from the white holes of the clay pits and is suddenly gone away towards the headlands below St Austell. I have been into one of these old clay pits at dusk and along the powdery roads and felt the utter whiteness of them like a song or a poem by Blake. A black man would be a ghost here.

They have this curious effect of belittling you and exalting you at the same time, as if being here you no longer had anything to do with that other world outside, the world of the buzzard, of spring just now breaking out in the hawthorn hedges with wild garlic beneath, the world of great seas on the nearby shores. In the last of the sun, falling on these high white hills, it is almost as if an angel was present.

One of the reasons for this complete desolation of mind and body is that within this fortress world of hills all noise is cut off. You are in a whirlpool of quiet, at least in the older pits. Yet, when you turn a corner of the road and look up, a light is gleaming from the pits further off where men are still working. A trolley runs up its deposit hill, in the night, to let fall its load. It is still for a second and then comes tearing down the slope again.

This landscape is the exact opposite of that of Samuel Palmer's Kent into which I was born and spent my early years, where the trees are smudged only by summer's dust, the moon harvested the corn with its yellow sickle and rolled up and down the valleys in and out of the sheep's heavy fleeces. At that time the rescue lay in nightingales and larks and abundant grass.

I came down the main Maidstone road with my brother Philip,

on our bicycles, into the villages of Farningham, Eynsford and Shoreham where Palmer had come, also, in the early 1800's. Here he saw and painted those chunky skies and cloudscapes which still hold over Kent, over the harvest fields and above the river Darenth. Here we would picnic and bathe in the stream amongst the water meadows when the trees were in full leaf, or hang over the bridge at Eynsford, or gaze at the horse-shoe shaped curtain wall of the ruined castle.

The village had seen its great days under Henry II. Indeed, the question as to who owned the church was the reason for Henry's last dispute with Becket. The Archbishop fell out with William de Eynsford over the patronage of the church and the King took the part of the layman. But it did no good for William. Once Becket had been murdered feeling ran high against his enemies. De Eynsford was excommunicated and left the village and his castle for ever. It fell into ruin.

Such a gentle landscape as the valleys under the North Downs was unlikely to prepare me for the desolation of the clay mines. It needed a complete reversal of one's soul to contemplate this new beauty of barrenness where there are no trees. I was not born to Cornwall and to such naked beauty as the clay hills. I came into it to live at a time in life when visions of the past are mixed up in everything you do. At a time when a man will put flesh on the tiny skeletons of the past who, in my case, were still standing in suburban houses outside London where I was born, and try to solve the enigma of their beginnings and endings. And still, in love and Time, to go on creating my own personality.

And although I could see and feel the beauty of the clay mines and, indeed, stood in awe at some of the landscapes revealed here, I could not stay for long. Not all beauty is comfortable. I turned off, with relief, down a steep lane to the Holy Well at Menacuddle. I went to escape the visions in clay and the desolate wonders. Here, in the groups of twisted trees, past granite blocks cut into seats and over the bridge which spans the white waterfall, stands the Holy Well. Still the river was running white like cream, throwing slabs of light into the darkness of the leaves.

This spot had been hallowed in the middle ages. A chapel stood here once beside the Well in its wooded gorge. Horsemen and wagons had cut the dry dust of the roads above. Now lorries roar away along the metalled surface, in and out of St Austell, and the poetry has gone. The Well itself remains. Built in the late fifteenth century, with two arched entrances opposite one another, it has a small window in the west wall. The Well itself is one of the most beautiful in Cornwall.

Weakly children used to be dipped here to give them strength and to cure their rickets. This disease was so prevalent in the middle ages that one imagines that half the population were cripples. Lovers, in dusklight and again at dawn, sought for the faces of their lovers and, in their sickness saw, perhaps, what they took to be the Devil. This was an age of superstition in which an owl hooting out of hours was enough to predict the end of the world. The east wall, dead in the natural rock, is of granite too. From beneath, springs up that well of holy water where cripples came to be healed and where men with fifteenth century faces worshipped God and thought of Heaven in the skies above the moors.

God is gone. There is now only the tourist, the orange peel, the ice-cream carton, the indestructible plastic container — unless you come here in winter or early spring when the cigarette ends have been eaten away by frost. Yet still God is gone. He is no longer in the soft places easily reached or, in autumn, in the carpet of beach leaves on the road to this Well. Nor is He in the rat runs from the mill close-by, or hanging in the holly trees and the purple deadnettle or the white wild garlic, as He was to fifteenth century men with their superstitions of warts and birthmarks and the runes of disease.

No one now thirsts for God at Menacuddle. For all that a personality could be born here beside the white river, the riven rock, the coloured leaf carpet which have seen centuries of pauperism and pomp. For, away from the flashing light of the clay hills hanging over the road, diamonds of landscape, impossible artifacts of an uncreated creation from the bowels of the earth, one is released backwards. The air here, by the Well, is still full of poetry and necromancy and potent with the witchcraft of forgotten hamlets.

Colan lies too deep in its shelter of elm trees to be much affected by the wind off the sea, too deep to be blown through by the clay dust, too deepdown for the clay hills to be anything but the wings of some monstrous white bird, a signature in the sky about it. If the white hills were to fall they would not engulf Colan. For Colan is a hamlet never torn out of its medieval quiet, supported by the spells of witches, existing in a cauldron of demons and monsters and faces behind tiny, curtained windows.

Its few farmhouses are a hundred years behind the times, with middens before the back doors on which the chicken scratch. Here is a mill-house dropping into ruin, the ancient wheel clinging to a side wall, static, covered in green fern. Colan is an anachronism, a bird-nesting hollow, swallows and night-jars, lying between the springboard of the airfield, within walking distance of Newquay with its brash holiday carnival crowds.

One expects, round every corner, a beggar covered in sores, a friar with his pockets stuffed with Indulgences, a knight exiled from the Court. Colan absorbs such things along with the countryside in which it lies forgotten. It holds secrets no one can now understand, its cottages are hieroglyphs as difficult to interpret as Ogham script. Lepers could have lived here. You seem still to hear the melancholy of their warning bells, above the voices of thrushes and blackbirds.

Forgotten, too, the ruined house, Fir Hill, in the Colan Woods which must once have seen the last of Edwardian gaiety, the young girls and men gone forever. This was the family mansion of the Figg-Hoblyns who owned the whole of the Colan estate. Now, its falling roof and walls are surrounded by banks of sodden leaves, the compost of time. In the garden blue-grey slates, beneath ages of leaf-mould, lead to the house. The French windows, all glass gone, the wooden frames black and brown with rot, bruised with decay, are a gap into the drawing room and the bedrooms above.

When I first saw it the house still had a roof. Now, so much of it has gone that the sky is clear right through. Drowned Calvaries of sad cloud float above it. Creepers vibrate to the noise of planes on the airfield, warming up or passing overhead. A robin is perched on an unbreakable mass of brambles. Its thin, sorrowful song is a commentary on the ruined scene.

Yet the story of the house only goes back to Victorian times. Fir Hill is no ancient monument, however ruined. The present confusion as to who owns the estate is due to a family settlement drawn up by the original owner, William Paget Hoblyn. The estate, on his death, was to go to his son William. But he died childless. The heiresses, after William, were his four daughters and any children they might have. Three of them, Wilhelmina, Frances and Zoe, lived and died in the decaying house.

Rosalind, however, fell in love. It was unfortunate, in those days, that her lover was the family coachman. They were sent away to Canada. By 1889 she had a family, though exactly how many is not known, though reports speak of 'infant children'. She herself was killed in an earthquake in the States. Until her children are 'revealed' by law, the confusion will exist.

Now nature is taking over. Great saplings of sycamore and ash are bursting the walls of the ruined house; rooks have torn mortar from the eaves letting in rain and the falling sickness in those parts which are still standing. The house is too melancholy, too left, too overgrown. It is dissolving into firewood. The young of Newquay come and, in their frustration at decay, inflict new wounds upon the corpse. In breaking glass and pulling down stones they proclaim themselves the masters.

Great swags of ivy branches are clinging menacingly to the tops of once tall roofs. The thick stone walls of the original are ugly and cloven with a menace of their own. They are the prison walls, a tomb in themselves being, as they were, but an inner shell of the house to which facings in brick were added. Their antiquity — these stones quarried from the moors — was clothed then in modern building materials which may have hidden the power of their frontal attack. Now, in their derelict state, they are once again naked and powerful. All stones are alive and, in this falling back of the house into Nature, they are exposed, reaching out their power to the giant hemlock rioting in the garden, enclosing, frightening, suffocating.

Did these stones come from the vast quarries on West Down, near Lanivet, which were famous but are now as deserted as Colan and Fir Hill? Would the wagons not have come here at the turn of the century and trundled away down the long lanes with the everlasting granite? Who now would come into these wide-open graves of brown stone, colossal gaps in nature beyond the hamlet of Lamorick, given over entirely to ravens and wild flowers? Water lies below the bare, riven sides of the quarries, deep silent pools. The roots of ivy are twice the size of a quarry man's arms. The enormous mouth of these quarries are black and forbidding. Those whose sweat gouged them out and ran the stone in tubs along the overgrown rails still to be found, here and there, are long dead. You imagine the noise of hammers and bettles within the dark shadow of these walls as tall as a cathedral, but it is only the ravens croaking. It is now no more than the home of foxes which, in the safety of these stone tunnels, bring their prey back to devour it before their holes.

In the depths of the fields, not far from Colan church which all the Hoblyns must have attended in Victorian and Edwardian times, coming down the long drive from the house in their carriage, is another relic of the past rarely visited today. Here, at Lady Nance, approached down a farm track, is this little Wishing Well.

It is deep in grass, gently bubbling and running with silver water and not more than two feet deep. It has no particular dedication but it is one of those secret 'sacred' places which were lit, for people of former ages, with a peculiar light and veneration. It is the place of Pan. They came for love-tokens. And down this lane they came to the well to bathe their sore eyes and offer tiny gifts or 'sacrifices' such as bent pins, in the hope of having their future revealed to them. Sore eyes were, of couse, a constant source of suffering in those days, probably due to living in low cottages from which the smoke of the fire could not escape properly.

Who actually declared this water to be 'holy' is not known though it was, at one time, used exclusively in Colan church for baptisms. Perhaps this is why, even today, there is a law that no cattle be allowed to drink from the well. Yet it must be used by countless numbers of small wild creatures from foxes to field mice.

As I pull the weeds aside, dip in my hand and draw the cool water to my eyes, the wing tip of a huge plane is reflected in the tiny silver mirror. It has just got up from St Mawgan airfield and is so low that even the long grasses tremble at its passing.

2. The Cathedrals

The approach to Truro from the south is from Pendennis Castle which, for all its greatest days when in the Civil War it withstood, under the command of Sir John Arundell, a Roundhead charge, is remembered these days for the colony of cats which thrived here in the thorn thickets. The ancestors of these fierce creatures arrived during the last war, being deserted by their owners, and were looked after by soldiers. Their numbers increased at an alarming rate. The whole headland became their domain. They roamed wild into the gardens of Falmouth at night and returned at dawn to sleep off the excesses of the hotels' dustbins. Yet, at feeding time — since any number of people after the war brought them scraps and regarded them as the town's mascots — they came out again to the bowls and papers of fishbones put down for them. But there was no approaching the animals which were regularly culled by the authorities.

I have lain in these thickets and watched. The whole colony seemed to be ruled by a large ginger and white tom which had only one eye. Whether he was 'king' or not, none of the others touched the food put down until he had eaten. His ears battered, his face scored from countless fights, he would lie curled up all day in the deepest hollow of these thorn thickets, emerging only for food and for night-prowling. The sound of fighting could be heard in the hotels along the front. Now they have all gone, the only colony of 'wild' domestic cats in England.

Across from Pendennis Castle, on the Penryn river, is Flushing and the walk to Mylor and, so across Mylor Creek, to Great Wood in the centre of this sub-tropical landscape which is in such sharp contrast to other parts of Cornwall, over the ridge-back of the A30. The walk from the house Great Wood to the Pandora inn is one of the most beautiful of all those in south Cornwall. This is the rich land of small boats and large houses; of expensive hotels and the deep woods of Roseland on the other side of King Harry's Reach. Yet few come up this narrow lane to the inn with the river below which, in spring is a paradise of wild flowers and tall gunnera raising their huge umbrella-like leaves across the path. Escallonia flourishes here. The cottages beside the path are alight with early flowers, the blue of the estuary forming a frame to their own blue slate roofs.

Beyond the Pandora inn, said once to have been a Priory, is a pittosporum farm. When I first came to Cornwall I was told that if you had an acre of this curious tree you need never go hungry because it always commanded a good price. Perhaps it still does, this evergreen, in the London markets at Christmas. Or when it sets off, in spring, the mimosa of these wet, warm lands.

This is, indeed, the green, lush land near water, where the trees come down to King Harry's Ferry, lining the Tresillian river running east of Truro. A warm land about the crushed stone heaps of the moors round Stithians which is hard and dry and full of ruined mine stacks. A green belt running into Truro with the cathedral as yet hidden in its hollow.

Along the rhododendron lanes into Perranarworthal I have sat and watched a fox cross from one thicket to another without being disturbed, and picked handfuls of early purple orchis. Bluebells were here almost an embarrassment, the pubs about Mylor and Penryn full of bowls of them. These long ponticum-hedged roads are, in winter's dusk, like the aisles of cathedrals; in summer they hum to the masses of insects, flies and mosquitoes, in the avenues of trees and bracken, no more than a stone's throw from the main road from Truro to Helston. Much of the farmland through which they run has now been sold off for very sophisticated houses, hidden behind the trees until you come, once more, to the main road and the beech woods of the landscaped gardens of Killiow at St Kea. And so down the hill, Lemon Street, with the statue of Richard Lander high over the cathedral towers below.

Richard Lemon Lander and his brother John are early romantic figures, the kind one finds in any Jules Verne story. They were unneurotic, sure of their place in the world, Victorians. Their exploits are commonplace today when explorers rush to all points of the earth with the most complicated and sophisticated equipment. But when the Lander brothers discovered the source of the river Niger they had nothing more to guide them but a common compass. Like the great Cornish inventors they were men of extreme courage and imagination, sons of a Truro innkeeper.

Richard, when he was only eleven, went to the West Indies as servant to a trader. He was away for three years and then joined Hugh Clapperton's second expedition to West Africa. Unknown Africa had as much fascination for the men of this age — Richard was born in 1804 and died in 1834 — as the moon has for us today. When on this expedition Clapperton died near Sokoto in April 1827, Lander went on to Kano and the Hausa states, and returned with Clapperton's journals which he published with his own journal of his adventures.

The Government then commissioned him and his brother to go back to Africa with the idea of planning the course of the lower Niger river, which was as much a mystery as the source of the Nile. They landed at Badagry on the Guinea coast on 22nd March, 1830, and set out into the 'unknown', in canoes. It is a classic Victorian expedition. They discovered the Benue river; were captured by the Ibos; ransomed by 'King Boy' of Brass Town and took passage to Fernando Po.

For all his success Richard could not keep away from Africa. He led his last expedition organised by Liverpool merchants. While upriver he was wounded in a native attack on 20th January, 1834, and died at Fernando Po on 6th February. His brother John died on 16th November, 1839. Now Richard stands immortalised by Burnard on his tall column overlooking Cornwall.

The Cathedral lays too heavy a weight on Truro. It is, in fact, a heavy piece of architecture with no subtlety at all. The blue roofs of the city below it do not rise up to it; they are crushed beneath it and the tolling of its great bells. It is a modern stranger in an antique land; it is not yet adopted by time and the thousand accidents of daily life. It is a symbol not a legend.

The new concrete Chapter House only increases this feeling of weight and oddity and helps to close in implacably the one really lovely piece of architecture in the Cathedral, what is left of the church of St Mary which was incorporated into the building as the Lady Chapel. One wonders what possessed the architect to leave this precious gem to confront the modernity of his new act of glory to God.

Indeed, it is this impression of weight which destroys entirely the intention of the architect, J.L. Pearson, to create a building which was to soar to heaven and lift the soul. The 'new Gothic' as it is called is unsuitable for Cornwall. The Cathedral gives the impression of being built from a box of bricks on a nursery floor and lowered complete into the heart of the town. In fact, it took much money and great devotion to complete.

The building, although it is in a hollow, dominates the City from any angle. Whichever way you come into it, it is the same. From the fields, up the long winding hill at Tresillian; up the hill from Falmouth to the edge of the saucer in which Truro lies; from the warm south of shipping and the Carrick Roads, or from the sands of Perranporth, this building compels your attention to such an extent that the rest of the City is ignored.

The building has an air of sadness about it as if it were a stranger who will never be accepted. People shuffle round it, through these stone caverns, and only a thousandth part of it is ever touched. For this is important, the touch of human hands is what brings warmth to stone, creates a building, makes for intimacy which, alas, the Cathedral lacks. The fact that its towers and spires can reflect the rising and setting sun in oblique beauty is not enough to give it warmth. It is a building without any warmth at all, the stones of which have never come alight as are the stones of certain country churches. It lacks a spiritual glow beneath the skin. Its sadness is not that of all great buildings, the wearing away of time and human use. It is the sadness of failure. You cannot pray here with any sense of intimacy, it is too new, too gauche. All you can do is to slip from its gigantic cold grasp into the Lady Chapel and wish that authority had left well alone.

This massive ecclesiastical shell encases you. You have the feeling that it was built to increase hierarchical magnificence and with no thought of the humble worshipper. Not even the couple being married under the high walls of granite and Bath stone can bring life to this building. I stood for a moment to watch the ceremony, to hear their vows, to hear the organ and, at last, the titan bells rocking God out of steeples and joy from the towers over and under the courts and corridors of the City beyond its confines. But still life did not come into these stones.

Yet there must have been hope and excitement the day that the scaffolding began to rise in the cleared space before the old church, in that last age of belief, before two great wars destroyed the meaning of an old God. The stones, then, in their wooden cradles, began to swing up over the horse traffic and one day, in 1880, Prince Edward came down from London with his silver trowel and, with regal pomp, laid the foundation stone. He did more, he laid two. Accompanied by his wife and their two young sons, Albert Victor and George, he moved from the nave to the north-east corner of the choir where he laid this second stone, as if by so doing the building would remain level against the fierce Cornish winds. With him went the Bishop of Exeter and, specially brought over by ship, the Bishop of Madagascar, Dr Kestell-Cornish, who was born at Kenwyn. A choir, gathered from various parts of Cornwall, chanted the psalms and hymns. The City was beflagged; it was a holiday. And suddenly something that was not, was. The old trees in front of St Mary's church were swept away along with the Assembly Rooms and this shell began to emerge. It has remained a shell ever since.

I walk swiftly into the south aisle of the fifteenth century church which is now the Lady Chapel. Here is religious sophistication of the highest order. My heart is released. I pass quickly from the swaying pile of the Cathedral, haunted by vergers, into the mysticism of the old church which is light and numinous and fragile with prayer, with centuries-old supplication and the open hands of God. Away from the Cathedral into an older Truro divorced for ever from the new ring roads, the hospitals and the factories.

Into that Truro seen in old engravings such as one taken from the village of Kenwyn which was old before Truro was new. In the distance the river Fal opens out between low hills. Where the Cathedral now splits the air, the spire of St Mary's now rises in the exact centre of the view in front of the viaduct. A line of oak and elm separates the town — for it was not a City then — from the churchyard at Kenwyn. Here, amongst the sparse graves, the flat altar tombstones, a man is working. It is high summer, leaves are languid on the trees, a green pall over bones. If you take a glass and look closer into the picture you can see that the man is digging a grave.

That was over a hundred years ago. Then, this grave-digger was alive in a Thomas Hardy western world. If I were to go to Kenwyn today, with this picture in my hands, I could identify the grave he is digging a century away. Thus time between him and myself is destroyed; it has ceased to exist. I, alone with him, and the person lately dead in the cottages of Kenwyn. I wonder, looking at the picture, what his name was.

And that is what I did. I went to Kenwyn with this picture and came upon one of the most romantic churchyards in Cornwall. Whereas, in the picture, the grave-digger is working in an almost empty field, as it were, today the whole area is full of tomb-stones, urns and shields, flat altar grave-stones and those odd tomb-stones shaped like coffins. These are the numerous dead of Kenwyn which join me to the grave-digger over time's one hundred years. It is a subtle, dumb, unlighted thread.

Two Council workmen were clearing away ages of rubbish from between the trees which had not even been planted when the old picture was drawn.

'It was like a jungle when I came into it,' the younger man said as we stood and talked in the cold February afternoon, glad of the fires of leaves and branches which he had lit over the sloping graveyard. The red painted clock on the fifteenth century church tower struck three. The fires spurted flicks of golden flame. Smoke was blowing over the new buildings of the Cathedral Choir School below. He went on to tell me that he had to cut his way through brambles 'as thick as me wrist' and seedling trees, even to begin to see the gravestones. 'Going to turn it into a kind of park,' he went on, 'the

Council is.' It seemed to me very fitting for this large ground, bisected by asphalt paths, high over Truro to the north.

Between the trees I could still see the viaduct and the river and away to the moors at Stithians. Yet here is all the elegance, in these memorials, which the Cathedral lacks, for all the Bishop of Truro has his palace in Kenwyn. It is not only that time has worked upon the stones but craftsmen. If there is, inevitably, a feeling of sadness and mortality here, there is also repose which, too, is lacking in the Cathedral.

Back in the great building for, at least in size, it is great, the wedding guests were leaving in their Moss-suiting and their garden-party hats, the brims holding the mauve light from the stone, the hanging candelabra, the sheen of glass. There goes the bride in her white and orange blossom, with the booming safety of the tall walls about her. The bells begin and the mighty wedding building sways to the joy of union. In flesh, in mind.

Truro must always have been an elegant town. It is described, about 1778, in *The Modern Universal British Traveller*,

> The town contains about 600 houses, many of which are exceedingly handsome; and the streets are clean and well-paved. It is a place of great trade, having a very extensive wharf, with the commodious quay capable of receiving goods from ships of 100 tons burden.

It was a Stannary town then. A parliament was held here by the Lord Warden of the Stannaries, at which laws were enacted for the government of the tinners. Indeed, in those days 'the principal trade of the town consists in the exportation of tin and copper ores. Of the latter there are several mines in the mountainous track between Truro and St Michael's which are wrought with considerable advantage.'

Truro was elegant when the soldiers and their horses were here in the Napoleonic wars, in the houses at the top of Lemon Street. It is still elegant from the downsweep of Lemon Street, below the Lander column, through what is left of the cobbled streets, to the by-ways about the Cathedral up and down which the wedding bells are booming now. From the lanes and the twittens which remind me of *The Tailor of Gloucester*; from the splendid front of the old City

Hospital, down Cathedral Lane and along the narrow streets to the Station.

Here the City is bounded by the railway viaduct and, then, suddenly, like all Cornish towns, is country. From the axis of the Cathedral all Cornwall stretches out, to the sea and the great rollers at Perranporth, to St Michael's Mount with its shell-strewn causeway, to the Dodman and danger. Again to the sea at St Agnes and Padstow, and away north to Boscastle and Bude. Echoes of St Ives and the Land's End ring off the last seastone cobbles left in Boscawen Street.

Archives of Cornwall, room after room, are stored in fine buildings beyond the flow of traffic and women hurrying home with fish caught that morning in Port Isaac Bay; old newspapers fill corners with their tales of murders one hundred years ago. Along the shelves of the Museum Benin bronzes look wide-eyed at you longing for the heat they were ripped from, and a stuffed chough is permanently gouging out the eyes of its prey behind a glass case. It no longer tastes the blood. In thin drawers row upon row of Cornish shells repose away both from their shelving beaches and the City dust. Cases of minerals glow in the sunbeams; the records of a thousand years suddenly come alive.

That evening the City was humming with traffic and lights were bearing up Lemon Street and before the Cathedral and what is left of the Assembly Rooms with its garage under. In the gentle curve of Walsingham Place the main tower of the Cathedral could be seen between chimney stacks. The stars were beginning to spin off the pinnacles in the frosty air.

Truro Cathedral now overshadows two other churches which were thought of as cathedrals in their time, though one, that at Altarnun, called the 'Cathedral of the Moor' is more a term of affection than anything else. St German's, however, was the Cathedral for Cornwall from Saxon times.

The Borough stands on the higher reaches of the estuary of the river Lynher, with the old quay south of it, just above Sheviok Wood. This cathedral church dominates the village and is impressive. Although in a hollow its two towers, both built on

Norman bases, the south of the thirteenth century, the north of the fifteenth, form a bastion against the beech woods of Port Eliot, with its fine 'prospect' laid out by the great gardener Humphrey Repton, in 1792.

Because St German's is between two main roads, and although the railway passes through it, it is almost impossible to think of it as Cornwall. It is so retired and peaceful, so caught in its own angle of the land, so by-passed. It is, nevertheless, a seagull land; they follow the plough in the fields, they perch on the cathedral and the beautiful almshouses lower down in the village, swinging in from Torpoint up the river past Erth Hill and the track of an old railway line which perhaps came down to float its stone across to the quay opposite, and up from the sea at Downderry beside the river Seaton. So that, in effect, one is on an island. All the year this vast building holds the music of the Bach Festival held here in early summer. The notes of Brandenberg concertos are woven into its purbeck stone.

We know all about the day Prince Edward came to Truro to lay the foundation stones of the present Cathedral, probably to what he was wearing, the lunch he ate, what he said after the lunch and the number of cigars he smoked. But there is nothing recorded of that day, in 430, when the great missionary, St Germanus, of Auxerre, came to Cornwall to found this church on this spur of land up the estuary of the Lynher, not even if the weather was fine. All we do know is that he created St German's the cathedral church of Cornwall, set beside a Priory on which the present house, Port Eliot is built. We have to wait until 936 before the first recorded mention of St German's. Then, on 5th December, Athelstan sailed up the river, having conquered Cornwall, and set up 'Conan as Bishop in the Church of St German's.' One other thing is known; the tide in those days swept much further inland, right past the church to the gates of the Priory beside it where, in 1358, a great day occurred.

Relics of St Germanus who had, of course, since that day in 430, gone from Cornwall back to Auxerre, suddenly arrived by boat at the Priory to be stored in the Cathedral. The monks were waiting to receive these relics as the gulls flew ahead of the boat hoping for ecclesiastical tit-bits. They formed a procession to place the casket in the fourteenth century chapel specially built for it beside the then great east window. They moved slowly up the nave with the splendid Norman doorway of the west behind them. St Germanus, or certain unnamed parts of his bones, had returned to his second home. A great sigh of relief went up, in oceans of incense, from the monks of the Priory, for there is nothing quite like having the bones of a Saint close at hand. It confirms the importance of a Priory and is as great a comfort on a Feast Day.

At The Dissolution, in 1539, the Crown claimed the choir (and naturally destroyed what was left of St Germanus's bones) which says Henderson, 'was converted to a base use.' What this means I'm not quite sure, but certainly this upheaval allowed the parishioners, without proper advice, to do a stupid thing. They moved the stupendous east window of the choir to the east end of the nave. The work was so hurriedly done, their cement not properly mixed, that, in 1592, it all fell down. The historian Carew writing about this fateful day says

> A great part of the chauncell, anno 1592, fell suddenly down upon a Friday, very shortly after publick service was ended, which heavenly favour of so little respite saved many people's lives, with whom immediately before it had been stuffed, and the devout charges of the well-disposed parishioners quickly repaired this ruine.

This is a small peninsula in great waters. From the towers of the church you can look out to Whitesand Bay which was dangerous in the days of the sailing ships, which were often trapped by south west winds as they made for Plymouth. It is a bay of four miles of sand below cliffs which rear up over two hundred feet, though these cliffs are even higher at Rame Head to the east where coastguards have their look-out beside a fourteenth century sailor's chapel.

These waters are, today, renowned for sharks. One wonders if they swam round into Cawsand Bay that day, after Waterloo, when Napoleon put in here on the *Bellerephon*, on his way into exile. It was a day as famous as that on which the Prince came to Truro, for hundreds of sightseers rowed from the villages of Cawsand and Kingsand to try and get a glimpse of 'the Ogre.' They went even further. News got about that Napoleon's friends were on the point of having a writ served on him which would have meant his return to London, instead of being exiled to St Helena. On hearing this, and before such a writ could be served, the villagers towed the ship out to sea. It was a notable victory!

From the towers, too, you can look over the remains of the stone quay. Today it is deserted, it lies before the acres of tidal mud below the railway viaduct which helped to destroy its trade, which must have been considerable. It dealt mostly in stone. You can look into the rocky reefs off the beach of coarse grey sand at Seaton, or that other beach of silvery sand in front of the holiday village of Downderry, or the former pilchard-fishing port of Portwinkle where the sand is grey. Or across the small river, north-east, to Saltash and the famous new road bridge.

Yet it is the cathedral which finally attracts you back. From the splendid dog-tooth Norman doorway, heavy with centuries of salt in the depth of the carving, to the monument by Rysbrack, of 1722, to Edward Eliot, in Roman dress, it is a place which has been touched by many hands. A perfume of magnificence and blessing rises from its interior.

Penpont Water flows past the 'Cathedral of the Moor' and joins the river Inny at a place called Two Bridges, some miles away. It is essentially a lost moorland stream and would hardly be remembered if it were not for Altarnun through which it runs. If you come to the village from Lesternick Hill on West Moor, over Trewint Downs, the tower of the church is a steadfastness beside the rushing traffic of the A30, only two miles away. Indeed, Altarnun takes a peace to itself from this enormous and impressive building standing above the stream and its two bridges, the one humped and ancient, the other modern and concrete.

It is, nevertheless, a comfortable building to come into from the roughness of the moors. Comfortable in more ways than one since the carved bench ends are so homely. One particularly which represents sheep grazing; they look more like hedgehogs. The church yard is full of slate tombs some, like that of the Isbells who were John Wesley's hosts at Trewint nearby, carved by Nevill Northey Burnard who was born in Altarnun, became famous and died in the poor house. Charles Causley wrote the best biography of this sculptor who learned his trade with no other tools than nails, in his poem which begins:

> Here lived Burnard who with his finger's bone
> Broke syllables of light from the moor stone.

It is the light from the moorland, reflected from the surface granite from which the pinnacled church tower is built, which is so noticeable here below the rook-filled elms of what was once the vicarage. You can take your shoes off and walk down the shallows of Penpont Water and come, past a lane leading to an even older earthwork, to Laneast, to the church of St Sativola and St Gulval, made of dark polyphant stone, which is a kind of countryman's version of the 'Cathedral' at Altarnun, and no one will disturb you all day.

3. The Stone Peninsula

Great seas roll round the stone peninsula. All summer and winter they are biting grotesque shapes from the rocks, wrecking ships, shoaling on the Doom Bar at Padstow, booming in the deep caverns of Trebarwith Strand. At other times these seas run smoothly into estuaries where fishermen take the tiny succulent dabs or fine bass, where swans nest under the shadow of fourteenth century bridges; they run safely over the sands in Church Cove near the Lizard, or over the supposed buried treasure at Gunwalloe.

The tide washes in and out, up the river Camel, about Bradford's Quay in Wadebridge, opposite the now deserted railway line. It washes across the sandy mouths of Hayle; and into Lamorna Cove and St Ives Bay. Strings of oyster-catchers weave between gulls and shags. The cormorant divides the circle of bays all round the stone peninsula. All have seen the great ships and swung down to observe the tangled wrecks. Crabs and lobsters have picked out drowned men's eyes and torn the flesh from their limbs.

Gently, too, at times, the tide washes in and out of small beaches like that of Greenway, or rolls into the summer beach at Polzeath under the headland of Pentire. The wide sands are dotted with children's sandcastles, built and sucked away and built again, in endless patience, between breakfast and supper. At six o'clock the sheep come down the valley to Shilla Mill as they did when I was a boy. In those days this coast was comparatively empty, waiting for the developers and tourists who have changed the character of the coast entirely. Nothing can change the great seas.

In winter these hard-to-get-at, long, sandy beaches are lonely and frightening. Such a beach is that at Tregardock; or the

Strangles. The farmsteads above the deep clefts downward to the beach have no relation to the fortress-like seas building up beneath them, rolling in ceaselessly, crashing into the rock of Cornwall, pounding the sand into even finer grains, roaring against an off-shore wind, a choir of nature.

These seas pound driftwood up the sand to the foot of the cliffs. They carpet the sand, at low tide, with razor shells and dog whelks, with Venus shells and common cockles. Here, in a tapestry of shells, are the fascinating *turritella communis*, the tower shells, the flat periwinkle and the limpet, mussel and great scallop shells. Their deep blues and subtle pinks, the interior opalescence of some shells and the intricacy of cowries, are patterns on the floor of the world.

All such beaches are subject to gales and coastal currents and so, at times, have no shells; at others millions. A great sea will shift vast quantities of sand and reveal shell ledges previously covered. Such gales, making massive seas, can remove a whole beach inland a few feet and cause the death of millions of sand-living molluscs. In the after-calm the thick shells of the tougher species will line the tide-line; the more delicate will be crushed to powder.

Only the gorse blooms in winter along the path to the cliff edge. The hedges are January-cold and bleak and the roar of the sea can be heard as far off as Bodmin Moor. A dog fox goes quickly into the spindle covert, over the fields already ploughed, on towards the farm and the ricks, making for Davidstow Moor and its home in the rocks under Kilmar Tor miles away. Or had he come from Tintagel where there are many foxes of whom, as Carew the historian says in his *Survey of Cornwall*;

> The fox planteth his dwelling in the steep cliffs of the seaside, where he possesseth holds, so many in number, so dangerous of access, and so full of windings, as in a manner it falleth out a matter impossible to disseize him of his ancient inheritance.

The deep gulleys to the low-tide beach are edged with sharp sloe bushes and dead honeysuckle. Yet, even in January, the primrose leaves sheltering in the mauve rock beside the shrouds of sea-holly and stonecrop, are alive. These bare rocks will be the gardens of spring with the lark rising overhead. Beyond now, and from this

The Chapel of St Clether beside the River Inny

(Ray Bishop)

Truro Cathedral

height, is the jut of Cambeak and Crackington Haven with its stone beach and its striated ledges like fingers into the sea, deep blue with mussels. In a half mist far out to sea, Lundy Island swings and sways its shadow into Hartland Quay.

Sculptured birds pose on the rocks, shags and cormorants, shivering in the cold wind. This is a foodless time of year when a flock of herring gull embroiders the low tide, spinning up and inland and out again to their fishing grounds. No one has been here on the sand. Only high on the cliff edge a girl on horseback stays to look down. The winter sun shines from her stirrups. The melancholy of all winter beaches creeps down the short afternoon into the spinning of the lighthouse at Trevose Head and the sea is a vast world of sadness, of wrecked ships, of oil slicks, of endless motion and the folding wave. All the way to America the sea is deserted, all the way is this vast water of fishes and the fear of night overlaid with carpets of brown seaweed coming in, perhaps, from the Sargasso Sea. Now even the horse-woman has gone back to the turnip fields and shelter.

This shore is littered with great stones which, in some odd way, are aware of my coming. The cliffs crumble and deposit loads of slate and soil above the tideline. To walk from one great stone to the next, on supple unspoiled sand, is to be in a world freshly created at every tide, a world which is never the same twice. Bells are ringing in the slit caves. Here is a sound of music as the everlasting rollers pour in, up and down their chromatic scale. A black-headed gull goes over, in the evening light, to its standing ground in the shallows of Trebarwith Strand. There, on the hot rock ledges of summer, my Mother is still sitting, though she is dead, waiting for me whenever I come. Time then and time now are forever one.

The long climb up to the landtop, through thorn hedges and gorse, begins to darken in its own shadow. The land is cropped with ferns from the sea spleenwort in the mouths of caves, dying in the first frosts, to the hart's tongue with its narrow polished leaves, the lady fern and maidenhair combed through by the endless wind. It will be a winter's night of long hours and winking lighthouses. The washed stones will darken and lighten again as the moon whips across the beach. Long skeins of brown seaweed are already entangled into heaps for the eggs of flies and sand-hoppers.

Spring comes. The cliff top is a Preraphaelite picture of wild flowers, a frame for the low stone hedges. Pale blue blossoms of spring quill are hidden in the green turf beside trefoil, trailing St John's wort, beneath speedwell, fairy fox, pearlwort, stonecrops and milkworts. Meadow grass is green for the spring-bite of the cattle turned into the cliff fields. The sun begins to lengthen, spinning over a calm evening horizon and colouring the mist of spindthrift. The lazy roll of summer seas is not far off.

Liners pass into the English Channel. Oil ships, like castles on the horizon, plough their way towards Wales past the great 'heads' of Cape Cornwall, Gurnard's Head and St Ives. Seals are calling in the caverns of Stinking Cove under Trevose. They lift their heads to gaze into the depths of Cathedral Cavern at Porth, or laze the summer away on the low-tide sands of Bedruthan, snoring in the shade of giant rocks.

The seals roll in and out of Fox Cove, near Padstow, under and over the wreck of the *Hemsley II* which struck on a foggy night four years ago. She was a small and very old tanker on her way to Rotterdam to be broken up. In the fog (and perhaps a drinking party on board) the captain thought (he said) that he was off the Lizard. He steered his ship round that headland, only to find that he was on the north coast. It was too late to save the ship. The bows of the *Hemsley II* were firmly gripped between two massive outcrops of rock beneath the cliffs of Fox Cove.

The noise she made when she struck must have echoed off the caverns opposite, though there was none but the crew to hear it. Her destruction altered nothing in the cove or in nature about her. The vixen still ran in the thickets below Winnard's Perch inland from the cove; the lighthouse on Trevose Head was still winking when the crew came ashore over the slippery rocks and made for the nearest habitation. All of them were unhurt.

And there the rusting hulk, ungracious at low tide, stuck for months, the seas banging into it, rocking its gear, slamming fo' castle doors, a brown, black, waif over which fulmars float, the seals sing, washing over the stern in breaking waves. The young wheat comes up in the fields above its mast-tip and maidenhair fern embroiders the stone hedges at the lip of the cove.

All Cornwall came to gaze on the wreck, until paths were worn over the headlands where no paths had been before. Pasties and pies were brought in vans to feed them, until contractors came and broke her up. When she was gone nothing had changed.

In 1875 it was still possible for ships to be at sea and nobody to be aware of it. Only weeks after the East Indiaman, the *Jonkeer*, broke her back on the rocks of Men y Grib near Mullion on a night of terrific storm in March, was she officially identified. She was homeward bound from the East Indies, carrying coffee, sugar, spices and some tin. Her cargo was valued at between £40,000 and £50,000. Her captain was Klaas van Lammerts and though his widow offered £5 for the recovery of her husband's body, it was never found. Only one survivor managed to reach the cliffs. He was a Greek sailor who could speak little English and had no idea of the name of the ship which he had joined in Batavia, or of her captain's name.

Three women were drowned and a baby who was wearing 'its little nightdress and a cap and a coral necklace' when it was picked up. The mother died, too, wearing nothing but 'drawers and stockings.' She passed as the captain's wife. Her baby had been born on board. One of the other women was about fifty and had 'nothing on but two stockings, both of these on the left leg.' The third, a woman of twenty three, with dark hair and fine features, 'with but drawers and stockings on,' was wearing a gold clasp-ring and a gold, heart-shaped, locket, containing the photograph of a young man, Herr M of Utrecht, whom she was to have married shortly. One of the mysteries of the loss of the *Jonkeer* is what she was doing on board at all.

Now, after the storm, their bodies were lying on the beach surrounded by quantities of coffee beans and sugar baskets made of split bamboo, washed off the wreck. They were carried to the churchyard at Mullion and there buried, while the ship broke up entirely. She lay in pieces in 'Poljew' Cove.

The voyage had not been a happy one. The Greek survivor,

named Buffani, explained later to interpreters that, at an early stage in the voyage, two English sailors had died off the coast of Africa and another, sick, was put ashore at St Helena.

On Saturday, before she went on the rocks, she was off Falmouth, 'which port we might have entered but did not.' They battled on, coming into Mount's Bay and 'tried to get out.' The Mousehole pilots spotted her and said that 'she missed stays' more than once off Mullion Island. They added that 'she was flying no signs and that unless she was very well manned, she would find it difficult to round the Lizard.' Buffani explained that when the barque struck everyone was on deck and that the captain 'cried bitterly'. Buffani with two other sailors, was on the jib-boom. They jumped for safety, but only Buffani was saved. The *Jonkeer* broke up in twenty minutes.

Cornish bays are littered with the bones of wrecks. Here, in Booby's Bay, at very low tide, are the fangs of a German ship lost in the 1918 war. And now, this day in 1960, the sea in the bay was so low that you could almost walk to America, three thousand miles away. The tide had so far receded. It had been, as it were, sucked from the land. Birds were already swallowing the low waters, diving into rock pools. Mussel-bound rocks were deep blue, razor-edged. Things were being uncovered that were only uncovered twice a year, when the tide fell so far away as if it were leaving the land for ever. The old wreck of the German ship looked like some agricultural machine left in a stubble field after harvest. A hedge of sand was about it, boldering up into the rocks which, too, were covered at other times of the year.

Here three people were standing on the sand looking down at the body huddled against the brown rusting iron of the wrecked ship. It seemed to be curled round the iron stays as if, dead, it was yet making a desperate effort for love and warmth. It was not apparent, then, that the dead body was that of a young man; the flesh appeared grey, mottled here and there with deeper purple of bruises. The drowned human flesh was deceiving the onlookers, for it hardly looked like flesh at all. We had waited over three weeks for the sea to return this body of a young man drowned in Treyarnon Bay while on holiday.

Only the shape of the curled thing — it could hardly be called more — made it human. That and the hair which was swinging back and forth in the pool left in the sand, hair like brown seaweed. The toes, where marine creatures had begun to divest the bones of its flesh, were missing. Given but a little more time and only the skeleton would remain. There was yet something of comfort in its attitude, the corpse lying naked with its buttocks towards us, the flesh slack.

When the police came they heaved the body free of the sand-hollow against the iron ribs of the submerged ship. Water ran from its mouth and from the staring eye-sockets. Rolled off the bloated face as if it were relieved to go. The lungs gave a deep sigh when the body was lifted to firmer ground, beseeching, it almost seemed, to be left alone in its convenient grave for the scavengers to complete their task of cleaning. The hair, under the weight of water, flung itself free from the head and hung down, a forlorn tapestry. Three gulls, perched on the nearest rock, began their squawking requiem. The water sucked at the sand of the hole where the body had come to rest and, in a moment, all trace of its former occupant was lost. The upthrust of Trevose Head remained impassive, the phallic symbol of the lighthouse unmoving.

So the currents in Treyarnon Bay had gathered in another summer victim. He was a young man from the Midlands who, working all the year in a car factory, was unable to resist rushing into the sea the moment he saw it, so wonderful was it compared with what he had left. Who can blame him? The policeman took the shoulders and the feet above the ankles, afraid of falling flesh, afraid that before they reached drier land this flotsam would have fallen apart. The grey flesh was greasy in their hands used to lifting the dead from the sea.

The body was spouting water again, in gusts, as if it had swallowed the entire ocean, when the policeman manoeuvred themselves between the rocks and the brittle sand and the bright shells up to the tussocks of the first marram grass. They laid the corpse down on its back. One of them went to fetch a sheet to cover it.

The tide had turned. The sea, all this time anxious at the loss of its prey, was now encroaching along the whole series of bays from Trevone to Newquay. The rusty ribs of the old German wreck had disappeared while the corpse was coming to dry land. The rocks and sands were tidy again.

It is inevitable that so fierce a coastline should have romantic tales of smugglers and wreckers, that men such as Coppinger (who may never have existed) were raised to the level of folk heroes. Indeed, the first time I came to Cornwall, a boy of fifteen, his was the name I heard most frequently because we were staying at Mr Old's farmhouse on Pentire Head.

This was remote enough, but daily we went down to Sandy Bay, below the headland, where neolithic men had built one of their fortresses, and swam in the bay. When swimming palled we explored an enormous cave. It was known, we were told, as Coppinger's Cave. I did not see then, and do not today, how any smuggler could have used this cave for hiding contraband, and I have no doubt that similar inaccessible caves round the coast are also known as Coppingers.

Ths man Coppinger was apparently a 'foreigner' whose arrival in Cornwall was heralded by a fierce hurricane. In such a way a myth begins. He reminds me of that other myth figure Tregeagle, the giant who is always being pursued by the Devil because of his sins and forever being condemned to work at impossible tasks. Romantic such figures may be but infinitely sad and, today, ridiculous.

Coppinger, so the story goes, was the leader of a gang of smugglers who allowed nothing to stand in its way. He and his men would, today, be engaged in hi-jacking planes. Nevertheless, Coppinger was ruthless, once beheading a Custom's man on the gunwhale of his boat as a warning to others. He left Cornwall as mysteriously as he came, going off in a cloud of sulphur, as you might say, in a fully-rigged ship. I think he is probably a left-over from the days of the Danish invaders, a folk-memory of a fierce past.

For all that he is supposed to have made fortunes and hidden them in caves such as the one I went into when I was a boy. At that time the mouth of the cave was a long slit and could be reached only at low tide from the beach. A long dark slope fell downwards to the yellow sandy floor of an immense cathedral-like cavity.

We explored it with torches and, in a crevice in the rock at the far end of the cave which seemed to me, then, a quarter of a mile long, we found a rusty old penknife with the words *S.S. Madras* still clearly outlined on it. In winter storms the sea must have risen up the cliff-face and come thundering down into the cavern and so washed up this relic. If there had ever been any treasure hidden here it must have been washed out again in the same manner.

Though I am far from ridiculing these tales of hidden treasure. When we lived in Suffolk a field in Mildenhall was, for some reason, ploughed three inches deeper than usual. The result is the superb Mildenhall Treasure now in the British Museum, the great dish, the numerous other pots and silver dishes. It had lain here all these years and no one had known anything about it. But, and this is the interesting fact about its discovery, for hundreds of years the field in which it lay buried was known as 'Treasure Field'. So who knows what is buried in Cornish caves, or what, in some extraordinary gale, may yet come to light?

I was over at Pentire the other day and asked one of Mr Old's men to direct me from the farm to Coppinger's Cave. It was an alarming experience. For one thing the tide was in and we could not go round by the beach and the rocks. He took me over the cliffs, in deep bracken paths, high over the sea, striding ahead of me with great confidence. When the path crossed a knife edge of slippery rock and bracken, I'm ashamed to say that I called a halt and turned back. I would not have turned back when I was a boy, not for anything on earth. And the strange thing about it is that the cave, which the man pointed out to me, was no longer a narrow slit but had an opening square and wide. So much for years of storm and sea!

The harshness of the south is different from the north yet it is, the coves and beaches, a better place for smuggling. To come from the lush valley of the Helford river to the hardness of the Lizard is like leaving paradise to enter the mystic's Dark Night of the Soul. The river is tree-lined and very much like the river Fal at King Harry Passage, where the woods come down to the water's edge as if jungle spread back into the interior. A painter would put crocodiles here, sun-basking, and the roots of the oaks could be the roots of mango trees. Birds with elaborately coloured plummage could nest in these trees; an elephant would not be an impossibility.

But the interior behind the Helford river, southwards, is not jungle. It is shaven land, rock-strewn, gaunt with the wide spaces of Goonhilly Downs and the wind-born buzzard from Gweek with its private quay, right down to Lizard Town, a gold-rush town, a film-set Western cowboy town.

At Gweek coal boats broke the miner's strike in 1972 by unloading into waiting lorries. Much of this strike-breaking was going on in little ports, such as Padstow, it was said that the pickets who came from other places to try and stop the unloading, met with short shrift from the women and soon departed. No picket had ever heard of Gweek.

Goonhilly Downs, in this flat heathy country, with here and there a prehistoric tumulus, standing stones, and windswept pines, was exactly the right place to put the two hideous G.P.O. dishes or Earth Satellite Stations, for it was near here, at Poldhu, that Marconi started it all. In a sense they distract the eye from the other hideous aspects of the long road from Helston to the Lizard, the caravan parks, the petrol stations and even the gauntness of Lizard Town itself.

But, then, who ever comes here for the beauty of Lizard Town? The beauty lies, or used to lie, entirely in what is below the land, the bays at Housel, Church Cove, Coverack, with it sombre plaques to those drowned here let into the rocksides of the small harbour, and Kynance Cove.

Kynance was still breath-taking when I first saw it. Now the shallow earth paths of the cliffs have been worn away by the countless feet which use them every summer season. The tourist, in such hordes, walking down to the cove and along the cliff path to Gunwalloe, is inevitable destruction. Gone now is the bloody cranesbill and other wild flowers.

An old guide book describes the Lizard as being ten miles by road from Helston. A bus used to take you there from the G.W.R. station above the town.

> The rugged peninsula south of the Helford river, is known as the Lizard, derived, as some suppose, from 'lezard' or 'lazar' — the old name for a leper. In years gone by lepers were banished to this remote spot. Lizard Point is the most southerly point of England and certainly one of the most dangerous to mariners. Kynance Cove, one mile north-west of Lizard Town, was much admired by the late Lord Leighton. Here may be seen the famous series of caves known as 'The Kitchen', 'Parlour', 'Ladies Bathing Pool', 'Devil's Throat or Mouth', also his satanic majesty's 'Drawing Room', 'Letter Box' and 'Devil's Bellows'.

No wonder Lord Leighton admired Kynance and the whole peninsula since, in late April and early May, the carpets of wild flowers create, over and above the beauty of the bays themselves, the kind of picture he painted. At every tiny stream or pool falling down the cliffs into the sea, you expect to see Ophelia floating as Millais painted her bedecked with flowers. Or that Tennyson, who was here with Palgrave, Holman Hunt and Valentine Princeps, in September, 1860, was inspired to write 'Queen Guinevere'. Valentine Cameron Princeps became an R.A., and his picture of Queen Victoria, as Empress of India, was later hung in Buckingham Palace. He exactly suited Cornwall. Holman Hunt describes him, in his memoirs as

> A burly, handsome young athlete, with breadth of shoulder and girth of limb that made him the admiration of Cornishmen, who by their wrestling bouts looked upon strangers as their forefathers did upon any new knights appearing in the jousting field.

Another visitor who admired the stone peninsula was the diarist Francis Kilvert who first came on a 'tour' of Cornwall in the same year as Thomas Hardy came to restore the church at St Juliot, 1870.

Kilvert records that he left Chippenham at 11.35 by the down mail with a tourist ticket for Truro on Tuesday 19th July. The mining country about Hayle and Camborne was stark and windswept and once his Cornish friends, Mr and Mrs Kockin, with whom he was staying, reported seeing;

> At Godrevy . . . a fearful battle between a seal and a large conger eel. The seal had got his teeth into the conger and the conger had coiled his folds round the seal's neck and was trying to choke him. The seal kept on throwing up his head and trying to toss the conger up out of the water that he might have more power than the eel. It was a fierce and dreadful fight, but at last the seal killed the conger. The Vicar of St Ives says the smell of fish there is sometimes so terrific as to stop the church clock.[1]

So he and his party go to Mullion and the 'Serpentine District' as he calls the Lizard, where he says:

> Roads were made of marble, the dust of which looked like coal dust. At last we got off and drove to Kynance Cove. The carriage was left on the moors (or Croft as it is called here) above, and we scrambled down into the Cove. The tide was ebbing fast and it was nearly low water. We wandered about through the Dining Room and Drawing Room caves, and amongst the huge Serpentine Cliffs and the vast detached rocks which stand like giants guarding the Cove. I never saw anything like the wonderful colour of the serpentine rocks, rich, deep, warm, variegated, mottled and streaked and veined with red, green and white, huge blocks and masses of precious stone marble on every side, an enchanted cove, the palace of the Nereids.[2]

It is, indeed, as I have said, a paradise of flowers. F.D. Hanson writing in *The Lizard*, a magazine of field studies, in 1957, says, 'here, in these few square miles are to be found a greater variety of unusual plants than in any other locality in Britain, with the possible exception of the sub-alpine regions of Scotland.' He goes on to name and describe some of the more unusual flowers to be seen here, the quillwort, Hottentot fig, hairy dyers greenweed, hairy birdsfoot, Balbi's trefoil, soft downy broome grass and many others, their names a poem in themselves.

---

1 *Kilvert's Diary*, edited by William Plomer. Cape, 1947
2 Ibid.

4. Burial Grounds and Ghosts

No magnificence attaches to the Quaker burial ground at St Minver. None was intended and the pomp of the Bishops of Exeter who, in 1383, had a manor and chapel at Pawton, near Wadebridge, is far removed from this flat lawn enclosed by stone walls beside a country lane. It is the epitome of the quiet and rest of the grave, with nothing but birdsong to disturb it and the sound of the sea over Daymer Bay. As they were quiet in their worship, so are they serene in their last homes, a scarf of cloud above them in their granite demesne. Yet it is hard to believe that anyone is buried here in this rectangle of quietness beneath its fir trees where, at night, I have watched owls preening their feathers into a full moon, and where the winds drive in from the Camel estuary, into Pityme and beyond, to St Endellion and the moors.

I had come down from London to stay at the farmhouse next door to this burial ground. I had come from Paddington to Bodmin Road Station and arrived there, to change for Wadebridge, late on a January afternoon, in 1934, when already farmers were lighting gorse fires on the Moor, when the last of the herring fleet was sitting quietly in Padstow harbour.

I was twenty five and recovering from an illness contracted in London while I was working in the old Mudie's Library warehouse in Southwark Street. I was very much alone for although I had often been in Cornwall before, for holidays, this was different. For one thing I had never been here in January. Above all I had not been to Cornwall alone and able to do exactly what I wanted at any time of the day or night. I had never been in Cornwall when Cornwall itself was lonely and deserted. I was to see it as completely different from holiday times.

Cornwall, then, hit me, created me, forced me into self-observation as a person existing in nature. I was no longer the young man who was born in the climate of a London suburb. In the glaring moments of January sunshine my pointlessness was exposed almost to suicide. Poor faded ghosts of my suburban desires and hopes came with me to the farm at St Minver and shivered with me in the shadows of the burial ground and went down into oblivion, as they should at nights, in the farmhouse bedroom. I faced a personal despair in which this burial place appealed to me. It would be so easy . . .

Cornwall, which first exposed myself to me in this gaunt time of year, now rescued me. I think it was entirely because it (and the people I met) existed without me and could go on existing without me, that, as my convalescence increased to full strength, I became determined that it should not exist without me. Something in its hardness of rock and land, in its brilliant, majestic seas kindled a fire in me and did not fail me. I had only, I felt, to put myself against its implacability and I should survive.

Cornwall was to test that idea of survival. One afternoon I went from St Minver across the sands at Polzeath and walked up the deep ravine to the farmhouse on Pentire Head where I had so often spent holidays from London. I spent the afternoons about the farm and was given an enormous tea of saffron buns and cream. I decided to return the same way, but across the rocks at the head of the beach from Pentireglaze to Polzeath. I was strong enough now to face anything.

Or so I thought when I saw that the tide had come in while I was at tea and was fairly raging into the rock ravines I had to cross. So that when I came to the really deep cleft in the rocks, wide and black, with the full sea now tearing in over covered sand, I slipped down the north face, waited a moment as the sea receded for a second, and flung myself on to the south face, tearing the skin off one hand.

Now that the tide was in, this was my only way home. In short, I was cut off unless I wanted to go back to the farm and walk some ten miles along the road back to St Minver. I flung myself against the black rock and began to climb away from the sea, not realising that I was still weak.

No one was within miles of me, that January evening. I was completely alone on the rock face which, in truth, was hardly very high. To me, then, it was like the last few feet of Everest as I lay panting against the cold, wet, hardness unable to move. The last rays of the sun were beginning to touch the horizon and the sea to make more fearful noise. If anyone had been walking on the headland they could not have seen me in this dusk light and hidden in this ravine.

I do not know to this day how I managed those last few feet, except that the noise of the sea below, licking its lips for me, was so frightening that it gave me strength. I believe, actually, that that strength came from anger at the thought of being trapped by my own self-confidence. I was alone here merely because my body was weak. As the sun set I managed it. I fell on the headland grass and lay gasping for breath and thought of the peace of my burial ground and refused, with the sea birds still hovering, to die.

I grew mentally between that Quaker burial ground and the small church at St Enedoc, between the sand of Polzeath and Pentire Head; between the loneliness of my room in the farmhouse and the meadows of Pityme, where mint was growing in the ditches and already primroses and snowdrops were blooming, and the then deserted hamlet of Port Quin. Above all, I came back to health and sanity in the touch of a calf's tongue.

I knew nothing about animals, I had no contact with them, except for a cat, though as a boy I lived in what was then a kind of refined countryside on the outskirts of London. I knew of cows and horses; my experience of them was less than nothing. In my present state of depression it came as a revelation actually to be in such close personal relationship with a farm animal that it was licking my hand.

I had gone with the farmer (he and his wife were as young as I was and struggling cheerfully against economic odds) to look at his week-old calf. He showed me how, once the calf was away from its mother, he made it drink by putting his hand in a bucket of milk and letting the calf suck it, gradually lowering his hand into the milk. He gave me a bucket. Half afraid I approached the calf. It was eager for it, its tongue came down into the milk for my fingers. I can still feel that leathery tongue on my hand and hear the soft sucking; I can still see the calf, in soft velvet of white and black, and its mother at the back of the byre, the yellow hay, the grey stone farm buildings; I can still smell that January farmstead. All of these things and the fact that this small particle of life needed a human being (and while I was holding the bucket, needed me) to help it, were recuperative in a way it would be impossible to explain.

All day I had nothing to do but walk, return to the farmhouse for meals (the cream was cream in those days), and walk again. This way I began to exorcise the burial ground or, at least, to change it into something other than a suicidal idea in my mind. It was no longer the main focus of my walking in what was almost a deserted Cornwall but for the towns, like Padstow and Newquay.

St Enedoc church, once so neglected, the roof in ruins so that the surrounding sand blew in and filled the interior, stood beneath the great grass mound of Brea Hill where the Romans had a settlement. The path to the door of the church was, and still is, lined with stone bowls which I took to be ancient piscinas. Actually they are medieval domestic mortars used for grinding corn. The church bell came, in 1875, from the wreck of the ship, the *Immacolata*, wrecked off Greenway beach between Polzeath and Daymer Bay. One could look out from Brea Hill to the Rumps or Pentire Head where a cliff castle, or fort, of the first century A.D. still stood hidden under the grass and stone of a sheep-hedge, awaiting the excavation of twenty years later.

I would take the sand ferry at Rock over to Padstow and walk to Harlyn Bay without seeing a soul once I was out of the town. Here, in front of a small forest of macrocarpa trees, I would sit alone sifting the shells on the sand at low tide and listening to the sea breaking on the rocks below the fish cellars. Later, I would visit the Museum with its skeletons in cysts in the garden which Baring-Gould had helped to excavate from the sand. I would let the slate needles and other neolithic remains rest in my hands, and think about that strong man who was rector and squire of Lew Trenchard the other side of Launceston.

I would come home to the farm again with an enormous sun setting over the sea and banging its fiery head against Pentire and the island of Newland. I would lie awake at night when the sea mist rolled in, listening to the foghorn on Trevose Head, or stand at the window of my bedroom to watch the gorse fires which almost, I persuaded myself, I could hear above the low, contented voice of the calf and its mother.

I existed, then, in a land of burial grounds which, by their very number, were forcing me back to life. In this part of Cornwall there is no escaping them, from the churchyards at St Minver, Rock, St Endellion, Padstow and those older ones on the Rumps and at Brea Hill. These churchyards have their sophistication of carved stone; their memorials of those drowned and wrecked. Such exquisitely carved slates exist in the atmosphere of the golf links and the holiday rush at Polzeath which, today, has destroyed most of that landscape I knew when I was a boy. These slates are upright or slanted, gracious and beautiful and time-worn, side-by-side with the latest from the Co-op Society. They are the final handicraft, these old slates, and the last reward of dying, dug and polished by the men of the Delabole Quarry and carved by local craftsmen.

Yet only over the grass of the Quaker burial ground did the suggestion of souls hovering occur to me. In the funeral grounds of Harlyn Bay the tiny skeletons, with their heads broken by stones, were clearly visible. These little men had once lived, had once fished the sea beyond the sand dunes. But here, at St Minver, there was nothing but a 'green place', a lawn above the skeletons of the unnamed, invisible people, lovely in their invisibility.

Now it is 1974. Maytime. I live only five miles away from the Quaker burial ground at St Minver and have done so for years. I was there a week ago, in the lane where the farmhouse is where I fed the calf in 1934. So little has changed in the lanes themselves, though much in the surrounding countryside and seascape. When I was here as a boy, however, the burial ground was impregnable behind its granite wall and iron gate-door. I could not have climbed in even if I had wanted to. Today, a great hole was driven through one of the bastion walls.

I went in between clumps of wild garlic — white bluebells as the tourists call the flower until they have picked it — and red campion. The quiet was still the same, the quiet of birdsong and blossom.

Those who lay buried here when I was a boy still lie buried, only gone from this life that much longer. The melancholy was deeper. I came away and walked down the lane I had known so well and stood looking out to Brea Hill. The dead there are so far off in time that they are comfortable, they have the benign scent of history about them.

Yet in one way this Quaker burial ground is luckier than that outside St Austell which has been obliterated forever in a road-widening scheme. The bones of my St Minver Quaker companions of all those years ago are as yet undisturbed.

In such a remote county as Cornwall you might expect to be surrounded by ghosts of the past. The ruined mine buildings alone seem to provide plenty of scope for spectres. The Cornish themselves — though fewer live here than in the old days, so many having 'emigrated' — are a race reputed to be able to see beyond ordinary reality. Yet it is an odd thing that where one would expect the most potent and long-lived ghost to appear none does. For example, in the many castles, fortifications, ruined halls and so on attached to the name of King Arthur. None of them has a well authenticated ghost such as that of Ann Boleyn at Hampton Court. The small remote church at Advent, near Camelford, would be an ideal spot for ghosts, for here is all the loneliness of deep country, the crooked tombstones, the dark corners that any ghost could want. I have heard of none.

Nevertheless Cornwall has its fair share of ghosts. Whatever the reason for ghosts, whatever one may believe about them, they certainly still do appear to some people. Neither do they always appear in historical settings. A number of well-known present day cases of poltergeists and ghosts occur in council houses!

The seashore seems, too, to be a potent spot for ghosts. Fishermen dread to walk anywhere near where a ship has foundered. The souls of drowned sailors are said to haunt such places and the 'calling of the dead' has frequently been heard. Voices of dead sailors have been heard 'hailing their own names.' There is the curious story of the fisherman at Porthtowan who, one night, walking beside the small waves, heard a voice from the sea shout, 'The hour is come, but not the man.' This was repeated three times. The figure of a man, in black, appeared at the top of the hill behind the beach. It paused for a moment and then rushed headlong down a steep incline, over the sands and into the sea where it disappeared.

Some ghosts have gone forever — or have they? In 1665 a Launceston schoolboy was haunted by a girl called Dorothy Dingley. The boy pined away and was, perhaps, in love with the wraith which would not leave him alone. He was questioned by the vicar of Launceston, the Rev William Ruddle. Ruddle took the boy to a field in which he said he used to meet the apparition and there the parson himself saw the spectral Dorothy. Afterward he was able to show her to the boy's mother and father.

The next morning, with supreme self-confidence, for he had studied the matter, Ruddle proceeded to the laying of this particular ghost. The story is given in C.S. Gilbert's *Historical Survey of Cornwall*.

> The next morning being Thursday, I went out very early by myself and walked for about an hour's space in meditation and prayer in the field next adjoining to the Quartiles. Soon after five, I stepped over the stile into the disturbed field, and had not gone above thirty or forty paces before the ghost appeared at the further stile. I spoke to it with a loud voice, in some such sentences as the way of these dealings directed me; whereupon it approached, but slowly, and when I came near it, it moved not. I spoke again, and it answered again in a voice which was neither very audible nor intelligible. I was not the least terrified, and therefore I persisted until it spake again and gave me satisfaction. But the work could not be finished at this time; wherefore the same evening, an hour after sunset, it met me again near the same place, and after a few words on each side it *quietly vanished*, and neither does appear since, nor ever will more to any man's disturbance.

Mr Ruddle tells us that he learned Syriac in order to speak to Dorothy Dingley, because it is the language that ghosts understand. He attributed his success entirely to his ability to communicate in this way. What is so depressing about his story is that he never revealed to anyone, least of all to the parents of the boy, what it was he said to Dorothy which made her agree to disappear.

However the field called the Quartils is still there, in the parish of South Petherwin, next to the granite-built farmhouse where the boy lived. Although there is now a slaughter-house close by, it was reported to me when I was researching the story for my book *Ghosts of the South West* that a figure had been seen in the field as late as the autumn of 1972, a figure which was 'certainly not of any human being living round here.' Was it the same ghost that Mr Ruddle had exorcised three hundred years before? And, if so, why had it decided to return?[1]

These are, of course, unanswerable questions. What did interest me at the site of each haunting I visited was the persistence of such stories. Many of these ghosts had first appeared a very long time ago, as with Dorothy Dingley, yet the people to whom I talked, both in Cornwall and Devon, Dorset and Somerset, mostly believed in these wraiths. What was it they were believing in? I do not know, unless the appearance of such a ghost, the materialisation of someone so long dead, points to some kind of after-life? In so far as I can attempt to explain such materialisations I feel they must have something to do with time-traces or the accumulation of energy in some kind of cosmic battery about which we know, as yet, nothing. The fact does remain that there is a continuing, serious interest in the subject.

In Charlotte Dymond, for instance. She was a milkmaid at Penhale Farm in the depths of Bodmin Moor. On Sunday, 14th April, 1844, she was walking out with Matthew Weeks, her lover, in their time off. Charlotte was a young girl, no more than eighteen and would hardly have been heard of today if she had not been murdered in so horrible a manner. And Matthew was not really an ideal lover. He limped, he was jealous and he was, although Charlotte was unaware of this, vicious. Undoubtedly the fact that they all lived in the same farmhouse belonging to a Mrs Peter, in a really remote coombe of the moor, must have fostered his jealousy and viciousness. It is a lonely place today and took me quite a time to find. In Charlotte's day, although many of the moor's deserted cottages were then filled, it was even lonelier. People were thrown too much together.

1 For the full account of Dorothy Dingley and other Cornish ghosts see my book *Ghosts of the South West*, David & Charles, 1973

And on this Sunday — they both had two or three hours off in the evening, once a week — they walked to Roughtor and down the hill to the ford. When they reached a gate on the long hill up to Camelford, Matthew suddenly drew a knife and, pulling Charlotte's head backwards, cut her throat. It was a quite pointless murder since Charlotte had no other lover, though that was Matthew's reason.

A monument was erected to her memory at the bottom of Roughtor, beside the stream, which must once have been upright. It now leans towards the south. It was put up by public subscription. Matthew was caught on the Hoe, at Plymouth, trying to escape and was hanged in Bodmin Gaol on 12th August, 1844. The scene as given by Matthew, at his 'Confession' before his execution, and reported in the Royal Cornwall Gazette, is gruesome.

> I told her I had seen her in a situation with some young man that was disgraceful to her. She then said, 'I shall do as I like. I shall have nothing more to do with you.' I took out my knife and then replaced it. But on her repeating the phrase I made a cut at her throat from behind. She immediately fell backwards, the blood gushing out in a large stream and exclaimed while falling, 'Lord have mercy on me.' When she was on the ground I made a second and much larger cut though she was almost dead at the time. After standing over her body about four or five minutes, I lifted up one of her arms and it fell to the ground as if she were dead. I then pushed her body a little further down the bank. I afterwards took her bonnet, shawl, shoes and pattens and covered them up in a turf pit. Her gloves and bag I put in my pocket. In the road I threw away the knife.

It is inevitable, in the context of psychic revelations, that Charlotte would have been seen as a ghost; that if she were to be so seen it would be at the ford below Roughtor. Indeed, a stranger to Cornwall (no name is given in the reports) after a day's fishing on the moor, arrived at the foot of Roughtor, quite alone. He saw a woman walking across the moor in the direction of Penhale and called out good-night to her. She did not answer but walked on. When he told his hosts at the house where he was staying, near at hand, that she was the only person he had seen all day and described the woman as wearing 'a gown of many colours, a red cloth shawl and a silk bonnet' they declared that he had seen

Charlotte, for these were just the clothes she was wearing at the time of her death.

Like so many ghost stories it is unsatisfactory because it lacks the substantiation of names and dates.

Whatever one may think of such stories the fact is that Bodmin Moor — perhaps any moor — is an odd place at the best of times. At dusk it can be frightening. Anyone might see what they took to be a phantom. Animals, for example, roam all over the moor, and the 'ghost' which this man saw could have been a brown and white pony with a long black mane, especially if there was a low mist at the time. I know myself how easy it is to make a mistake in such mists, which are frequent on the moor, and how the trickling of shallow water under the old clapper bridge at this spot could be mistaken for a ghostly voice.

For all that Charlotte must have been greatly loved to have a monument erected to her memory since, only in her death is she at all memorable. In time, no doubt, she became a 'folk' figure, the young maid done cruelly to death. For maid she was. The doctor who examined her body when, after a week, it was discovered in the shallow grave where Matthew had buried it, declared that she had not been interfered with in any way. And, as I've said, such remote places as this can foster the most remarkable legends. Charlotte may well have been an innocent who became, for the parishioners of the little chapel at Higher Town which she attended with her mistress, Mrs Peter, 'a guilt' figure on to which they could shift their own sins. For the preaching in such chapels was mostly of the 'sin' of premarital sexual intercourse and the possibility of hell fire.

Her story, when it became fully known from newspaper reports of the trial, would have been that of a 'shining white maid' who had been martyred by 'a Devil', in Matthew's form. And so a monument was erected that she be remembered for all time and as an example to others of the same religious persuasion. For, today, we are unable to realise fully the effect of such preaching upon the minds of such simple folk as then lived on the moor.

Now, just below the spot where she was murdered, china clay mines are in operation. The tall white spoil heaps reach almost as high as Roughtor — a fitting shroud for the dead girl!

Another lover who died and returns is Kate Penfound. She was the daughter of Arthur Penfound of Penfound Manor, near Poundstock. In the seventeenth century she fell in love with John Trebarfoot, son of the owner of another manor house close by. The Penfounds supported the King; the Trebarfoots Cromwell. For the parents of these children a marriage between the two houses was out of the question.

So John and Kate decided to elope. On the night of 26th April (the day on which Kate is supposed to re-enact her death each year), Kate came down the stairs from her bedroom to meet her lover at the main door where he had horses ready. Unfortunately her father got wind of the elopement, intercepted them, and is supposed to have shot both of them in the courtyard. Another story — very unlikely I think — has it that John and her father fought a duel and Kate, trying to separate them, was killed. Whereupon they fought to the death and both were killed.

I have often been to Penfound Manor — no longer open to the public — which is the oldest continuously lived-in manor house in England, going back to 1045 when Edith, Queen to Edward the Confessor, owned the estate, and I have never experienced anything but peace and quiet. Yet the tradition of Kate 'walking' still persists. It is almost, as in the case of Charlotte, as if the villagers take a personal interest in this girl who lived so long ago, as if she were one of the family and her 'return' a reason for some kind of celebration.

Just outside Tavistock, which is almost in Cornwall, is Kilworthy House, attached to which is another story of a 'fated' lover who died long ago and has been seen recently, although the apparition which appeared to several people had no face. She is the daughter (so it is supposed) of Judge Glanville, a formidable Elizabethan, who built Kilworthy House, outside the town, as a fitting place for so 'magnificent' a person to live.

I was at the house while I was writing my book on ghosts of the South West, because a figure thought to be that of Elizabeth had appeared in one of the dormitories in the house which is now (or was when I was there) a school for mal-adjusted children. Mrs

Bray, the wife of the vicar of Tavistock in the middle 1800's, wrote a series of letters to the poet Robert Southey in which she described the house as it then was and the fate of poor Elizabeth.

The Judge, her father, refused to allow her to marry the man she really loved, George Stanwich, a lieutenant in the Navy, and ordered her to marry 'Old Page', a goldsmith of Plymouth. This she did. Mrs Bray, in her book *Borders of the Tamar and the Tavy* (1869) finishes off the gruesome story.

> She took with her a maid-servant from Tavistock; but her husband was so penurious that he dismissed all the other servants, and caused his wife and her maid to do all the work themselves. On an interview subsequently taking place between her and Stanwich, she accused him of neglecting to write to her; and then discovered that his letters had been intercepted. The maid advised them to get rid of the old gentleman, and Stanwich at length, with great reluctance, consented to their putting an end to him. Page lived in what was afterwards the Mayoralty House (at Plymouth), and a woman who lived opposite, hearing at night some sand thrown against a window, thinking it was her son, rose and looking out, saw a young gentleman near Page's window and heard him say, 'For God's sake stay your hand.' A female replied, ''Tis too late; the deed is done.'
>
> On the following morning it was given out that Page had died suddenly in the night, and as soon as possible he was buried. On the testimony, however, of his neighbour the body was taken up again; and it appearing that he had been strangled, his wife, Stanwich, and the maid were tried and executed. Judge Glanville, her own father, pronouncing her sentence.

While, no doubt, the most famous Cornish ghost — and the most contemporary — is that of the vicar of Warleggan which I mention in my chapter on vicars, there are many other tales of fragmentary ghosts, such as the ghostly bells which are heard out at sea off Forrabury, near Boscastle. Local people have seen phantom ships and crews rowing silently to a spot where a ship is supposed to have been wrecked. In a sense this is a similar story to the sighting of the drowned city of Lyonesse and may be due to a particular light over the sea at a particular time, or to a mirage created by a reflection from the cliffs.

Then there is Stanbury Manor, near Morwenstow, where the poet Hawker was vicar. At one time recently this house belonged to a Mr T.A. Ley. He owned a haunted chest thought to have come to England with the Spanish Armada. Poltergeist manifestations occurred wherever this chest was placed in the house. Indeed, it has a story of its own which may account for the manifestations. It belonged originally to two ladies who lived in the village. Once the chest, placed in their bedroom, opened without any human aid. The sisters went across to look inside and 'what they saw was so horrible that they were both struck dumb on the spot.' They never revealed what it was they saw, but the story persists locally.

When I owned a house near Wadebridge, called Treneague, I was inundated with stories of ghosts attached to it and also treasure. Buried treasure does often go along with ghosts turning up to point out the spot. At Treneague monks were supposed to sit on a bench built against one wall of my work-room. Although I saw nothing at any time this was not an impossibility since the house had once belonged to the Manor of Pawton, just up the road, which was a seat of the old Bishops of Exeter.

While below, in the woods about the Hay stream, was another cottage, Lower Treneague. Alone, at night, in this cottage it is just possible that a small cold hand can be put into yours. Such a thing did happen to a friend of mine who owned the cottage and lived alone. Another friend, Miss Wood, of Newquay, wrote to me about this girl ghost who lived and died on St Breock Downs just above this cottage. I think this ghost is one of the most tender of all in Cornwall and that the letter is worth quoting here;

> A long time ago three sisters lived somewhere on St Breock Downs. They were very poor and made what they could by cutting brushwood on the moors (they would certainly have come down the thickets of the Hay stream) which they made into brooms and sold in the market town. (Wadebridge).
>
> Eventually the younger sister married and moved away. After a few happy years she was left a widow with one little girl. Then she died and the child was left alone.
>
> The two elder sisters felt they must have the little girl to share their home, although they did not want another mouth to feed, or the worry of a child about the cottage. Life was not happy. It was terribly hard and the girl had to take her share. She was taught how to make the brooms, prickly work for soft fingers. On market days she was left alone with strict orders to have so many made by the time her aunts returned.
>
> One afternoon when they came back, instead of a tired, lonely child, she

was singing and laughing and very happy. They were instantly suspicious.

'What have 'ee been doing? Have 'ee made the brooms?' They asked.

'I've done 'em all,' the little girl replied, 'I was sitting working on the 'epping block, and my mother came and helped me — 'tis all done.'

The women looked at each other. 'What do 'ee mean? Your mother's dead.'

'Yes I know, but she came, I wasn't lonely any more.' After that things were better, kinder words were spoken, the work was not so hard. The aunts were ashamed — did their dead sister really come? They did not have long to practise their kindness for, in a short time, the child joined her mother across the Gulf of which love had been the bridge.

Is it this child, one wonders, who comes into the cottage, so near where she lived and died, and holds your hand when you are alone?

It is undeniable that the Cornish are interested in their ghosts, as I have said, almost as if they were family. But the general present-day interest in ghosts is due, I think, to the decline of organised religion. A hundred years ago everyone, more or less, believed in a Christian after-life — in heaven and hell.

Now that that belief has largely gone we are still left with a desire for paradise and a longing for something after this life. And belief in ghosts is one way in which this desire seems to be assuaged. If Charlotte, or Elizabeth, if the little girl at Lower Treneague returns, then why not me? No doubt this longing runs counter to the best scientific opinion which assures us that when we die we return to dust and ashes — and nothing more.

Apart from this being a hideously pessimistic, typically scientific and not necessarily true summing-up of Life and Death, such an opinion gives rise — because we repudiate it within ourselves — to the climate in which ghosts can exist and be seen. He or she thrives on our very human desire not to be returned to rubbish; thrives on our sneaking certainty that not *all* of us dissolves into dust, that certain parts of us, whatever the scientist may say, do survive.

You do not need to be a scientist to know that the body returns to dust. But what of the spiritual integument which has no definite location in the body? What of memory and the soul? It is with these that the ghost clothes himself and is made manifest.

The ghost — if it does nothing else — assuages our longing for immortality. At second hand we can enjoy the sinner's guilt being punished (walking lonely and miserable in spectral form); we can enjoy paradise when a ghost is happy because capable of journeying from paradisal boredom back to 'normal' life and haunting people (what fun this can be only a ghost can know); and the very possible suggestion of an after-life in which we may share. Above all, we are terrified of the unknown. But unknown only to us. To ghosts our 'unknown' is now very well known indeed. And this, too, is shattering and frightful. 'As we are so shall you be' is as good an epitaph for a ghost as it is for a tombstone.

On the other hand our times may be more propitious for ghosts than any other. Especially in Cornwall with its Telstar on Goonhilly Downs, electronics, microwaves, radar, to mention a few new means of communication which allow modern ghosts to move about with a great deal more freedom than they used to do. Such modern marvels may well breed a new race of phantoms more terrifying than the old. Familiar ghosts, like those found haunting ancient rectories, mansions, ruined abbeys and deserted woods, may soon be a thing of the past. Somehow one felt that one knew how to deal with the grey wraith waiting beside the Holy Well. One was almost meeting a friend. The possibility of electronic ghosts is, however, not comfortable at all.

5. Pools and Inventors

All land is full of pools. On Greenaway beach, halfway between Daymer Bay and Polzeath, the pools above high water are purple and mauve, pink and grey and aquamarine, because the rocks which hold them are these colours both from the stone and from the marine creatures, anemones and others, living there. Whoever lived on Brea Hill, centuries ago, must have seen the same pools, the same colours as I do today. Nothing in so hard a landscape, could have changed more than a millionth of an inch, unless it be that a forest was where the long sands to Padstow are now.

In the woods at Carnanton and in the deserted thickets of Colan, in little Hay Wood running up to St Breock Downs, are ruminate pools of rainwater, still and black where birds and insects drink. On the moors over Zennor are greater pools, pike-infested, changing colour with the skies. Here the badgers come from their ancient rock fortresses on Zennor Head to drink.

I have had, for a number of years, a recurring dream. I will be walking in a grove of thick laurel hedges, dark and carpeted with dead leaves. I come to where there are two dark pools of water, still and black and deadly. I know, as one does in a dream, that the water is very deep. The pools lie side by side, long wide stretches of oily water, the colour and texture of molasses, encased in brick sides. Like two large swimming pools. Nothing moves on the surface of the waters which are divided by a raised brick path. As with all dreams I know what is about to happen. One moment I shall be on the path; the next I shall be in the water.

The more I have the dream the better I understand what is to happen to me. The horror, at first, was that no one had thrown me in. The second horror is that, once in, I shall not be able to get a handhold on the slippery sides of the brick surround. I know that I ought to be able to do so as the mortar will surely have decayed between the bricks. For one thing is certain, the pools are very old indeed. Old and deserted. No one, I know, ever comes here.

But now the sides of the tanks, for in my dream they have become huge tanks, are turned to marble. And with this absolute certainty that no one will come to my help, I wake up covered in sweat and shivering.

For years now I have come across such deep, dangerous, black tanks of pools in actual reality. It is true to say that I cannot go exploring into strange and deserted places without coming across such pools like that at Maidenwell in the moor, a disused clay mine pool beyond a tall house on Cardinham Moor, or the equally mysterious pool (for it is little more) of the Tamar Reservoir in the narrow lanes behind Kilkhampton, or again the pool at Slaughter Bridge where lies a massive stone said to celebrate the last battle that King Arthur fought. These are all lonely, unvisited places.

Even more lonely is the marshy area to the north of the Wadebridge to Padstow road. It is haunted by the isolated industrial block in the hamlet of Edmonton which was the home of quarrymen in the 1850's. On Saturdays they used to go across the fields to the inn beside St Breock Church and carry on their feuding with the townees, since the church, though some way from the town, is the mother church of Wadebridge. The inn has gone now (it is a private house) but the ghosts of the quarry men still haunt the lanes which were once the ways through the Bishop of Exeter's deer park when he had his summer pavilions at Pawton.

You come into this lowland, sloping down to the river Camel, down a lane to Lower Halwyn, to Oldtown Cove and the railway line. This is now ripped up, overgrown, desolate, looking across to the old quarries on Cant Hill, opposite which are the more frightening quarries of Bodellick. You get into them through a long corridor from the riverside where, in the old days, barges loaded slate. The wooden quays are still there, rotting and dangerous with green slime. The massive wooden piles which supported the quayside are hung in seaweed of a black and blistery kind, bladderwrack. It is like an early Chirico painting.

The river Camel here makes a wide sweep and, at high tide, looks exactly like a lake. But as soon as you have crossed the shale surface of the quays you are in a stone landscape in which these deep pools exist which are so exactly the pools in my recurrent dream. Even now it is not easy to find them for the great open space which had once been slate, is a desert of weeds and low scrub, of betony and hawkweed, nettle and thistle and sloe bushes. In these corridors of slate rats are running unceasingly. They are large shaggy rats with red eyes in the dark places of the slate and along the rusted railway lines which run eastwards into the heart of the quarries.

The fallen slate rises in vast piles of rubbish. The huge blocks, in many cases weighing over a ton, are flung down haphazardly, forming grotesque shapes and overtoppling threats. Sharp edges protrude into the air like canopies of anger, or lie inert like antediluvian beasts. Acres of slate have been torn from the deep beds, in some cases a hundred feet below the level of the surrounding earth. The residual slate lifts itself in impossibly high columns, motionless, ageless. In the deep holes foxes live and hunt. Higher on the terraces the holes of caves can be seen where the quarriers dug into the slate or blew deep shafts with gunpowder. It is like being at the bottom of some hell painted by Gustave Dôré.

Further into the quarries you come on the relics of cottages. Below the low brick hovels — why brick one wonders? — grass is now growing. An old apple tree hangs dejectedly in one corner. Here is the first pool. The surface of the water is as dark as its surroundings. There was no lapping noise against the side of the pool, it was dark dead water. It is the pit of my dream, with brick and cement sides, impossible to grasp once one was in. I could have swum in the deadly coldness to the far side of the pool. This would have been even worse for here the edge is nothing but the smooth enamelled face of the quarry itself going up in a glassy wall. The pool is a smooth, oily, glassy nightmare at the end of labyrinthine tunnels in slate.

Much later than my first dream, when I was gardener to Mrs

Raymond at Belchamp Hall, in Essex, I came upon my dream pool again and the effect was as shattering as going into the Camel quarries.

There was, at the Hall, a large walled garden, away from the house itself. It was overgrown with years of weed, a jungle of blackberry and giant hemlock, a wonderful bird sanctuary. Mrs Raymond told me, when she asked me to work in it, that she herself had not been near it for years.

I went into it, in a white shirt and grey trousers, a billhook in my hand, to attempt a clearance. To get, in fact, at the raspberries which were planted and fruiting well somewhere inside the tangle. I described what I found in my book *Sometimes into England*.[1]

> The sight which met my eyes was frightening and alarming for, as I've said, the mighty hemlock was standing everywhere and I had no idea, as I ploughed my way amongst it with a billhook, hacking at the large tubes, that I would come on water. Mrs Raymond had not mentioned water at all. Suddenly I was standing on the edge of what must once have been a long, wide, oblong, ornamental 'lake' with water-lillies on the surface and urns about it. That was all gone now.
>
> The apple trees which once graced the gravel walk round the brick edge of the water were sprawling over it in abandon of leaves and fruit. The water itself was black and still; a bat was flying up and down in the deep shade, and a tree-creeper was nesting somewhere in the unpruned peach and cherry trees on the surrounding walls. A dead cat was floating silently in the centre of the water, as if, finally, to point the loneliness of the place.

This was exactly one of my dream tanks. This time I did not run away. I wanted to absorb myself in the haunting picture and, by so doing, to destroy my dream forever. This time there was no sound of muffled oars as I had once heard in the mist over Dozmary Pool, in Cornwall, on an autumn evening. This time I was unable to confront myself. In the loneliness of that overgrown walled garden I might well have been waiting for God to speak to me. And then a plane flew over and children were laughing in the lane outside the brick wall of the garden.

One of the larger Cornish pools is the man-made reservoir at Siblyback. The river Fowey comes off the moor where the Withey

1 Cassell, 1970

Brook almost joins it. The reservoir stretches below Tregarrick Tor on the southernmost aspect of Bodmin Moor, and is much used as a sailing centre. The river flows free again at Trekeive Steps. A mile below is one of the loveliest places, of deep pools and tall trees, in Cornwall.

Golytha Falls is easily missed unless you come across Draynes Common into the congregation of dark woodlands with the Fowey winding down to Two Waters Foot. The entrance, beyond the bridge, known in 1362 and mentioned by Leland in 1535, carries a very ancient track from Caradon in the direction of Bodmin and was 'probably the first bridge over the Fowey'[1], is by an avenue of splendid beeches beside the river. And down through these woods to the green cascades. Here the brooding air of the moor is funnelled into a dark gorge, secret and with traces, here and there beside the winking water, of large, destroyed buildings. What was stored here? And when? Who raised these unroofed structures, ruined amongst roots of ash and oak with spindleberry bushes in the close thickets? Or used the small passages downwards beside these low-stepping cataracts?

In this green darkness of lichen and fern only half the sun-light penetrates. Westward the earthwork of a fortress, Bury Castle, which belonged to the Earls of Cornwall, commands this entire landscape of steep valleys. In the woods of Golytha must have run the hunted boar for shelter and water, or come King Doniert to speak to a hermit who had his place here, or to be drowned in 875 A.D. He has a commemorative stone not far away, consisting of two granite monoliths, one a shaft of a Celtic Christian Cross.

To go down into the depths of these mossy falls is to come into a landscape of primeval lichened scrub with the sound of water over stones all the ways. Birds fly ahead of you. It is to be in the heart of Cornwall.

In the south of Cornwall is Loe Pool, the large tract of water behind Helston, some two miles long and two or three hundred yards wide. The water of the river Cober, which forms the pool,

---

1 See *Old Cornish Bridges & Streams*, Charles Henderson & Henry Coates, Bradford Barton, Truro 1972

would, in ordinary circumstances, run smoothly down the valley and out to sea as do the waters of all rivers and streams on other beaches. But here the sea has thrown up a bar of sand and shingle at the mouth. This fresh water lagoon mirrors the woods of the Penrose estate towards the town of Helston.

In the old days when, in winter, the valley was flooded, the miller used to cut a channel in the sand to let the water run away. Nowadays a proper pipe has been inserted in the land to let the water off. A subterranean channel cuts the end of the Pool to a point where the water can flow out from the face of the cliff across the beach.

Wilkie Collins was at Loe Pool in 1850, before the railways were built in Cornwall. It was not difficult, then, to find unknown places, or spots on the cliffs where the chough still bred prolifically. He describes what he saw.

> The banks of Loo [sic] Pool stretch to either side for the length of two miles; the lake, which in summer occupies little more than half the space that it covers in winter, is formed by the flow of two or three streams. You first reach it from Helston, after a walk of half a mile; and then you see before you, on either hand, long ranges of hills rising gently from the water's edge, covered with clustering trees, or occupied by wide cornfields and sloping tracts of common land. So far the scenery round Loo Pool resembles the scenery around other lakes; but as you proceed the view changes in the most striking and extraordinary manner. Walking on along the winding banks of the Pool, you taste the water and find it soft and fresh, you see ducks swimming about in it from neighbouring farmhouses, you watch the rising of fine trout for which it is celebrated — every object tends to convince you that you are wandering by the shores of an inland lake — when suddenly at a turn in the hill slope you are startled by the shrill cry of the gull, and the fierce roar of breakers thunders on your ear — you look over the light grey waters of the lake, and behold, stretching immediately above and beyond them, the expanse of the deep blue ocean, from which they are only separated by a strip of smooth sand.

He goes on to relate the legend attached to Loe Pool which is supposed to explain the forming of the bar.

> It is said that the terrible Cornish giant, or ogre, Tregeagle, was trudging homewards one day, carrying a huge sack of sand on his back which — being a giant of neat and orderly habits — he designed should

serve him for sprinkling his parlour floor. As he was passing along the top of the hills which now overlook Loo Pool, he heard a sound of scampering feet behind him; and, turning round, saw he was hotly pursued by no less a person than the devil himself. Big as he was Tregeagle lost heart and ignominiously took to his heels; but the devil ran nimbly, ran steadily, without losing breath — ran, in short, like the *devil*. Tregeagle was fat, short-winded, had a load on his back, and lost ground at every step. At last, just as he reached the seaward extremity of the hills, he determined in despair to lighten himself of his burden, and thus to seize the only chance of escaping his enemy by superior fleetness of foot. Accordingly he opened his huge sack in a great hurry, shook out all his sand over the precipice, between the sea and the river which ran into it, and so formed in a moment the Bar of Loo Pool.

If King Arthur had never lived he would have had to be invented, as Voltaire said of God. And Loe Pool, in certain lights, is exactly right for the other legend, the first appearance of Excalibur, just as Dozmary Pool is for its final disappearance. To reduce Arthur to a general, at the end of the fifth century, of royal armies fighting in South Britain, is to take away not only a large part of Cornwall but to destroy Tennyson, Matthew Arnold and many other poets who have written his romance.

> There likewise I beheld Excalibur
> Before him at his crowning borne, the sword
> That rose from out the bosom of the lake,
> And Arthur row'd across and took it — rich
> With jewels, elfin Urim, on the hilt,
> Bewildering heart and eye — the blade so bright
> That men are blinded by it — on one side
> Graven in the oldest tongue of all this world,
> 'Take me', but turn the blade and ye shall see,
> And written in the speech ye speak yourself,
> 'Cast me away!' And sad was Arthur's face
> Taking it, but old Merlin counsell'd him,
> 'Take thou and strike! The time to cast away
> Is yet far off.' So this great brand the King
> Took, and by this will beat his foemen down.

Romance indeed! But part also of the grain of Cornwall, as are some of the greatest English inventors. Indeed, the giants of invention were possibly the last Romantics, following the unknown men who discovered the wheel, or Archimedes (so the story goes)

The wreck of the *Hemsley II*, off the North Cornwall coast

(Richard Hawken)

The weir over the River Camel, at Dunmere

(Ray Bishop)

with his cry of 'Eureka', as he sprang from his bath and rushed madly, naked, through the streets of Syracuse, on discovering one of the fundamental laws of hydrostatics.

The great inventors of the 18th and 19th centuries were men who confronted massive engines, the power of steam, the elements. They were men of sweat. Later inventors might be called the Sophisticates. Some of the inventors who flourished during the Industrial Revolution, a period stretching roughly from 1750 to 1900, made their fortunes; others died penniless. Nevertheless, all the world over men were being freed from the shackles of medievalism by these men of muscle and brain, by Watt, by Davy and by Henry Trengrouse. Westward the land was very bright indeed.

The figure of Henry Trengrouse haunts Loe Pool. He was a cabinet maker of Helston. He still stands watching the wreck of H.M. Frigate *Anson* on Loe Bar, in 1867, with the loss of one hundred lives. His shade is, in a sense, the epitome of these Romantics. For he used his own small fortune of £3,500, his time, his comfort and his health in inventing the life-line which, later, in the shape of the breeches-buoy, was the means of saving ten thousand lives between 1870 and 1920.

Wrecks were nothing new in Cornwall, of course. What was new was that the right man was in the right place at the right time. This is the basic principle of all successful inventions and discoveries. As Henry watched the drowning sailors struggling vainly for shore (so near) and being dashed to pieces; as later he watched their bodies being shovelled into a common grave on the cliffs above, with no proper burial service read over them (the usual practise in those days), he remembered the rockets which were fired when the King's Birthday was celebrated on the green at Helston.

Why not attach a rope to such a rocket and have it fired from the doomed ship to helpers on shore? The idea was brilliant and revolutionary. Many dead men would have been saved if it had been adopted at once. But the Board of Trade, to whom Henry sent his idea, hummed and ha-ed for many years before it actually ordered twenty sets of the life-preserving rocket. The Board paid Henry fifty pounds, the calculated amount of the profit he would have made on the order. In fact, all he ever received in compensation was this small sum from the Government; the large silver medal of the Royal Society of Arts and thirty guineas — all of which money he spent on further investigations of his idea — and a diamond ring from Emperor Alexander I of Russia. The Emperor tried to persuade Henry to go to Moscow where he would, he said, be properly appreciated. But Trengrouse was a Cornishman and a patriot before anything else. 'My country first,' he cried, and died penniless.

When one comes to consider inventions and inventors what an enormous effect Cornwall has had upon both. Even men like James Watt who was not born in Cornwall. He invented the steam engine at the Boulton works in Birmingham, but it was first put into operation in Cornwall. Watt was the gentlest of all inventors and Cornwall, it turned out, was too tough for him.

'Of all things in life,' he wrote, in one of his fits of depression, in April 1769, 'there is nothing more foolish than inventing.' When he was a boy Watt was dogged by migraine. Like so many future inventors he was reported to be 'dull and inept' at his first school. Yet, in his spare time, spent in the workshops of his father, a carpenter and shipwright, he was very bright indeed, making models of such things as cranes and barrel-organs. His father was chief magistrate of Greenock and, in the fear and excitement of the '45 rising was suspected of hiding Prince Charles. His house was searched from top to bottom without success.

James was put to the trade of mathematical instrument maker. Within a short time he left Greenock to work in Glasgow with the master instrument-maker, Mr Morgan, to whom he paid twenty pounds and gave his work free. But shortage of food and long working hours, only increased Watt's headaches, toothaches and back aches. To add to his miseries his mother, whom he adored, died before his training was over. However, things changed a little for the better when, in 1764, he married his cousin, Margaret, who 'drew out all his gentle virtues, his native benevolence and warm affections.'

The great day arrived (the right man in the right place at the right time), the turning point of his life. He was, then, running his own business in a small and unprofitable way, making quadrants and organs, violins, flutes and guitars, when he was asked by the College of Glasgow to repair a small working model of an 'atmospheric-steam' engine which had been made by the famous engineer, Newcommon. Nobody else wanted the job. Newcommon, as it happened, was a West countryman, born at Dartmouth.

Watt solved the problem of its break-down at once; the model was repaired. But it was one thing to understand the 'theory' of the best use of steam, quite another to 'invent' a way of putting it into practice. In fact it took him two years before he hit on the solution. Then, one Sunday afternoon in April 1765, when out for a walk, the answer came. He had made the greatest discovery in the history of steam power. In his own words, 'It occurred to me that if a communication were opened between a cylinder containing steam and another vessel which was exhausted of air and other fluids, the steam, as an elastic fluid, would immediately rush into the empty vessel, and continue to do so until it had established an equilibrium; and that if that vessel were kept very cool by an injection or otherwise, more steam would continue to enter until the whole was condensed.'

But though Watt knew that he had solved the problem he had no money to exploit his invention. To support his family he gave up his small business and became a land surveyor (about which he knew less than nothing) in various parts of Scotland. While working as a surveyor he was sent to the House of Commons to discuss the Bill for the Forth/Clyde canal and reported back, 'I never saw so many wrong-headed people on all sides gathered together. I believe the Devil has possession of them.'

Watt was a shy man who hated taking risks. His luck, however, changed again when, on his way back from London, he met Matthew Boulton, the Birmingham industrialist, who was cheerfully prepared to take risks on his behalf. He moved, on the death of his wife, to Birmingham, in May 1774. It was eleven years since he had had his idea for a steam engine; now he could develop it with success in Boulton's works.

The first orders came from the tin mines in Cornwall. Watt, who came down to supervise the installation, neither understood nor got on with the fierce, sometimes brutal 'mine captains.' To them he was a foreigner. He was so unhappy that he begged in one of his letters for 'Peace of mind and delivery from Cornwall.' This delivery was soon forthcoming with the help of another inventor, William Murdock, nicknamed 'old Iron Skull', whose mighty fists soon put the captains in their place.

In 1800 both Watt and Boulton decided to give up their successful partnership and hand over the business to their sons. James retired, after remarriage, to his workshop at his home on Handsworth Common and devoted himself to other ideas. As he grew old and frail he needed a lot of rest. The difficulty was to get him to go to bed. A friend has left a picture of his wife's stratagem to force Watt to retire. 'At a certain fixed hour the door of the dining-room opened; an old servant appeared and, altogether disregarding the great presence in which he stood, with a few active evolutions swept out at once the fire, the lights — and his master'.

James Watt died on 19th August 1819. He left a fortune of £60,000. But he had not always been engaged with 'monster' engines in Cornish mines. He made the first copying machine, the Bi-grapher. He invented a machine for drying lines of muslin and an instrument for determining the specific gravity of liquids. He began to invent an arithmetical calculating machine which was never completed.

William Murdock, who had come to Watt's help with the Cornish captains, was another of the great inventors of the age. It was, in fact, a simple age and they were simple men. Yet they bestrode their world. Murdock, as we have seen, solved all his problems in his own way, either by his mind or his fists.

On one occasion some Cornish mine captains came to his workshop in Camborne purposely to run down him and his machines. He answered by challenging the beefiest of them to a boxing match and knocked him out. They agreed he was right.

How beguiling is the picture of these giants of invention (Trevithick, of Camborne, a pioneer of steam locomotion, was another) wrestling with their problems in huge, grim workshops. And then going home and building toy models of steam engines (as

Trevithick did) which amazed everybody by carrying small household objects about the room. How fundamental to this simple age the picture of Murdock's mighty steam carriage on its first road test! Murdock lit the flame under the boiler and the whole contraption — for it was no more in those early days — dashed off ahead of the inventor who was unable to control it. He heard cries for help and running up found the vicar of the parish paralysed with fear. He had mistaken the monster tearing towards him, hissing and belching steam, for the Evil One who had come to fetch him to Hell.

The man who finally put it all together, the locomotive and the lines to run it on, in short the railway, was, of course, George Stephenson, renowned in his youth for feats of great physical strength and as a wrestler, which would surely have endeared him to Cornishmen.

Stephenson worked at a number of occupations before he was 19, when he first wrote his own name at evening school, the fees of which were paid for him by his work as a plough-boy and a cow-man, coal-sorter and engine man. His chance came (like Watt's) at Kinnington Colliery, near Newcastle, where he was employed. A new pump-engine had failed. No one wanted to have anything to do with it. Four days after he was given permission to try his hand at the hopeless task, the engine was in running order again. It is obvious that Stephenson had not been wasting his time at night school.

The idea of a locomotive connects him with Watt, of course, and later with Brunel who joined Cornwall to the rest of England by his famous bridge over the river Tamar. Stephenson began to work on his idea for a locomotive in 1812. Twelve years were to elapse before he could try his engine, the *Active*, on the short line between Stockton and Darlington then, by Act of Parliament, under construction. This steam locomotive drew six wagons of coal, a passenger coach full of directors and their friends and twenty one wagons of ordinary passengers, 450 of them. It took sixty five minutes to cover ten miles. On the return journey the coal wagons were replaced by more passenger coaches, on one of which an orchestra was playing!

It was only the beginning. To get a railway built at all a Bill had to pass Parliament. There had been opposition by land-owners to the Stockton and Darlington Bill, now, in the House, Mr (afterwards Baron) Alderson declared it to be 'the most absurd scheme that ever entered into the head of a man', and Sir Isaac Coffin, in reply to William Huskisson's Bill of 1826, made himself absurd;

> What, he asked, I should like to know is to be done with all those who have advanced money in making and repairing turnpike roads? Is this House aware of the smoke and the noise, the hiss and the whirl, which locomotive engines, passing at the rate of 10 or 12 miles an hour, will occasion? Iron will be raised in price 100 per cent or, more probably, exhausted altogether.

Nevertheless, against all non-reformers, Huskisson's Bill was passed. On 8th October, 1829, the *Rocket* won the competition for £500 which was run over twenty-two miles of the Manchester to Liverpool line, near Rainhill. One competitor had the bright idea of concealing a horse in his engine — it was discovered and he was disqualified; three other engines were severely damaged as they got up steam. Only *Rocket* achieved 30 miles an hour without, as it was thought possible 'rendering the passengers insane with speed' or the driver being killed by air pressure. It was ironical (if nothing more) that at the inauguration of the line, a year later, the first railway accident occurred.

It is a pathetic story. The Duke of Wellington, then Prime Minister, was someway up the line sitting in the State coach of the special train which had brought him and other eminent politicians to view the opening of the line. Huskisson, the MP who had championed the Bill, was amongst them. But, till this moment, he and the Duke, who was against reform of any kind whatsoever, were not on speaking terms.

Now Wellington, seeing Huskisson amongst the others who had left their seats and were strolling past the Duke's carriage, called to him, opened the door of his carriage and they shook hands. They were reconciled. It was at this moment that *Rocket* came tearing down the line. The spectators were yelling 'get in, get in' to the party beside the Duke's coach. Some flattened themselves against the side of the coach; Calcraft jumped into one compartment and Prince Esterhazy was hauled into another.

Only poor Huskisson who was suffering, as Crevey wrote later, from a complaint brought on by long confinement in St George's Chapel at the King's funeral' which had the effect of paralysing one leg and thigh, lost his balance and fell. The passing wheels crushed his thigh and, although he was put on the train and taken to Eccles, he died soon after. But nothing could hold back the railways. By 1846 London was linked by rail with many of the principal cities in England.

Stephenson, at sixty, retired to his home, Tapton House, near Chesterfield and became a country gentlemen growing grapes and melons and peaches in his huge glasshouses which he designed himself. On 18th August, 1848, he died, aged 67, leaving a fortune of £140,000. His conclusions on life in general were summed up in his not very original words, 'I've dined with princes and peers and commoners, I've made my dinner off a red herring in the hedge bottom and gone through the meanest drudgery, the conclusion I have arrived at is this — if we were all stripped, there's not much difference between us.'

Besides the steam engine he was also the inventor of another safety lamp which competed with Davy's for a prize and took second place. Of the inventions of his spare time were a mechanical scarecrow and a self-rocking cradle and an alarm clock for waking colliery workmen. Best of all, perhaps, he was one of the first to introduce a scheme for medical and sickness benefit for his employees.

That day in October, 1892, when Stephenson's *Rocket* tore down the line at 30 mph leads inevitably, as I've said, to the figure of Brunel the great engineer. It hovers still over the river Tamar, between Devon and Cornwall, where his railway bridge stands, in full use after one hundred years, beside the new Tamar road bridge. He died soon after helping to erect it. But he also invented the vessel *The Great Eastern*.

Derek Tangye, now living in Cornwall, has a delightful description of his forbears Richard, James, George and Joseph in his book *A Gull On the Roof* (Michael Joseph 1961). Speaking of his great grandfather 'who followed the plough in Quaker dress and broad-brimmed hat' he goes on to explain the triumphs of Richard and his brothers who became engineers. Their success, they used to say, dated from the occasion when Isambard Brunel's huge iron vessel *The Great Eastern* obstinately refused to be launched from the dock at Millwall, in 1858. It was then that the Tangye brothers produced their new invention, the hydraulic jack and, to the excitement of the watching crowd, the vessel slid into the water. 'We launched *The Great Eastern*,' said Richard, 'and *The Great Eastern* launched us.'

Poldhu Cove is a memorial to Marconi who, in 1898, succeeded in establishing wireless communication between England and France. He was reporting the races during the three-day Kingstown (Ireland) Yachting Regatta for the *Dublin Express*. The event came to the Queen's ears and, in the summer of that year, she gave orders that wireless communication be set up between Osborne House and the Prince of Wales who was in the Royal yacht off Cowes with an injured knee.

Marconi invariably erected his own aerials. He was helping to put up the masts at Osborne when the Queen passed by. Marconi raised his hat and said, 'Good morning, your Majesty.' The Queen was affronted at the impertinence of a workman and passed by without any acknowledgement. Marconi, offended at the rebuff, refused to go on with the work. The Queen, informed of the 'workman's' attitude, replied, 'Very well, then, get another electrician.' Someone had to explain to her that Marconi was not just 'another electrician', but the famous inventor. She relented of her rudeness; he was mollified and they lunched together. Later messages, naturally of the utmost importance, were exchanged between her Majesty and her son.

Indeed, Marconi was anything but another electrician. He was born the son of a wealthy father who never quite got the hang of what his son was up to. Marconi's first experiment, in 1894, for example, was to make a bell ring some thirteen feet away from the 'home-made transmitter'. It was, of course, revolutionary, but all his father said was that there were easier ways of ringing a bell.

Marconi, unlike other inventors, was never short of money.

Deciding to come to London, since the Italian government refused to have anything to do with his inventions, he was arrested with his 'apparatus' by the Customs who took him to be an anarchist. Anyone less of an anarchist, this man who later became a figurehead of the Fascists, is hard to imagine. He was, however, released on the advice of Mr Preece, the head of the Post Office, who was so impressed by the apparatus that he ordered Marconi's invention to be tested, first by sending a message between two rooms, then by transmitting a message from the G.P.O. to a building three hundred yards away and, finally, that his experiments be demonstrated to high ranking Army and Navy officers on Salisbury Plain. The trials were a brilliant success.

These crucial tests proved that sound waves actually bent and did not go off into space in a straight line. Marconi increased the range of his wirelessed messages until nothing was left but 'to cross the Atlantic'. He chose a spot on the cliffs at Poldhu Cove, near Mullion, in Cornwall. Here, in October 1900, he set up his elaborate transmitting plant and, a year later, sailed to Newfoundland, ten thousand miles away, where he built a receiving station. The agreed signal was the letter S or three Morse Code dots.

On December 11th, 1901, Marconi took up his position in a disused hospital at St John's, dressed in a belted tweed check coat and knickerbockers. A gale was roaring outside and he received nothing. On the next day the gale was so strong that the aerial kite blew away. Another was erected and, in the afternoon, it came, all the way from Cornwall, the signal he had been listening for.

Further triumphs followed and in 1922 the BBC was founded. Marconi was awarded the Nobel Prize in 1909 and he married his second wife, the beautiful Countess Maria Bazzi-Scali. *The Times* wrote of him on his death, in Rome, in 1937.

> When the early twentieth century comes to be surveyed by historians yet unborn, Guglielmo Marconi may be regarded as the supremely significant character of our epoch.

From Leonardo da Vinci (who probably knew it all anyway) to the present day men have always asked questions. Anyone can ask questions. The successful inventor is the man who asks the right questions and then proceeds to find the right answers. Allied, however, with the wonders of electronics, miniaturisation, transplant surgery and the like are the more diabolical inventions of the chemists, the nerve gases of Nancekuke, above St Agnes, in north Cornwall, and Porton.

Has man, with the suggestion of dropping a nuclear bomb on the moon, at last learned to invent his total destruction? In the face of such appalling inventions Benjamin Franklin's words take on a new meaning. 'You ask me,' he said, 'What is the use of this discovery? I ask you, What is the use of a new-born child?' Or as the poetess Ethel Jacobson put it:

> To smash the simple atom
> All mankind was intent,
>   Now any day
>   The atom may
> Return the compliment.

6. A 30

This is a winter landscape. No one can any longer come down the A30 — or go up it from the Land's End — in summer who does not have to, because of the crowds of holiday makers, the car jams and the noise.

At its far end, here at the Land's End, is the vision of Lyonesse where the road splitting Cornwall ends or begins. Here is the land of Arthur whose soul is gone into a bird, the chough. And the chough, too, has long since gone from Cornwall, except for the one old fellow who still haunts the cliffs above Newquay. I have seen him peering into Fox Cove and into Pepper Cove. But there is no Guinevere for him any longer.

The summer seas roll about the headlands out to the Longships lighthouse from the Wolf, and the summer people eat their ice-creams in the wooden huts, in the gorse on the cliffs, in their cars; even the sea birds are tamed with scraps. The souvenir-seller has come into his own. Secrets have retreated into the deep meadows and unreachable holes in the cliff-faces, into the far ends of caves and remain with the straying deer out beyond the bogs of the moors. The poetry is now in the wings of the buzzards who wait above the naked tors beyond such villages as Zennor, driven here by the vast quantities of litter which overlay their usual haunts.

In summer the Land's End is no land at all, its incense is the smell of fish and chips, the same smell which hangs over the towns of Mevagissey and Looe and which no sea air can sweep away until autumn when the woods hang red again. In summer the Land's End is nothing. It waits only for winter and the great seas that once, long ago, split the Scillies away from Cornwall and drowned the romantic land of Lyonesse on, so the *Saxon Chronicle* says, the 11th November, 1099. In summer, the smuggler who comes in at Sennen Cove is tamed, too. He becomes a fisherman or a tourist attraction or a man who runs a boat for trippers. There is contempt in his eyes which will not die until winter comes and, once again, he hears 'the calling of the sea'. He, too, waits for winter.

The A30 waits for winter before it goes, alone and cold and hard blue, over the deserted commons of Trevorian and Trevedra where, even still, the gorse is blooming, on its way to the town of Penzance.

It was a winter night that drowned Lyonesse, that epitome of all that Cornwall stands for, the treasure, the fish, the colour and the blue-eyed men and women. Two living creatures escaped the holocaust, riding before the huge mass of water falling upon that city of one hundred and forty churches, Trevelyan of Basil, near Launceston, and his white horse. He must have come down the whole length of that fragmentary road (if road there was) which is now the A30, though it has never been stated why he was in Lyonesse. Maybe, even then, King Arthur attracted admirers and he had come to visit the scene of his last battle, as Tennyson tells us. As fine a place to set the King's death as any;

> So all day the noise of battle roll'd
> Among the mountains by the winter sea;
> Until King Arthur's table, man by man
> Had fallen in Lyonesse, about their Lord
> King Arthur . . .[1]

though in another poem he gives the death scene as Dozmary Pool, on Bodmin Moor. But that is half the value of a legend, you can move it about to suit the people and the place.

I have dreamed of Lyonesse as I have dreamed of that other drowned township, in Suffolk, Dunwich, now under the sea with its fine collection of churches and its bells ringing when the tide is swiftly running. Bells ring here, at Lyonesse, calling the faithful to prayer still, or the modern fishermen to a miraculous catch of mackerel. They ring, too, in Bosham Harbour, in Sussex, where a

1 Morte d'Arthur

Roman Emperor's palace bells toll on winter nights.

Full fathom five at all three places lie the bones of fair women and the knights who rode those square-barrelled horses and wore their favours. Only at Dunwich you can still pick up the bones of the dead who fall to the shore from the last church to crash into the sand and be swallowed up. Only the shag which is a deep diving bird could really tell us if Lyonesse is still beneath the waves, for it might well have been in and out of the corridors of the houses, prying into unopened chests and the lockers of old women.

The poetry of Lyonesse (which is not of this age) has not gone forever. It is blown on the south westerly winds along the Gulf Stream to join the warriors of the Icelandic Sagas or southwards to the Balearics.

The storm which destroyed this fair land (a kind of Utopia and all men's dream) could also bring it to the surface again and join Cornwall to the Scillies.

So the treasures of that land would be laid bare and collected in museums; so would arise the walls of ruined churches and the gold chalices and the bells which fishermen hear mixed in with their catch of silvery herring at dawn; so would arise again the houses with their sea-worn tapestries, the roofs of which are reported also to be seen under a calm sea and a riding moon; so would the A30 be extended from the Land's End westward. Contractors would move in and destroy the romance as they have destroyed it elsewhere, so that only the unknown places are left, the unexciting-seeming places and the winter roads which are largely unused. May the knights and their ladies lie in peace! Cover the King with his shield and let the ocean drift over his deathbed!

For now, in winter, the sea birds are fishing the massive seas which run into the last land and beat upon the outriders of granite at Pordenack Point and you can walk on the cliffs and know what Cornwall is like. And though I have not been so lucky myself I know people who have stood on Cape Cornwall and, looking westward, have seen that city of Lyonesse, or its mirage, rise again from the sea as it was in 1099. They speak of marble bright with light and the peculiar green of the houses. Who can tell the truth of this magic?

So the A30 rolls across the moors of West Penwith, under the ravens and stormy-petrels, beside the gorse, past the village of Sancreed in the centre of its age-old monuments, its Bronze Age caves and forts and Celtic crosses, like an open-air museum or the pieces a modern sculptor has left behind to weather. A landscape of ancient Henry Moore's! The Blind Fiddler stands by the road, south of the church. It is a Bronze Age standing stone. In the centre of Carn Eung, an Iron Age village, the late winter afternoon air is luminous and full of voices. The wind rustles the few dead leaves in the wooded valley in which Sancreed lies, it blows across the reservoir at the junction of the Sancreed road and the A30. And away to the north is Gurnard's Head where the naturalist Hudson spent so much of his time and wrote about in his book *The Land's End*.

> The rocky forelands I haunted were many but the favourite one was Gurnard's Head, situated about midway between St Ives and Land's End. It is the grandest and one of the most marked features of that bold coast. Seen from a distance, the promontory suggests the figure of a Sphinx, the entire body lying out from the cliff, the waves washing over its huge black outstretched paws and beating on its breast, its stupendous deformed face composed of masses of granite looks out on to the Atlantic. I was often there afterwards spending long hours sitting on the rocks of the great head and shoulders, watching the sea and the birds that live in it; and later when April set the tiny bell of the rock pipit tinkling, and the wheatear, hovering over the crags, dropped its brief delicious warble, and when the early delicate flowers touched the rocks and turf with tender, brilliant colours, I was more enamoured than ever of my lonely castle by the sea.

And this 'castle by the sea' is as true today as ever it was in Hudson's time, provided always that you are there not later than Easter. Also the brilliant colour of the wild cliff flowers which blossom like gardens in Preraphaelite pictures before the inrush of holiday-maker's feet.

Now there is a suggestion of sand in the air driven down from the estuary at Hayle. Yet before that is reached the A30 is in Penzance which, even in winter, is a blue and white town, its flags waving in the direction of St Michael's Mount across the causeway. The living centre of this curious end-of-land town with its lovely Georgian terraces like Clarence Place and Clarence Terrace, its almost grotesque Egyptian house, is Morab House and gardens, looking out to the sea.

Occasionally someone goes into the house, under the splendid *Magnolia grandiflora*, which is a library, and potters through the delightful rooms with their collection of *Gentlemen's Magazines* and old newspapers and records set here in this gull-ridden sub-tropical landscape. Until either the train leaves for Paddington or the helicopter flies over on its way to the Scillies. Go down the narrow streets to the rock and sand coast and watch the *Scillonia* round the headland at Penlee Point and come into dock a little way from the collection of vast iron Trinity House buoys. You seem always to be walking, in this town, amongst hydrangeas and fuschias.

Penzance cannot have changed a great deal from the days when Humphry Davy was born here on December 17th, 1778. His father was a wood carver. At school Humphry showed no inclination to study science. What he really loved was the romantic Cornish scenery and poetry. He was forever writing verse. He is one of the 'great' men of Cornwall if not, in his fine temper, his power of invention, his compassion, of the whole world.

It was not until he met Dr Thomas Beddoes who had set up his Medical Pneumatic Institution (for the cure of diseases by the inhalation of gases) at Clifton, that Davy became really interested in science. It was at this Institute that he discovered laughing gas. He was then twenty. However much Sir Humphry Davy, 'abominated gravy, and lived in the odium of having discovered sodium', it is highly fitting that one of the happiest inventors should have discovered laughing gas, nitrous oxide. After a number of experiments he recorded his impressions;

> I existed in a world of new connected and newly modified ideas. I theorized I imagined that I had made discoveries. I exclaimed; 'Nothing exists but thoughts! The Universe is composed of impressions, ideas, pleasure and pain.'

How very like Aldous Huxley's impression after first taking mescaline which he recorded in *The Doors of Perception*!

Davy is of the second generation of Cornish inventors. Unlike those men of sweat, Murdock, Watt, Stephenson mentioned earlier, he no longer deals with vast machinery; he is the sophisticate. From experiment to experiment he progressed until, in October 1807, with the help of powerful electric batteries, he discovered one of the two things for which he is famous, sodium. He succeeded in isolating sodium and potassium. This was, of course, more a discovery than an invention. That day, says his cousin Edmund Davy, so delighted was Humphrey at his discovery, 'that he danced round the laboratory in ecstasy.'

Fire-damp was then the great enemy of coal miners. Its presence, indeed, prevented some deep seams from being worked at all. A naked light in such a place meant instant and disastrous explosions. The whole matter came to a head with the explosion at the Brandling Main Colliery, near Gateshead-on-Tyne, on 25th May, 1812, in which ninety-two men and boys were killed.

It was not until the autumn of 1815, however, that it was decided to ask Davy's help. He went to work and on 1st June, 1816, Mr Buddle, owner of the Wallsend Colliery, was already using Davy's new lamp with success and wrote to tell him so. It is a coincidence that at exactly the same time Stephenson invented his safety lamp. When the two inventions came up for financial assessment it was assumed that an uneducated man like Stephenson could not have produced as good a lamp as Davy, who by contrast was learned. The result was that Davy was awarded £2,000; Stephenson only one hundred guineas.

The satisfied Buddle now suggested to Davy that he take out a patent for his lamp. Davy, however, 'the gentleman of Penzance', with plenty of money, replied:

> My good Friend, I never thought of such a thing; my sole object was to serve the cause of humanity; and if I succeeded I am amply rewarded in the gratifying reflection of having done so. More wealth would not increase either my fame or my happiness. It might undoubtedly enable me to put four horses to my carriage; but what would it avail me to have it said that Sir Humphry drives his carriage and four.

It would be superfluous to comment on such a letter. Better to think of Coleridge's overstatement of Davy's qualities as a poet. 'If he had not been the first chemist, he would have been the first poet of his age.' Nearer the mark was his brother John who said that Humphry 'was the most successful angler I ever saw.' Yet Southey, going to Portugal, left his poem *Thalaba* for Davy to revise and publish. One cannot think of a higher compliment than this, unless it be that of Wordsworth who asked him 'to look over *The Lyrical Ballads* correcting anything which you find amiss in the punctuation, a business of which I am ashamed to say I am no adept.' In 1820 Davy was elected President of the Royal Society. He resigned in 1826 and died at Geneva on 29th May 1829, where he is buried.

In Penzance, too, before the present road was macadamised, lived Charles Valentine Le Grice who was a friend of Charles Lamb, visited Wordsworth and died in Penzance where he was vicar of St Mary's. Le Grice is one of the 'forgotten' characters of the literary scene of those days, a small offshoot of the Romantic Poets.

Le Grice was born, the son of a clergyman, in Bury St Edmunds Suffolk, in 1773. He went to Christ's Hospital school, in London, in 1780 where he knew Lamb, Leigh Hunt and Coleridge. He took his degree at Cambridge, in 1796 and, at once, went down to Penzance, to tutor the son of a wealthy widow, Mrs Nicholls, of Trereife. It must have been something of a shock to his friends who expected him to stay in London and bring out some major work. In fact he rarely left Cornwall and the only work of any substance he did produce was his translation of *Daphnis and Chloe*.

He always refers to Trereife, after his marriage to Mrs Nicholls, as 'his Seat' and not long after his arrival he wrote the poem.

Sonnet on Mount's Bay
Bay of the Mount; whose op'ning coasts are spread
From Mousehole island to the twin-starr'd Lizard,
Whose waves are speckled with the mullet red,
From head to tail all good — except the gizzard;
Whose sons the patriotic flame display,
Which arm'd the breast of Hampdens and of Sidneys,
Whose sloping headlands with potatoes gay
Bloom with the scarlet robe, and silvery kidneys;
O land of yellow ling, and powder'd hake!
O Cornucopia of clouted cream;

> O Nurse of matrons skill'd the pie to bake
> Beneath the furze-filled kettle! Not a ream
> Of folio paper from the stores of Hewett,
> If I could write thy praises,
> Would give me room to do it.

'Two-starr'd Lizard' refers to the two lights formerly at the Lizard lighthouse; 'clouted' is another word for 'clotted', and Hewett was, then, the only bookseller in Penzance. This verse may stand as an example of all those occasional pieces which Charles Valentine Le Grice wrote which have Cornwall as their setting and which he had printed off to give away to friends. He died on 24th December, 1858 and is buried in Madron Churchyard next to his 'enemy', in print and theology, Sir Rose Price.

Godolphin Hall lies to the south-east of the A30. One of the sad things about it is that Margaret Blagge, who married Sidney Godolphin, never saw it in the flesh. She came here, it is true, in 1678, but only in her coffin. That must have been a tremendous journey, in September, from London to Cornwall, the last part of it being along the road which is now the A30, if road as we know it existed in those days?

Margaret's body might have been taken round by sea. It was the usual custom. Indeed, she, herself, before she died, suggested this as the most economical way. It was decided, however, to come by road, a very much more expensive matter. The costs of her funeral were about one thousand pounds which, in those days, was a colossal sum. She was 'carried to Godolphin, in Cornwall, in a hearse with six horses, attended by two coaches of as many, with about thirty of her relations and servants'. Each night the coffin was taken into a convenient house and surrounded by tapers, the cortege had to be fed and all the funeral formalities attended to. In fact, although she was not buried each night she must have had something like thirty 'funerals' on the way down. It was almost a Royal Progression with the nightly prayers and obsequies! The last thing poor Margaret, who hated all formality, would have wanted.

Today great woods surround the house to which she was finally brought. It is a building, long, two-storeyed, mostly of the seventeenth century. How Margaret, who hated London and the Court where she spent most of her time, would have loved the granite north front, the old stone walls with pillars forming a loggia, the box-edged walks, the gardens. At least she was finally buried in the fifteenth century church at St Breage nearby, with the rare wall painting looking down upon her.

The diarist John Evelyn wrote her life. He called her a Saint which, no doubt, in the perfumed atmosphere of the Court, she was. Evelyn was the only one in the secret of Margaret's marriage to Sidney, in May 1675, at the Temple Church in London. But Sidney was an important diplomat and so often out of the country on the King's business that Margaret had little more to do than to 'walk in the Fields or Gardens to contemplate the works of Creation.' Until, on 23rd September, 1678, she gave birth to a son, Francis. Six days later she developed 'a Feavour, with lightness in the Head.' No amount of 'the *Cupping* nore the *Pidgeons*' could help her and she died. In John Evelyn's Diary he recounts how he was present when Sidney Godolphin (he received an earldom in 1706), hurriedly summoned back from Europe, arrived and was 'struck with unspeakable afflictions and fell down as dead.'

The A30 crosses the river Hayle with the railway beside it. You would have to leave the main road at the town of Hayle to come down to Godolphin, but it is worth it. At Hayle itself the sands or towans are particularly eerie at dusk when the road is sometimes covered with blown sand and slippery.

These towans stretch a long way from St Ives right round to Godrevy Point and the lighthouse.

The history of the Hayle estuary goes back into dim time. In far off days the river Hayle reached almost to Mount's Bay, and was a natural harbour and trading centre for merchants who built trackways along the river valley. Here they bartered the Cornish tin to other merchants who came over from Ireland or up the Channel. Today the estuary is silting up, but if you stand on the sand dunes, at dusk, you can still see the shapes of small men in small boats. Who they are no one can tell, except that this is Cornwall and visions, like the vision of Lyonesse, is no uncommon event. In summer no one would take the least notice of such visions. Indeed, they could not be visions at all — but holiday-makers. But, in winter, from that small bridge over the Red river inland from Godrevy, in the acres of blown sand, who can say who these figures are?

Even the blood-red river is a portent for all its colour is due to the residue of tin still staining the surface and washing the banks from the mines close to its source. Who shall say whether these 'ghosts' of the sands have not risen up from other ruins now buried, such as the Oratory of St Gothian, who gave his name to Gwithian parish, where is a little granite church amongst the windswept trees? Once past it and the collection of 'modern' bungalows, you are into the deserted towans. Across the Red river are tall, lonely cliffs, one hundred feet high, coming down all the way from Portreath, past Samphire Island and the Crane Islands which add to the remoteness of the shore below.

The lanes inland run into the woods about Tehidy House which is now a sanatorium. The best part — it escaped the fire of 1919 which destroyed the old house — is the eighteenth century stable block which visitors to the hospital rarely see. It is in granite with cupola and corner turrets still just surviving. The house is reached through the woods which, in the evening, retains the impression of the times when the Bassett family lived here. One of these Bassetts became Lord de Dunstanville whose monument at Carn Brea, built in 1836, overlooks the A30 as you come back to it at Camborne and the rush of 'industrial' Cornwall. This Francis Bassett, who died in 1835, the last peer, was a patron of the arts and of science. He befriended Opie, the Cornish painter, who was one of his coffin bearers at St Paul's Cathedral where he is buried. The column, so dominating the area, and with splendid views over West Cornwall, stands on the 740 foot high Carn Brea. Near it is a kind of Gothick Folly of a hill fort.

What was the 'old' road, even before a road was, ran through Redruth and Camborne. Now the A30 passes through this mining area, by-passing the town of Redruth. From Carn Brea it is possible to look down into Gwennap Pit, a place to be seen in winter or early spring when it is nearly always deserted. It is now nothing like it was when Wesley paid his first visit in September 1762. Then it was no more than an 'irregular 'sink', a mine subsidence, with old surface mine-workings about it. In old engravings it looks like the mouth of Hell. Perhaps this is fitting since Hell was so often the subject of the preachers who attracted crowds to the Pit. In those days religion was black and white. The established church had sunk so low that is needed a man like John Wesley to bring the heart back into the people. Even they rejected him at first. The history of Wesley, in Cornwall, is the history of the softening of a rude people who, once they saw that someone cared for them and their immortal souls, warmed to him. No wonder that Gwennap Pit is still a holy place!

Its great virtue, in the early days, was that it was admirably sheltered. It was remodelled in 1806, to make a circular pit some 120 feet across at the top; thirteen terraces were cut and levelled and turfed. It is impossible to understand Cornwall and the Cornish without understanding Gwennap Pit. For the hardness of it as it was originally is the basic hardness of the Cornish who, at the time, lived mostly out of doors unless they were employed in the mines underground. So that there is a definite attachment between those men and women and the granite cliffs, in that they bore hardship manfully; a certain relationship between their souls and the birds flying overhead. It is the hard poetic reality of the Cornish soul which has never been broken. Whatever one thinks of later manifestations of non-conformity (and in the 1920's it became very nasty, destroying Anglo-Catholic churches and turning out of their vicarages parsons who disagreed with it) it is the voices which issued from Gwennap Pit, at the end of the eighteenth century, which are authentic.

Even if the accent was wholly on penitence, even if this penitence bears some relationship to the great white hills of china clay refuse (the penitent's white sheet) today, the accent is, for its time, deeply authentic. In no other way could the worship of God have continued; in no other way could the souls of the impoverished and often brutalised miners have been 'saved'. It was no mean thing to know that, even if you were starving here, after death, which did not delay coming often and swiftly, there was a Heaven where poverty did not hold sway. It is useless to accuse Wesley and the others of bribing children with toys; they were, these people, children and little else. For all their brutal ways they were innocent. The concept of Heaven after life may be poetic; it saved a great many people.

In the days when Wesley came into Cornwall Gwennap, the parish, was one of the most highly populated areas in the country, due to the prosperity of the mines. The bleakness of the Pit is still hard and uncompromising. Today, with the abandoned Cathedral Mine close by, it still has an air of prayer and strength. From this spot, one feels, it was possible (and perhaps still is) to take Heaven by storm.

The A30 goes off at Chacewater towards Bodmin, while the A390 goes on to Truro towards that other holy place, the Cathedral which, unlike Gwennap Pit which goes down into the earth, rises its spires high into the clouds. In a sense one is coming out now along the roads of mining Cornwall into diocesan Cornwall. Yet the road is still through small villages with a sea wind blowing in from Perran Sands. In these sand-dunes is a concrete building which houses as holy a place as Gwennap Pit or the Cathedral. It is the dry walls of St Perran's church and a stone altar which were buried by sand for three hundred years and only revealed, in 1800, when the mountains of sand shifted.

Perranporth is one of the loveliest bays in Cornwall, providing, once again, you are here in winter when enormous seas build up the entire length of the sand, coming in like moving fortresses upon the distressing holiday town in front. Here, above all, one can stand and be mesmerised by this vast extent of water which is held back — by what? One wonders why it does not crash in and devour the town, so that the gentle stream flowing off the land across the bay, to be absorbed into the sea, seems only the trickle of tap water compared. Here, the full length of the sand, groups of black-headed gulls stand amongst herring gulls; the cormorant dives into the winter sea and the rubbish of summer is drawn out and split into fragments. Shells are banging together and being reduced to powder and the shape of the sands altered immeasureably. The rollers ride in unceasingly.

The road runs into and out of the village of Zelah which now-a-days no one notices, they are so quickly through it. In the old days coaches would have stopped at the 'Hawkins Arms', to put down passengers who wanted to get to St Agnes. The coach brought letters from Wordsworth and Leigh Hunt, in 1842, to Valentine Le Grice, the vicar of Penzance. The miners from the Blue Hills mines, at St Agnes, with their wives and daughters, the 'Bal maidens', as they were called, came to watch the night coach arrive and depart for there was nothing else to do, though they were mostly too poor to travel on it themselves except in extreme emergencies. These women the 'Bal Maidens' wore a wonderful white headdress of cotton which made them look like abbesses. They worked on the surface of the mine, breaking the ore which had, as they said, 'been sent to grass'.

Zelah is not the most beautiful village in Cornwall. Yet it has its decaying beauties. There is a haunting here in the Bible Christian chapel built about 1800 and closed for worship in 1931. Its fine windows look directly on to the A30 and the traffic whizzing past. It is now used as a hay and straw storage depot. Behind this chapel are the great 'mundick' burrows on which the fortunes of the village were, it was hoped, to be founded. Alas, this red sand when used for building ate into the other building materials wood, brick or stone, and when applied to the land as fertilizer, it killed the crops because it contains a high percentage of arsenic.

St Allen, a mile off the A30, is the mother church of Zelah. It, too, has pathetic memorials to young dead miners. Thomas, son of Thomas and Mary Bishop, was drowned in the Easter Wheel Rose Mine, on 9th June, 1846. He was twenty years old. William Henry, son of James and Mary Lampshire, also drowned at the same mine, in the same year, aged eighteen. Another Bishop, Simon, aged forty two, was killed in the East Chiverton Mine just up the road on 30th May, 1873. These names make a tragic poem. A blackbird was sitting on the headstone of William Henry, and its nest was in the hawthorn by the vicarage gate.

These boys, for they were little more, waiting for the water to rise in their deep tombs, are portents of greater mining tragedies and have nothing to do with the appalling vulgarity of the A30 at this point. For if you go north-east from Zelah you come to Mitchell and then to Fraddon which is infested with petrol stations and the roar of heavy traffic. The fine Methodist Chapel, in the Georgian tradition, at Summercourt, alone breaks this vulgarity.

Yet above Mitchell, at Carland Cross, is a wonderful minescape of white clay hills which, at sunset, are red-tipped and like a Chinese painting. And so to Roche with its hermit's rock and to Goss Moor. Roche Rock is an outcrop of the St Austell moors. The hermit who lived here had a fine view, when he said his prayers in the fifteenth century granite chapel, of what is now the china clay country towards the ancient hill fort of Castle-an-Dinas and the dusty villages of Bugle and St Dennis.

The A30 roars past the Victoria Inn at Roche to Lanivet and Bodmin and so out across Bodmin Moor. It is now that the road opens up a beautiful landscape rolling towards the distant blue hills of Dartmoor.

7. Bodmin Moor

You will not like this shorn place unless your mind is attuned to the brilliance of loneliness and the hardness of nature. There is nothing of softness here unless it be the bogs and marshes all over the moor. A place, in its depths, inhabited only by cattle and horses, by wild bees in disused quarries, and the mounting skylark. A place lit by the light of wide skies and the colours of yellow lichen, milkwort, biting-stone-crop and the green of open space. A forgotten place of ruined cottages on the edge of civilization, crossed by horse riders, and a single jet plane overhead. A place of profound secrets and of revitalizing myth.

We have forgotten the importance of myth. We need such a place as Bodmin Moor to reveal ourselves to ourselves. Yet it will not receive you in a single visit. You need humility and courage to face this truth. You are broken down before it. And then, surviving, you are built up again under the fierce healing power of granite. Here is the last silence of unvisited pools and the haunts of neolithic civilization, when man had not lost touch with nature and spoke the language of cattle and grasses. And came to the green sedges and grey cromlechs to die and be buried in the nature he understood.

Wide over all is the expanded sky about the church towers on the moor's edge and the clapper bridges, like those at Bradford, where, at mid-day, the bulls come down to drink and to shake off the flies. They stand knee-deep in the cool waters of the De Lank river below the waterworks and seem to be listening to the chittering of a wren in the hedge opposite. All summer they wait for the moor farmer, on his pony, to round them up for breeding or for slaughter. The lush watermeadows are polished with buttercup, the may scent is heady over the walls of fallen farm buildings which were flourishing sixty years ago, when sides of moor bacon blackened in the smoke from peat fires.

Now the skies of the moor are the monopoly of God in summer or the wrath of His displeasure in winter, under snow, when the moor is full of tiny explosions of grasses, brittle and snapping under the weight of thawing frost. Grasses burnt by a one-eyed sun in the long days of August; the ash of grass in the sweeping salt gales of winter, when the lambs come and the colts hug the sides of their dams.

In this area of thin earth over granite are the faggots of history before history, amid the rough envelopes of moorland parishes. Fields stolen from rocks and rock-burdened still, full of the last remnants of copper and tin mines, the chimneys of their ruined engine houses upthrust against the modern television tower at Caradon Hill. Such ruins are the pathetic reminders of an early industrial age.

You walk on the diagram of a railway line from the pub at St Cleer to the immense mouthful of the Cheesewring quarries. This is a granite landscape, and the traces of the railway (there are no lines now) are those of the Cheesewring line, running down from the disused quarry to Caradon and Liskeard. It was opened in November, 1844, and, two years later, it was extended into the moor to serve the quarries, and the Kilmar granite quarries beyond. It was a gravity line, standard gauge, the trucks, full of iron ore, being returned when empty by horses. Before 1860, when passenger coaches were attached to the line, people could always get a seat in the 'mineral' waggons, by a free pass, if they paid for a parcel. Many of the inhabitants of the now deserted little hamlets must have so travelled to their shopping in Liskeard. The railway was abandoned on 31st December, 1916. The great days of the mines and quarries had passed. We are left with this trace of a railway line in the landscape dominated by the Cheesewring, forever toppling and never falling, the Turk's stone-cap pointing to the interior.

The setting out into the moor from the Cheesewring itself is like advancing into a sea of grass and deepest stones with the height of Brown Willy beckoning you on into the wilderness, to the long shales of its lower slopes. Behind you are the Hurlers on their green lawn, those upright stones which are supposed to be Sunday dancers, or players of the game of hurling, ossified for their evil ways. Whatever the mystery of them, they stand now immobile, decade after decade, watching posts for the stonechat and crow, as ungiving of their secrets as the great burial chamber, the Quoit at Trevethy, a little way off, of the Minions and the Celtic cross on the avenue of roads into the moor.

Immediately before you is a ruined farmhouse in the waste of stone and stone hedges, being sucked back into the moor by time. In the calm heat of a summer's day you can hear that 'winged chariot' with its blazing horses, charging from the quarry heights, and hear again the agonised lowing and bellowing of the bull which was once chained in the bull-house beside the farm itself, now given over, in its lower rooms, to fostering cattle against the winter. Amongst the litter on the stone floors are the pages of a copy of *The News of the World* for 1922. The empty oven holds the charred sticks of the fire which baked the last loaf of bread to be eaten here, when those who were leaving forever were packed and ready to go back off the moor and the hardness of their life. Such ruins epitomise the falling-into-nature of the moor. They are the modern scratchings of human beings who have failed, down the centuries, to leave anything but etchings on the moor itself.

From the hot summer stones (what Ice Age deposited them?) the chalk blue butterfly rises, the dragon-fly basks in the arbours of its greenness, the bracken seen through its diaphanous wings. A slow worm wriggles away between the dry stalks of grass hummocks, swimming in grass. There is nothing but silence. In the bird's wing of this blue day, the deep places of the moor are born. They are no different from neolithic times; only we are that.

You follow the river Fowey, here small and rushy, between Smallacombe Downs and Browngelly Downs until you come from the silence to the hiss of the A30, the great moor-crossing road, to Bolventor and Jamaica Inn. And you pass them by to stay beside the little inland lake of Dozmary Pool, where Mesolithic implements and flint flakes are still to be found, where King Arthur gave Sir Bedivere his sword Excalibur to cast away. At the poolside he heard

> the ripple washing on the reeds
> And the wild water lapping on the crag

and finally cast away, after a third time of asking, the magic sword. It was the end.

> Then quickly rose Sir Bedivere, and ran
> And, leaping down the ridges lightly, plunged
> Among the bull-rush beds, and clutch'd the sword
> And strongly wheel'd and threw it. The great brand
> Made flashings in the splendour of the moon
> And flashing round and round, and whirl'd in an arch
> Shot like a streamer of the northern morn,
> Seen where the moving isles of winter shock
> By night, with noises of the Northern Sea.
> So flash'd and fell the brand Excalibur;
> But ere he dipped the surface, rose an arm
> Clothed in white samite, mystic, wonderful,
> And caught him by the hilt, and brandish'd him
> Three times, and drew him under in the mere.[1]

And so, this being done, Arthur was carried, dying, to the barge and the three Queens who awaited him. As the boat disappeared into the mist over Dozmary Pool (or, perhaps, Loe Pool, who can tell?) the great Cornish legend of Arthur was born, the King whose soul passed into the body of a chough. When you stand alone by this evening water you can believe it, forgetting to ask where the barge could be going, since there is only moorland on the far shore. The cattle come in to drink from Deweymeads and Gilhouse, from the neolithic hut circles under Harrowbridge Hill. To the south is the lost hamlet of Temple, overshadowed to the north west by china clay pyramids.

Here, in the 12th century, the Knights Templar held a small area of Bodmin Moor. Here they had a church and a 'commandery'. When the Order was suppressed, in 1314, the Knights Hospitallers came into the property. In 1340, in order to give hospitality to

---

1 'The Passing of Arthur', Tennyson.

passers-by, a preceptor, one brother, and two servants lived here with a chaplain. From about 1744 Temple became famous as a sort of Gretna Green, where all 'sorts of irregularities were carried out with impunity,' Carew, the historian, wrote that 'manny a bad marriage is there yearly slubbered up.' The church was in ruins in the 1800's. It was rebuilt in 1883, but has now been declared 'redundant' and closed.

To be in the hamlet of Temple is like being in the Midlands at the time when the deserted villages were on their last legs. Ash, sycamore, oak and elm hedge-in the falling houses, owls call from the stone roof angles. A few more years and time will have dragged it back to the desolation of the neolithic hut circles about it. Or it will be swallowed up in the industry of Bodmin itself, or sucked down into the nearby bogs of Menridden and Stuffles.

From Sharp Tor farm, near North Hill on the east moor, a track will lead you into the marshy valley of the Witheybrook, a tributary of the river Lynher. This is remote land indeed, crossed by the track of yet another deserted railway line, closed when the mines on Caradon went bankrupt. The line runs into a cutting and stops. Beyond is the heart of the moor and the treacherous bog of Redmire. It was here that Sabine Garing-Gould nearly died;

> All at once, [he says], I sank above my waist and was being sucked further down. I cried to my companion but in the darkness he could not see me, and had he seen me he could not have done anything for me. The water finally reached my armpits. Happily I had a stout bamboo, some six feet long and I placed this athwart the surface and held it with my arms as far expanded as possible. By jerks I gradually succeeded in lifting myself and throwing my body forward, till finally I was able to cast myself full length upon the surface. The suction had been so great as to tear the leather gaiters I wore off my legs, I lay full length gasping for nearly a quarter of an hour before I had breath and strength to advance and then wormed myself along on my breast until I reached dry land.

But now it was winter. As I stood with my back to the old quarry, a mile from Redmire, the horses came. They were a vision in the cold, so unexpected, so masterful, so utterly beautiful. There were six of them, chestnuts and one grey. They were coming up over the line of the disused quarry workings towards a ruined cottage, amongst the massive grey chippings, charging into the cold moorland air, their manes blazing wildly in the weak midday sun. The grasses, under this weird light, had taken on an unearthly greenness.

The horses, in their whirling charge, their bodies leaning half sideways as they cleared the stones, thundered on. Their heads were held high, their exquisitely polished hooves, sure and swift. It appeared, from where I was standing, that they actually came out of the earth; that their bodies were flying through the air. They owned the winter moorland. The cattle, gathered about the cottage below, were aware of their coming and turned to regard them. Banners of grey breath streamed from their straining nostrils and off their shining backs.

They came on, past me, at great speed, straight at the back of the cottage, spun out into two groups as if they were used to the exercise and the route they were taking. It was a ritual charge up from the low levels of the moor to the hill and down to the brook. By their galloping these magnificent wild animals proclaimed their dominance of the other cattle, of the skies, of the whole moorland climate. It was a superb exhibition of their power.

When they reached the buildings of the cottage they tore past them in an agony of beautiful action and strength. Their passing was a stream of chestnut light, a flash of spinning cream manes, each single strand visible, their feet poised like equestrian statues as they breasted the hill above me. Then down again, their heads bowed to the moor, to be lifted in piercing neighs of pure delight in their strength and knowledge. The thunder of their hooves faded, their bodies gone down into the valley, to stand quickly, necks arched, in the winter landscape.

Suddenly the wind changed. There was a warmth in it. The snow would soon melt. Primroses would appear at the base of stone hedges, the snowdrops open fully. A buzzard, its wings curled by the wind at each tip, was hovering over the river below. At my back, some miles away were the granite hills of Rough Tor and Brown Willy. Between the two hills were the ruins of an ancient chapel now beyond the confines of time, not to be reached by a modern mind, touched only by storm and sun and the wall pennywort growing in the crevices of their last stones. But this moment of the charging horses was to be in the heart of the modern moor, with the granite closing in on your body and mind, with the chattering of ancient men about you across the long, deserted, meadows of Twelve Men's Moor. This was to be out of touch of civilization and, perhaps, immortal.

If always Brown Willy and Rough Tor draw you into the moor by their height and remoteness, there are other ways than their lower slopes to enter. St Breward is a village high on the edge of the moor, an outpost of grey Cornish stone cottages, a pub and a church in which is the carved slate, showing a former vicar, in 1607, Lewis Adams, his wife in a high-crowned hat and full-skirted gown, kneeling behind him. 'This worke,' says the inscription, 'was made at the cost of John Adams, his sonne, in 1609.'

These moorland villages have about them a closed-in air, self-sufficient, standing upon the hopes of ancient cultures, steadfast, indestructible. Their lanes are often full of cattle, farms are at their centre and the sheep dog growls in the hot sun, guarding a memory as old as the moor. All Cornish farms are haunted by the past of stone and bear the hieroglyphics of age in cracked granite. If not so old as the neolithic remains everywhere on the moor, these farms seem never to have changed. They are bound into the landscape by the greyness of stone and the surprising colours of roof leeks and stonecrops. They exist in a haze of blue slate and yellow lichen on the roofs which might have been here in Tudor times. The grey, liana-like lichen on the gnarled thorn trees beside the farm is part of a mistletoe past, wind-shorn, cutting the gales in half.

Pack horses crossed the clapper (from Latin *clapperius*, great stone) bridges laden with ribbons and trifles for Launceston Fair or Liskeard market, or Bodmin, their long legs reflected in the water of strong, still streams, peaty and brown, down moorland chines.

From St Breward lead off a number of roads into the moor. Once on the moor itself they peter out into the traces of the old trading tracks which ran northward to the Midlands and north west to Wales. One of these lanes leads to the De Lank Waterworks, discreetly hidden above the small clapper bridge over the river. To the right, also hidden from the bridge, are the quarries at Hante-Gantick, in the rock grandeur of its valley and the Hannon valley where two moorland crags, the Devil's Jump, flank a ravine.

Lease cottage stands on the edge of the moor, raised up from amongst the great stones where sheep shelter in winter, not far from King Arthur's Hall. Anything out-of-the-ordinary in Cornwall is labelled with Arthur's name, from Tintagel itself to any mysterious heap of stones. There is even King Arthur's Bed, a rock basin on Trewortha Tor. But this large open space surrounded by stones (you can see, indeed, that it was once a hall or meeting place, or store) was built by the Beaker folk when they came into Cornwall from Wiltshire. They used it for a storehouse, though some have suggested that it was a reservoir. All Cornwall, from Chysauster, near Penzance, with its clearly defined village, to Bodmin Moor with its stone and hut circles, was populated by these people in about 2,000 B.C. Even then the citadels of Rough Tor and Brown Willy must have seemed impregnable fortresses to them, or god-places, the sun spinning off their summits in summer; the moon, in winter, split by the ragged granite. To such people these mighty hills were their 'history', pin-pointed on the map of their descent.

Above Leaze cottage is a small stone quarry, unused for a hundred years, where pools of greenish water create, in spring, tiny gardens of wild rock plants in full flower. Below this quarry, with its split granite blocks still shaped and left, is a perfect stone circle, halfway to Garrow Tor, which must have been connected with the great store house at King Arthur's Hall. The sun roasts their unreadable signatures. You can stand in the centre of this circle, the long grasses above your ankles, and it is easy to imagine such 'temples' filled. Was the sun both their god and their magic?

One thing is certain, they must have carried water up from the De Lank river, and bought their fish from other Beaker folk who lived beside the sea at such places as Harlyn Bay and, perhaps, came carrying bass and herring, lobster and crab inland to sell. To them, as to us, the leviathans of Bodmin Moor's two tors would seem to be moving under the sun's shadow, and God to speak out of the clouds which rolled inland to enclose their summits.

Rocks at Penally Point, Boscastle

(*Wolf Schroeder*)

The water wheel at Hingham Mill, near Wadebridge

(Ray B

These people would have carried their dead to tumuli in the burial grounds beyond their hearths. What language did they speak to each other? In the silence of present-day moorland you can still catch faint murmurings of their voices from the stones which they raised and the stone fire-places of their almost disintegrated homes, so little has anything changed in the remote wards of Bodmin Moor.

With the De Lank river behind you you can walk to another cottage at Mount Pleasant, rarely used except in summer, with Garrow Tor rising before you, its lonely shepherd's hut a kind of entree to Brown Willy beyond. Garrow is dotted with hut circles about King Arthur's Downs. And so by valley stream feeding the river, by cattle-tongue and the spring flower to another completely deserted cottage now in ruins, and so down the long meadows to the foot of the 'mountain'. From its fairy castles you can see, across the valley where St Petroc is said to have settled, the strange bastions of Rough Tor. It will take you an hour to reach them, with the Stannon stone circle on your left and the silver plate of the new reservoir at Davidstow on your right.

Upon the summit of Rough Tor you seem to be standing at the heart of Cornwall, with the land spread out below you, the sea on both sides of you and Dartmoor in the distance. You are pinpointed on a large scale Ordnance Survey map of landscape, the centre of a topographical puzzle completed and all pieces in place before the world began. To the north west are the tall cliffs of Crackington Haven. There is Beeny Cliff, near Boscastle, where Thomas Hardy courted Emma Gifford, who lived at the rectory of St Juliot, the church which Hardy came, as a young man, to restore. To the south east, across the brown wastes of the moor, are the sun-white clay pits about St Austell and the rivers running creamy with clay effluent right to Carlyon Bay. As the land narrows like a pencil you seem able to see even the Scillies.

There are other ways into the moor, through the doors of deeply tunnelled lanes, down the long strides of Altarnun and the wide woods of North hill, seered by valleys. The church at Altarnun is the glory of Bodmin Moor, the tower tall and pinnacled and built of surface granite from the moor itself. Here, too, is the Georgian

Wesleyan Chapel. Over the door is the most famous effigy of John Wesley, carved by Nevill Burnard, the Cornish sculptor, who became famous and died in poverty. Two stone bridges cross Penpont Water, below the church, and the stream leads backwards, through fields and farms to the slopes of Bray Down and Buttern Hill. Now Brown Willy is to the south, dominating the scenery.

So the moor is bounded and edged and rimmed by the soft villages and meadows, by St Neot with its magnificent glass windows in the church, by Cardinham with the foundations of the motte and bailey of its castle built about 1066 by Richard FitzTurold, the first Lord of Cardinham, by the hamlet of Warleggan, which church is supposed still to be haunted by a former vicar, Frederick William Densham who died in 1953.

It waits to reveal itself and its inner places beyond hawthorn hedges and in the cemented roof-tiles of hedge farms with honey for sale, and the bold horns of bulls who peer at you over the granite escutcheons of the outcrop of moorland, inviting you to enter through the gates or through dolmens and border grass, challenging you to the effort of the moor and the hard-booted walking over the shale to its summits.

We used to come, when we were boys, my brother and I, for holidays to Mr Old's farmhouse on Pentire Point, north of Padstow in the late '20's and early '30's. We came from London and, naturally, we came for the sea, the caves, the loneliness of such places as the beach at The Strangles. I had only to look backwards from the heights of Crackington Haven and there were the wide stretches of Bodmin Moor, dominated by its twin tors. Yet we never went there except that on the way down and back again, we crossed the Moor in the three-seater Citreon car belonging to my elder brother, Jack. I am convinced now that, as we sped along the road from Launceston, we all closed our eyes against the bleakness on either hand.

It was a mistake. We missed what to me is, now, the finest part of Cornwall. Perhaps we were too young, then, to appreciate the experience, physical and spiritual, of the moor places where the birds sing with more ecstasy and the buzzards stand taller to the wind. I was not ready then, as I have been since, to confront the wolf and bear in their stone moorland caves. To have looked at the mask of a fox in Sydney Woods, in Kent, near my home, was enough.

In the early years of the century two of my father's cousins kept a bookshop in Camelford. My great uncle was vicar of the tiny parish of Tresmeer, to the north of the moor, for nine years to 1900 when he died and was buried in the churchyard. In a sense, then the moor is in my bones, for I think my cousins twice removed (if that is what they were?) must always have known the places on the moor like Altarnun, Cardinham and St Breward. Would they not, in high summer days, have walked out of Camelford along the straight road to the bottom of Roughtor and taken their picnics on the slopes and among the hut circles, or even below Charlotte's Monument? It was a great day for walking.

I remember them only as two straight-backed, thin, rather severe ladies concerned more with envelopes and writing paper than with the books they sold, flitting about their dark shop (which is now a Bank) with feather dusters. But they were wearing sensible shoes (it might well have been boots) and I am sure they were walkers at week-ends or on early closing day.

My great-uncle must have driven out into the country, past the ancient Crosses and through deep stone lanes into Launceston to church functions if for nothing else. He was Edward Jones Hardy (therefore on my mother's side) and he was born in September 1835. He married Laetitia Ridler of Portarlington, in 1864. When she died, in 1884, he came, a lonely man, to Tresmeer. He was only forty-nine, and to come to so small a parish at such a young age seems unreasonable. Perhaps he was already ill and had been advised that the clean air of the moors — and not much work — would benefit him. For he died six years later of 'a decline', as one of his parishioners, now living in New Zealand, a very old lady, informed me last year.

I see him as a tall man, like my uncle John, who was also a clergyman, who preferred the 'civilization' of such places as Launceston and Truro to the solitude of the moor, because at one time he lived (and may have been born at) in Falmouth. He built his vicarage at Tresmeer looking out over the mild landscape towards Dartmoor in the distance.

The branch line of the Southern Railway was incorporated in 1864 but not at once completed owing to lack of money. But, no doubt, my great uncle drove his pony and trap to Tresmeer station on 28th July, 1892, when it was finally opened, to go to Plymouth or London via Exeter. I was lucky enough to travel over the same single-track line before it was closed for ever by the Beeching axe. Until we reached Tresmeer we were, the driver and myself, the only people on the train.

Then the two carriages were suddenly filled with Cornish men and women returning to other little stations, and to Wadebridge, from a wedding in Tresmeer village. In their happy laughter (it had obviously been a good reception) I seemed able to re-create my great uncle's figure, who must have celebrated at similar functions in his day. But for their clothes I doubt if the people who attended this 1966 wedding were very different from those he ministered to. Now he lies in a corner of his churchyard, between the shadow of his church tower (which is gradually falling down with damp and rot) and the roof of his vicarage, across the lawn.

The long road from Davidstow drives across the moor towards Launceston through State forests of pines on the left and right. Just before Wilsey Down forest you turn off into the parish of Davidstow itself which is full of stone lanes which are rarely visited by anyone but the local people. The hamlets have lovely names such as Lambrenny, Treglasta, Woolgarden, Trevillian's Gate and Doney's Shop. You turn to come south again over Davidstow Moor between the new Crowdy Marsh Reservoir (a haunt of water birds) into Lowermoor and, beyond, the clay pits at Stannon Downs. It is a picture you can hold in your hands, framed by the small villages and the gracious unbending churches until you come to Bodmin itself.

Bodmin, chief of moor towns, is a dark place, overlaid by pain and sorrow. The gaol stands in a hollow to the north-west and though it is closed, it is a kind of 'fate' over the long town street, the small cottages and the narrow lanes. It possesses a human shame not made any better by turning the gaol into a Night Club, and encouraging people to drink cocktails in the condemned cell. Human misery, even the memory of it, is not washed away in gin like this. So that Bodmin is a town for early morning. Seen, then, from Cardinham Moor, in the rising sun in its valley, it is like a brown jewel. Seen from Cardinham, itself, with its two ancient Celtic Crosses and its blackberry fields, it shines with a veneer of medievalism. Behind Bodmin are the woods of Lanhydrock framing the town.

But now, in autumn, the sun shines upon the altar tomb of Prior Vyvyan, who died in 1533. It is made of dark blue Catacleuse slate, with its vested effigy on top. The sun gleams upon the slate warming it with the last glow of summer. Warming, too, the elvan stone of the small town cottages up Fore Street. Now, before the lorries have begun their parade up the A30, there is nothing in the streets but a cat going from one house to another between the main street and the ring road, stopping a moment to drink from the little well above the car park with its legend Eye Water. Was this some healing well like that of Saint Guron west of the church? High on the far hill is the monument erected to commemorate Sir Walter Raleigh Gilbert, who was born in Bodmin and created a baronet for his services in the British Army in India. The hangman could see the tip of it as he knotted the rope round a victim's neck and laid his drop.

Such absurd memorials, such miseries, are forgotten in the long night of the autumn moor. Already the hollows beneath the stone plinths are beginning to turn purple, the few gorse flowers to swell into yellow globes, dying in the last of the night, as the moon comes riding up over the sea above this vast granite shelf, and whirls skydown between St Agnes Head and into the Edwardian terraces of Bude. It crosses the shadow of night birds. The owl hoots from windshorn branches of a meagre tree, its noise only increasing the silence below the curious stones of the Cheesewring. When the moon rolls down between the moutains (backwards and forwards it seems to go, up one side, down one side, up one side) the granite splits into fragments, borne deep into the chalice of the moor, splintered on horned cattle and lowly weeds, rest-harrow and self-heal and scarlet pimpernel.

It begins to be cold; heat is being withdrawn from the long meadows. Sheep pull their fleeces about them, a slight wind blows into and out of the holes of stones and disturbs the green algae on the secret pools. The night begins a low whistling on Garrow Tor, winding up the spindles of marsh reeds. The great clocks of dandelion seed float outwards from the gardens of Camelford and Launceston, of Wadebridge and Bodmin. The day's last beetle bangs its horned case down the corridor of Shallow Water Common under Hawk's Tor and the mist floats, like a handkerchief, over Dozmary Pool where, they say, the giant Tregeagle is still trying, after centuries of punishment, to bail out the water with a leaky limpet shell. How long, one wonders, will it be before another legend attaches itself to the new reservoir on Crowdy Marsh?

Under the night hours the moor increases, the mountains become taller, more majestic, dangerous, spirit-inhabited. The sound of the sea is clear, running over the sands of The Strangles, and the moorland seems to slip away to meet it as you wait for the sun to rise and the whole land to breathe again in the pink light. Colour is coming back into nature.

8. Temples

Some light still hangs over the temples of the 'Saints' who came into Cornwall from Wales, Ireland and Brittany, even if they themselves go back into the twilight of a legendary past. Some of then, at the end of the fifth century, came over from Ireland on 'boats' as varied as millstones and leaves. Such modes of travel were part of the climate of innocent holiness they shed about them. It would not have done to come by ordinary ship. It was a miracle in itself that they came at all. They needed an extraordinary myth to support them.

Innocence is about them like the beginning of the world. The eyes and minds of ploughmen and cattle-minders regarded them as wonders and saviours. These 'Saints', in their engaging simplicity, were in touch with a God who could not be reached by other means. They lived in a climate of peculiar sanctity now forgotten and overlaid with sophistication. Their staves, sandals, ragged clothes were the toys of an unmethodised divinity. Before the days of copes and mitres their words held all the dogma there was.

They were, of course, the first homeopathic healers, curious in the properties of plants and the virtues of clean water. Their power was concentrated in prayer and contemplation. They were aware of the value of withdrawal from ordinary affairs and people. They created local centres of healing and were as much in touch with animals as with human beings. Indeed, very little but speech separated human beings from animals in those early days. Their case-books dealt mainly with sores and rashes and the lunacy of idiots.

The stories of their travels and miracle-workings were used to hush babies in the rushes of hovels, and to dispel the fears of older children whose companions had been eaten by wolves or carried away into remote, enchanted places in the moorlands. If they existed besides these shrines which are still standing they, too, were children. They are part of a texture of fairy story.

St Austell, for example, was the pupil of St Mewan, who once killed a dragon. When St Austell died, St Mewan was so broken-hearted, that he died within a week. They decided that he should be buried in the same grave as his tutor. When they opened the grave to put St Mewan in, they found that the old man had moved over to make room for his body. St Neot, for all he was the cousin of King Alfred (and therefore hardly needed a mill-stone to get him to land) was only eighteen inches high and lived on the miracle one-fish-a-day from the well in the meadows below the church. St Crantock possessed seven belts of which he was inordinately proud, and St Minver frightened the devil down a hole in the cliffs and put a large stone over him.

So the credulous talked and talked over the fires in their hovels, explaining away the great cliff chasm down which one of them had fallen (driven by the devil, no doubt) and, later, went to bathe their sore eyes in the local saint's well and thought they were cured. And came back to their small fields to plough in the blistering cold winds and to look at the family lunatic (epileptic?) mumbling in the hearth corner. The problem was to get him carried down to St Nonna's well, at Altarnun, and have him bowssened or dipped. The banging of his head against the walls of the well, while he was in a state of holy wetness, was generally regarded as being capable of curing his lunacy. As well as much else, one imagines.

The ricketty and the children with whooping cough came to the wells with their mothers. Those who wanted to ensure that their children were not hanged later in life had them baptised with the water from Venton-Uny well, near Redruth. If you wanted urgently to know how your absent friends were getting on you visited St Gulval's well at Penzance, on a special day in May.

Centuries of superstition (St Samson killed a woman with a curse) rolled down to the present day when these small temples exist beside lanes, deep in woods, or beneath the main road with the traffic roaring over them, mouldering away, or reconstructed and mouldering again, pin-pointed as curiosities, their patron saints laughed at, their homeopathic cures (for they had nothing more than clean water, plants, berries or leaves for their salves and ointments) smothered in the latest miracle pill or abortion clinic. Yet these shrines were the doctor's surgeries of those days. And were much concerned, too, with love and the success of marriage. St Adwen is the patron saint of lovers, when the Easter birds sing and the lanes are bordered with wild garlic.

St Keyne's well, near Liskeard, though concerned with love, had a different virtue in its waters. St Keyne, as befits a woman, was on the side of the bride and kept a watchful eye on what was going on in the church above. Here, by the laneside, the poet Southey must have stood and later wrote:

> If the husband of this gifted well
> Should drink before his wife,
> A happy man henceforth is he
> For he shall be master for life.

So the newly-wed husband would rush from the church, down the hill, to drink from the well before his bride could reach it. But, as Southey goes on, he was not always as clever as he thought:

> I hastened as soon as the wedding was done,
> And left my wife in the porch,
> But i'faith she had been wiser than I,
> For she took a bottle to church.

St Keyne was a princess who lived about 900 A.D. Her well, restored by the Old Cornwall Society, under the guidance of the late Mr Glubb, still stands under the hawthorn trees and the thrush's nests, a monument to unsophistication; a blessing (of a sort) on the wedding bed!

Many of these temples, however, are no longer tourists' attractions. Who, for example, is going to shove their way through the jungle of fields and woods overgrown with bramble, to find St Pyder's well, at Treloy, near St Columb Minor? You need a billhook to follow the tiny stream in the darkness of the June woods, when pheasant call from the other side of the valley, or aircraft roar over from St Mawgan airfield. But the exploration is rewarded by one of the finest wells in Cornwall. Or it must have been after the Old Cornwall Society restored it, in 1953. Now a tree has fallen over its granite roof. The little stone building is covered in vegetation and neglect, its shell-roof cracked with ivy stems. Water still runs through it down to the valley below. You walk on carpets of decayed leaves and weeds to reach it, stung by tall nettles as your feet are caught in hidden roots.

Who could have come here, to what now looks much more like an eighteenth century folly built to worship Pan, than a holy place? It has, more markedly than other wells, a feeling of paganism. And this is not to be wondered at since paganism did not die out immediately on the emergence of Christianity. They existed side by side for a long time. Dark, not light, deeds could have happened here, the palms of pilgrims turning into knives of priests who worshipped only blood.

To stand on the large baptismal stone at the entrance of the well, to go in under the elder branches to the small domed interior festooned in ivy and honeysuckle, is like going into a cave, with the womb of nature here in the heavy canopy of leaves. No one comes here any longer and, in a few years, it will be nothing but a heap of stones. It may be gone before that because the farmer, on whose land the well stands, told me that he was going to have the entire woodland bulldozed and levelled. 'What's it benefit me?' he said, laughing at the absurdity of anyone attaching value to such a spot. Obviously he put his faith in antibiotics!

I have a feeling, however, that levelled and buried and made an open field, this land will still bear a magic, pagan or Christian, for all time, for the sorrow of those who came out from Newquay or down from St Columb and returned cured by the virtue of St Pyder in the fourth century. Man has never been able completely to destroy the power of the supernatural. And at the well at Treloy that power is very manifest, even in its ruinous state.

Some of these so-called 'holy' wells were never more than wishing wells and unconnected with 'Saints'. At Laneast, below a farmhouse in the wet meadows, is a well not unlike Treloy. It was very popular with American airmen in the last war who came, before a mission, and threw in dimes for luck. In this hamlet was born John Couch Adams, the astronomer and discoverer of the planet Neptune. He must often have bathed his face and hands in this clear, fast-running brook, when he was sent out from school to call in his father's cows to milking from the tall valley hills above.

In the old days (perhaps even today?) you could have walked the county over from one well to another, from Lady Nance well in Colan to St Gulval's well at Penzance, calling in at the wind-and-sand-driven well at Constantine Bay, near Padstow, which lies back from the bastion of Trevose head and the sand dunes of the bay. Here a stream takes you over the golf links to the well, past Parsons' hut, which is supposed to be haunted by Parsons himself, a smuggler who died in suspicious circumstances. The wind is driving the sand up from Booby's Bay, over the sandhills of marram grass almost to the village of St Merryn.

No one knows exactly who St Constantine was. One thing is certain, however, he was not the Emperor Constantine, though he may have been the King Constantine who ruled in these parts after Arthur. For many years his well had been marked on Survey maps of the district but all clues as to its real position seem to have been lost. The discovery of the well is an exciting story.

On August 25th, 1911, two local archaeologists, Dr Penrose Williams and Mr Charles Mott, began to excavate at a likely spot. They were lucky and came across the ruins at once. The well, when they actually got to it, proved to be seven feet below the present level of the sand. They were so hampered by surface water, as also from spring water from the well itself, that they had to leave the work.

Nothing further was done, after that first exploration, until 1919, when Dr Williams began draining the fields about the well by cutting new stream beds and making bridges. In all, he spent fifteen years in constructing the lovely bridges over the stream to the sea-cutting in the sandhills.

What might be called the 'Big Dig' came in 1921 when the well was fully exposed as we see it today. It is one of the best preserved wells in Cornwall, dating from the second or third century A.D. The roof and the slate approach were put up by the present owner of the golf links, Mr John Gammon. Doomsday Book mentions the well, where the water is ice cold and where, on the seats at the side, pilgrims sat to bathe their feet or even to spend the night, their eyes blinded by the swirling sand.

Just across from the well, running east and west, is the ruined church of St Constantine. Here, it has been suggested, in this fallen mass of masonry covered with brambles, was a Druid temple, now buried in sand. St Constantine built his church on the top of it. In 1390 it was rebuilt and, once more, fell into ruin. Exactly where the Golf House now stands was once the site of an ancient village which this 1390 church must have served. So that, in this one small area, there must have been a small community worshipping in the church, taking miraculous cures in the holy well and testing their good luck from the water itself before they went fishing in the still dangerous seas to the west.

These beaches, from which they must have launched their cockshells, are reputedly haunted. There was a neolithic settlement on the 'Island', a small piece of land jutting into the sea from Booby's Bay. When, in autumn, the seas along these deserted sands roll majestically into Mother Ivey's Bay, or crash into the bastion of Trevose Head, these places can be frightening. Stories of dark shapes seen near the 'Island'; of huge wheels which come hurtling out of the sandhills, white hot, only to disintegrate in the waves, of the ghosts of drowned sailors, can be believed. The fierce winds build up the monstrous seas which crack like whips against the rocks and throw their spume high over high headlands.

'There are more Saints in Cornwall than in Heaven,' it is often said. Most of them were early Christian missionaries who came into Cornwall in the 5th and 6th centuries A.D. They often took over the existing tribal system and preached from the many pre-Christian crosses still to be seen. Beside these bare emblems their white beards waved in the Cornish winds, their tongues tasted the salt blown inland from the sea and their gnarled hands baptised the hard granite. In their mouths was love, and the food their disciples brought them. Their crosses were both their altars and their restaurants. The fountains gushed permanently over their feet and in and out of their grass fonts.

They built baptisteries over the sacred fountains where the people had worshipped before they came. These springs now became Holy Wells, their waters having mysterious and wonderful powers. St Clether's well is one of the great Cornish wells. It is some way from the church, but the walk to it is a delightful expedition on a summer's evening. The church was originally Norman. The earliest record of it is its consecration, by Bishop Bronescombe of Exeter, on October 23rd, 1239. After the Reformation the church gradually fell into decay until, in 1865, it was entirely rebuilt and most of the Norman features which, today, we should treasure, were 'ironed out.'

The walk to St Clether's well is, in every sense, a pilgrimage to a Holy Place. By the church stile sticks are provided to help pilgrims along the half mile of green valley. Before you as you go over the fields, the roof of the Chapel appears in the distance above the river. All this part of the valley is, in fact, called Chapel Valley Park. How easy it is to imagine St Clether, son of a Welsh chieftain (he is supposed to have landed at Bude) coming over the hill in front of you, sometime towards the end of the 5th century A.D., rejoicing in the sight of the water bubbling from the rock!

And so he built his holy place for healing, this well, and his chapel for prayer and contemplation. The people came to him, with food, to be healed, and he fished in the river Inny. In winter he lay down with the sheep for warmth until he died 'at an advanced age' and was buried somewhere about here. Who can tell where? Here, beside the chapel where he lived with the sound of the river always about him, entangled in his prayers; here, where he healed and taught? Or does one of the rock chambers in the long hillside between the well and the church still hold his remains. Wherever he lies, the stillness at the edge of the moors hangs over him. Even today twenty four ancient crosses point the way, from the heart of Cornwall, to his chapel.

Gradually, with the decrease of belief in miracle-workers and the good effect of this holy water, the well fell into ruin. It was not until

1895 that the building was restored by the Reverend Sabine Baring-Gould, who did so much for Cornwall. Only the floor plan remained when he arrived, the foundations going back more than a thousand years. It was necessary to rebuild the upper parts of the walls and re-roof the building which was dedicated in 1900. Services are held here occasionally in summer and, it is said that Baring-Gould gave all the royalties on his hymn 'Onward, Christian Soldiers' to pay for the restoration.

Inside the chapel the water, from the well in the rocks outside, passes under the altar and then into a recess in the south wall also outside. There is a shelf above this second well where, it is supposed, pilgrims left their offerings. Below this pre-Reformation altar is another recess which may well have held relics of the Saint. The water running by was probably doubly sanctified by such relics.

Here St Clether lived, bowling his halo up the valley in the pure joy of an innocent life, and loving the animals with whose warmth he shared the winter's nights. Or singing as he washed himself in the river, while God came down upon his naked limbs from the clouds. Caught, as he must have been, in a transcendent joy, his body responded in curious gymnastics of pure health.

As an old man God would have spoken to him daily, but with less exuberance, for the leaves were falling by the well and food was scarcer. So he was gnarled like the winter elms and thorns. He grew a long beard like the lichen from a branch and fell, at last, into God's hands outstretched over the moorland, hands of which he must have been aware for a long time.

When they came to bury him they hung his halo, beside his well, high on a sloe bush. Maybe it is still there today!

9. A Taste for Ruins

Sacheverell Sitwell, speaking of ruined cathedrals and abbeys throughout England, says:

> The ruins are not even the corpses; they are the skeletons, and what little have these to do with the soul and mind inhabiting them when they were alive . . ? There is not the silhouette or shadow of a monk or nun in all the ruins. The stones were there, and the great cathedrals, but no sight of the monks and nuns.[1]

The same could be said of castle ruins and the remains of great houses. Yet, in imagination, it is possible, in the cleaned-up shell of Restormel Castle, near Lostwithiel, for example, to see the Black Prince, the first Duke of Cornwall, riding over Poston bridge that August day, in 1345, to come to his castle and Cornish home, even if today the shell no longer resembles anything but a Ministry of Works tourist attraction.

In spring, and again in autumn, when the tourist is gone and you can have these relics to yourself, it is possible to people the sheer-cut battlemented walls with soldiers; the chapel tower on the east with priests and acolytes; the rooms inside the circular walls with those whose business it was to run the castle, to attend the Dukes who had a park here until it was disparked by Henry VIII and they all, townsmen and Dukes, moved down the hill into the present Lostwithiel.

What would be the point, for example, of the ruined piers which once supported Brunel's wooden viaduct, seen beyond the modern viaduct over the Glynn valley, if one could not imagine Brunel

---

1 Sacheverell Sitwell. Monks, Nuns and Monasteries. Weidenfeld and Nicolson. 1965

himself here on the slopes of the valley with his measuring rod? Or of the long walk up to Lanhydrock, without seeing some former Lady Robartes being driven in her carriage to Bodmin Road Station on her way to London before the days of British Rail?

Ruins are more than a tourist attraction. They have a curious fascination and power, and have done so down the ages. Travellers in the eighteenth century would turn their carriages aside to visit a ruined abbey on every possible occasion. They romanticised about them later. They went even further; to the extravagance of erecting follies, mock castles and ruins, grottoes in their gardens. Such 'ruins' fitted into the landscape of parks and induced in them a melancholy for time and the passing of time. They reminded them of their classical past, and were a kind of visible self-pity against a world of change they resented and did not understand. They were unaccustomed to the barrenness of an untamed nature. By their mock ruins they were able to cultivate the wild and, at the least, give a point to a walk in the grounds.

Yet what is it that compels *us* to leave our cars to gaze at, even to touch, the walls of a ruin such as that of the church at Constantine Bay, near Padstow? What persuades *us* to cross a ploughed field to see the fragment of a ruined gateway to an Augustinian priory such as that at Pentney, in Norfolk? Is it more than idle curiosity?

This gateway stands quite alone in the fields, is two storeys high and gathers to itself, in the evening light, an air of romance and impossibility. The whole structure, small as it is, is embattled with wide and splendid archways and turrets reaching high above ground. Within the gateway, all that is left of the Priory itself, are ruined rooms with traces of hearths, and old stone stairways leading to turrets. The feel of the stone is now cold; yet this absconded relic was once reality. Where weeds grow and stones fall from the high towers was a flourishing community. If one were to stand here long enough there would also be voices from the past and the clatter of hooves. An abbot might have arrived.

Pentney gatehouse, in East Anglia, is to me, because of its vulnerability to weather, the prototype of all English ruins. It is one of those evocative traces that time has left on the landscape. Aesthetically ruins represent a perfection, a completed cycle, which now nothing can break. One can gaze at a ruined gothic window, such as in St Thomas's Priory in Bodmin, and not wish it to be restored to its former beauty. It is beauty enough where it stands, open to the sky. For ruins are, in one sense, stories in bricks and mortar and stone. They add more than one dimension to the figures of history.

When I visit the pathetic remains of a convent, such as that at Shaftesbury, in Dorset, I seem to be in touch with these figures of the past, whatever Mr Sitwell may say to the contrary. The pleasure is, I suppose, that I am not involved in their lives. Their stories, of love or hate, of cruelty, of vast wealth or abject poverty are complete.

They can be judged without argument, and to visit a ruin is rather like coming to the last page of a book. The characters, abbots, imperious abbesses, kings and queens, monks and nuns, are enclosed in the covers of time.

I am borne into ruins by a nostalgia for a wider life only to find that the characters I have drawn out of oblivion are figures of myth. I am searching, too, like the men of the eighteenth century, for a 'great' past of which I feel myself to be a part. I come to ruins like a lover to a mistress. The ruins of the past war were evocative in the same way, calling back to those who remember them, in the rosebay willow herb in the bomb ruins of London, a host of memories as touching and as poignant as those evoked by an abbey destroyed under Henry VIII. Or a ruined pill-box on the coast, with the figures of Home guard soldiers, waiting the night through for an invader who never came. They, too, those soldiers and civilians who died in the blitz, are figures of myth and seem further away from me — though much nearer in time — than the great historical figures.

This melancholy for ruins is, as I have said, no new thing. The poet Clare felt it, in 1820, when he looked at the 'Ruins of Pickworth,' a forgotten village, and wrote his poem;

> These buried ruins, now in dust forgot,
> These heaps of stone, the only remnants seen —
> 'The Old Foundations,' still they call the spot,
> Which plainly tells inquiry what has been —

A time there was, though now the nettle grows
In triumph o'er each heap that swells the ground,
When they, in buildings pil'd, a village rose,
With here a cot, and there a garden crowned.

How contemplation mourns their lost decay,
To view their pride laid level with the ground;
To see, where labour clears the soil away,
What fragments of mortality abound.

Since first these ruins fell, how chang'd the scene!
What busy, bustling mortals, now unknown,
Have come and gone, as tho' there naught had been,
Since first oblivion call'd the spot her own.

The man who first opened my eyes to ruins was a friend of my father's. I would see him striding across the long lawns which separated our boarding house from the sea at Tankerton, in Kent. It was September and we were, as a family, on holiday. We were in one of the tall houses at the turning in the lane which led from the sea to Clowes Wood. At that time there were only these two houses this end of Tankerton. In winter these tall houses must have rocked in the sea wind but now, in the St Martin's Summer sun, stood firm. From the windows one could slide out to sea to the distant horizon in dreams of ships and mermaids.

On the beach, far below the cliffs, were sounding shells and two absurd wooden huts in which we changed to bathe so that no one saw our nakedness. At low tide the ooze of the mud shore sucked between your toes and jelly-fish — of which that year there was an invasion — melted away to nothing in the hot sun. The cliffs stretched miles away to the west to the town of Whitstable.

He was a tall man, thin and wiry, with dark hair and a moustache. A long face and penetrating eyes, he carried a set of tools with him which fascinated me, small hammers and picks, measuring tapes and rods and sets of what looked like silver trowels. What could he want with all this apparatus? To me he was a man who came out of distant time, a time different from my own, and to whom ordinary life was of no consequence. His whole air of being removed from our frivolous distractions marked him out as a god rather than a man. I was drawn to him across the sunlight of holiday excitements and pleasures, for he did one other thing for me. He opened my eyes to time itself.

How far off in time are the ruins of the Iron Age village at Chysauster in its lonely field, halfway up the hill to Gulval Downs, near Penzance. I always feel comfortable here in this village street with the traces of the beehive houses laid out on the ground, in the same way as one can see the outlines of a Deserted Village in the Midlands.

Chysauster is really the oldest village street in England and the comfort comes, I suppose, both from its simplicity and in knowing that, but a mile away to the east is a hill fortress, Castle-an-Dinas. The people who lived here from about 100 B.C. to the 3rd century A.D. and farmed and smelted tin, were protected from upland invaders. The warmth of that protection still persists today. And though in winter it might be cold and raging winds blow everything about, in summer and early autumn it must have been perfection, with hunting in the long forests to the sea to the south, or fishing from the shell beach (once through the forests) between the mainland and St Michael's Mount.

Though the village, for the most part, was deserted — perhaps under Roman influence — around 300 A.D. you can feel the presence of these ancient people most powerfully. Is this because they must have come up the same hillside as you do today, or because, in the small terraces attached to each house, they cultivated gardens here above the now fertile fields which grow flowers early enough to rival the Scillies? Is it because they kept their stores in a cave to the south of the village, called a *fougou*, and must have gone 'shopping' down this high street to this communal market? Is it because we can see them rushing to this cave for shelter from invaders when the alarm went out from their castle-fort. It is all of these because, of course, the stones you touch they touched; the street you walk in they walked in with their fish for supper or their boar steak, and here the soldier on leave came from the hill-fort, or to make love. Here, the village girls walked in the latest fashions which might well have been trousers copied from the men who wore them to tame and ride the wild horses.

The village, today, consists of eight excavated houses (and nine not yet investigated), two rows of four each all of much the same design. At first it seems odd to have sited a village here, on this exposed hillside with no more protection than a line of hawthorn hedges. But, in the days when it was built, the valleys were less habitable and full of hunting forests. And, in those days, you could have walked the village streets and met cranes and buzzards and such odd birds which might well have been kept as pets in the houses.

You can go into any of the houses which now have no roofs and feel instantly at home. In one sense, since all the houses are of similar construction, it is almost like walking in a modern garden suburb. The front door faces east or north-east, away from the prevailing south west wind. A passage in the outer wall leads into a courtyard. They must have driven their cattle here and stalled them in the recess on the left of the courtyard. Immediately opposite this long entrance is the Round Room which because, in most cases, a stone with a socket in it was found, was the communal sitting room. Most houses had two other rooms, called by those who excavated the huts, the Small Round room and the Long Room. For water, channels were cut in the ground and laid in stone, passing through the entrance passage. There are kitchen recesses in most of the houses.

To the south east of all the houses is this garden terrace. And one house, No 5, has even a separate 'cottage' attached to it, set in the thick walls, in which traces of a hearth were found. Is it too fanciful to suggest that an aged relative lived here? For this village suggests one thing above all else, that the inhabitants were highly civilized. They would have looked after their old people. They hunted red deer, wild boar and probably wolves; they grew barley, made simple ornaments of bronze, and lived and died within the sound of the sea. And did they, one wonders, exchange visits with other Iron Age people in the similar village at Kynance Gate, not all that far away, near the Lizard?

Cornwall has forty or more hill forts from Maen Castle, near the Land's End, to the cliff castle on the Rumps, near St Minver, or Helsbury Castle in Michaelstow. Most of these are strongholds which used natural features, such as the sea, as impregnable defences and only needed to erect a rampart inland-facing.

Tintagel, which is very late, was a hill fort before the Normans built the first sketch of a castle there in the twelfth century. It stands on a headland 270 feet above the sea, this trace of a castle with a cell of Celtic monks who built here in the sixth century. When Leland saw it, in the sixteenth century, it was ruinous, 'the buildings of the castelle be sore wether-beaten and yn ruine, but it hath bene a large thinge.' At its building it must have been magnificent above the spinthrift of a double sea biting away at the Island from the mainland, and stretching away into an infinity at the end of which was America.

Yet, to me, each time I come here, the magnificence is clouded by terror. Indeed, at the best of times, the site of the Castle is frightening, even if you approach it down the long grass lanes of the cliffs from the church. For I first saw it when I was a schoolboy on holiday with my sister Mary and my brothers Jack and Philip. They are here, even today. We are alone, the four of us, on a Sunday morning in July, standing looking down into the swirl of water between the mainland and the Island. I don't think, then, it was the history of the place that engaged our thoughts, it was the sea below and the beach and the going-down into the tiny bay.

Once again we were lodging, as at Tankerton, with my mother, in a boarding house in the hamlet of Treknow and had walked out to see the castle. So the four of us went down the shaly slope to the little bay and threw stones into the sea, unaware of the towering columns of cliffs on which, still higher, rose the ruins of 'Tyntagel on its surge-beat hill.' It was holiday time and the sun was shining. London was miles away.

When we decided to come up again, Philip and I agreed to race each other up the slope to the top, perhaps fifty yards. The shale was loose and we did not notice pieces flying from under our feet as we ran and scrambled up the sharp incline. I forget who won, but when we reached the top there was no sign of Jack or Mary, whom we supposed were following us up at their leisure.

We went down again, after a few minutes, to find a tragedy, a double tragedy at the beginning of a holiday. A large piece of shale had flown down the slope from our running feet and aimed itself directly at Mary's head. My brother Jack, in throwing her down, got himself in the path of the shale and it cut like a knife into the calf of his left leg. It was a tremendous cut, deep and long, right into the muscle. There was little blood, but it looked as if the whole of the interior of his leg was opened. How he managed to get up that slope (even with us all helping him) and back to Treknow, is still a mystery to me, though I well remember the walk along the lanes. It must have been agony to him.

A doctor was fetched. In the low bedroom of the boarding house he put twelve stitches into Jack's leg without an anaesthetic. Our admiration of his bravery, when we heard this, knew no bounds. But, in those days, our eldest brother was our hero and we should not have expected a hero to act in any other way. The second part of the tragedy was that, being so wounded, he could not drive us about in the car. Yet, for me, it was lucky. I was now tied to walking about a small area of Cornwall. I began to relate the ruin that was Tintagel to other ruins I had seen. I began to people the ruins with figures from Tennyson and Matthew Arnold, Tristram and Iseult.

> A year had flown, and o'er the sea away
> In Cornwall, Tristram and Queen Iseult lay
> In King Marc's chapel, in Tyntagel old —
> There in a ship they bore those lovers cold.

I sat and reflected that perhaps on this very small shore where the accident had happened the boat bringing the dead lovers had come in.

A taste for ruins need not necessarily mean that one has always to be looking at monasteries, churches or convents. In Cornwall are other ruins such as sea-mills like those at Trevorrick, near St Issey. The mills, or what is left of them, are on the creek shore. In use until 1880, these sea-mills were used for milling wheat brought, before the railway was built, by ship from Padstow. They were driven by tidal water caught by a sea wall with sluices. Power came from a waterwheel driven by freeing the water at low tide. Now little remains but the grey water of the Camel sluicing in over the brown-green ruins, the vivid seaweed and the red-seeded dock standing straight in the marshes.

Other ruins are the romantic wooden viaducts of Brunel's first railway, seen behind the 'modern' viaducts over the wooded valleys, or the ruins of mine buildings such as at Blue Hills, or old cottages on the moors at Zennor.

Houses, too, can be ruined, can be romantic and set in romantic surroundings. As, also, those offshoots of ruins, follies, grottoes, caves and hermitages.

The most romantic house I ever came across is Hafod in Wales. It has haunted me ever since I first heard of it, but I was too late to see it in its full ruined splendour. When I arrived all that was left of it was a massive pile of rubble. I was told that it had to be blown up, so strong was the building.

This was the mansion of the estate that Thomas Johnes inherited from his father in 1783. He was delighted by the rugged surroundings — still rugged today and very much off the beaten track — and appalled at the poverty of the inhabitants of the mountains and valleys. He extended hugely the old, humble house and settled down to cultive the estate.

The new Hafod mansion was rich in Gothic style, with pointed windows and pinnacles, by Thomas Baldwin of Bath. In 1793 an octagonal library and a conservatory 160 feet long were added. The library Johnes stocked with Welsh and French manuscripts, including Froissart's *Chronicles* which he, later, translated and partly printed at Hafod.

Johnes was more than a scholar. He was an eccentric who loved trees. He planted over three million on the bare mountain-side, thus giving work to the peasants who were his tenants. Most of these trees were cut down during the two World wars.

One night, in March 1807, the house was gutted by fire. It has been suggested that it was the fault of the housekeeper who set fire to her bed with a warming pan. Whatever the cause the damage was very great. But Johnes was not overthrown. He was an enthusiast and engaged Baldwin to rebuild. In three years the house was habitable again.

After his death, in 1816, Hafod was empty until, in 1832, Henry, fourth Duke of Newcastle, bought the estate and continued to improve the land. The last owner left it over forty years ago and it now belongs — the demolished ruin of the house which Baldwin built and Anthony Salvin added to in about 1850 — to the Forestry Commission. Now the hills and mountain slopes are covered, once again, with trees as in Johnes's time, but today it is pine not oak. The site of the house, beyond the pile of rubbish, has become a holiday caravan park.

I took away a piece of carved stone, part of one of the gothic windows, which was lying in the rubbish. I brought it back to Cornwall, to my then home at Treneague, near Wadebridge, and built it into a new low wall in the garden.

10. Deserted Railways

One hundred years, more or less, and most of the railways, with the exception of the few main lines, have come and gone. Yet the oldest deserted railway in Cornwall is hardly what we should call a railway at all. It is the Cheesewring line, a small tramway for part of its length, running down from the disused quarry, past the remains of copper mines at Caradon and Liskeard. You walk along the traces of its course to reach the moors; you tread on the grass-grown, grass-interlaced granite sleepers leading into the heart of the quarries of light mauve slate, and into a corner of the history of early industrialism.

Few now living ever saw the trucks on these rails. Those who looked from the windows of cottages in such hamlets as Tremar and Railway Terrace, have all gone and, perhaps, were not even there when, in November 1844, the Liskeard and Caradon Railway was opened. Two years later it was extended into the moor to serve the Cheesewring Quarries and the Kilmar granite quarries beyond.

You came, and you still do, to the Cheesewring down a corridor of antiquity and medievalism, from the church at St Neot's, with its Holy Well in the valley below. Here, in this meadow below the church, the spring bubbles into its granite basin. Once it would have been full of bent pins. Here the little man (St Neot was a dwarf) tended his oxen with which he ploughed his glebe. Within the church above the valley are the fine windows depicting his life. They are a poignant biography. They were put up in the fifteenth century when the villagers rebuilt the church, and repaired by Hedgeland in 1824-1828. Their fine colour is probably due to an even later restoration.

Here is the story, then, of how St Neot resigned his crown (of Wessex) to his brother, took his vows as a monk, and came to the parish of St Neot. In the third picture he is paddling in the well reading his Psalter. Legend has it that he did this every day, standing up to his neck in the water which, if he were really only eighteen inches high, he might well have been.

Back in his little room over the church porch, an angel arrives to tell Neot that his supply of food is guaranteed for ever. It shall consist of one fish from the well each day. We can only hope that this poor diet was supplemented by the villagers with bread at least, for he was forbidden to take more than his ration of fish each day. If he took more, the food supply would be cut off immediately and for ever.

Alas, Neot fell ill. His servant, Barius, is ordered to bring him his daily ration of fish. But Barius, thinking his master needs building up, and knowing nothing about the one-fish injunction, catches two fish and brings them, cooked, to his bedside. Neot is horrified. He send Barius back to the Well, ordering him to return the two fishes. Instantly they touch the magic water they are uncooked and become alive again.

In the ninth picture Neot is fully recovered and off to the glebe to plough, only to find that, while he was laid up, someone has stolen his oxen. It so happens that one of the villagers with his boy is ploughing another part of the glebe with stags. With their help the saint finds his beasts and gets to work. Finally, here is Neot receiving the Papal Blessing, though it is not known how he got to Rome or what happened to his parish (and the daily fish) while he was away.

The fact that St Neot is always referred to as a dwarf seems to point to a Christian take-over of the Scandinavian mythological figures of elfins and goblins who lived either in mountains or in the depths of the earth. These creatures were reputed to be 'kings; of metals and mines, a conception well in keeping with Cornwall. Furthermore kings and queens have, down history, often been attended by dwarfs. The Akka race of Africans thrived at the courts of the early Pharoahs. Philetas of Cos, about 330 B.C., who was tutor to Ptolemy Philadelphus, used to wear tiny leaden shoes to prevent himself being blown away and Julia, the niece of Augustus, owned a dwarf only two feet four inches high and a maid, Andromeda, no taller. And, of course, the British tradition of dwarfs begins in the very appropriate-to-Cornwall ballad, 'In Arthur's Court Tom Thumb did live.'

There are other brilliant windows in St Neot's church depicting the life of Adam and Eve, the Flood and Noah's Ark, St George and the Dragon. High over the parish hangs Brown Gelly, a round, bare hill (which could conceal a dragon, indeed! Or a family of dwarfs!) on the remote southern part of Bodmin Moor. In the churchyard is one of the tenderest epitaphs of the many which abound in Cornwall. It is to a young man who died, in 1850, aged twenty five:

> One of the best friends, he died
> and they have laid him here
> Tread lightly on a hallowed bed
> for Death has made it dear.
> How soon my youth has faded
> and hastened to decay
> Disease my heart invaded
> and took my life away.
>
> No medicine could restore me
> no drug could do me good
> The hand of God was o'er me
> And grief my only food.

Out of St Neot's parish towards, Liskeard, you might miss the tiny left hand turning which takes you up into the farmyard of Higher Trengale, and so by gully lanes to Golytha Falls and the deep antiquity of this part of Cornwall. All remote Cornish farms have about them the quality of a small village or hamlet. They look self-sufficient, cut-off, boldly standing into a persistent black wind, enclosed on their secrets, full of the dead. Their ricks are crowned with crows and jackdaws; stonechats fricker on the gorse-topped moorland hedges of grey stone running to the Falls, and there are kingfishers in the shallow river Fowey, speeding under the squat, firm bridge at Trenant.

King Doniert was a ninth century Cornish king. Two stones

mark his place. One a half-shaft Celtic Christian cross and the other inscribed, in Latin, 'Doniert prayed for his soul.' But there is nothing here in this commemorative semi-circle of stone and grass to rival the melancholy of the ruined mine chimneys the railway served, nothing but the roughness of the granite on your fingers, nothing royal, nothing of grandeur but the landscape.

The grandeur is in the Quoit at Trevethy, a neolithic tomb chamber, the giant lid one massive stone lying at an angle on five uprights pitched like an immense surf-board riding the moorland winds. These stones are like the bones of a giant picked clean of their shroud of flesh. The Quoit stands in an oasis of its own quiet beside the road and modern cottages, nibbled at by sheep, approached by a bramble bank. Grand and still, impressive with its strength in its two tomb chambers, the skeletons of aged chieftains scattered in the ash of centuries grass, potent at touching, an epic poem, a stubborn memorial.

Here before civilization; here after civilization passes away, are The Hurlers northward on the moor, the twelve Sunday dancers who were turned into stone for their wicked frivolity, when a pagan god rode his horse into the black skies of the deep moor and caused the ancient stones to move and to take on life which were, to ordinary eyes, inert, unliftable masses of granite.

So, by ancient Celtic crosses, wan and lonely, to the doorway of the moors and the long railway walk to the Cheesewring itself, through the deserted copper mines and beneath the steel spire of the television mast at Caradon Hill. You are passing through a deserted civilization based, much nearer our own times, on the cracked chimneys of ruined engine houses, of torn engine houses themselves, of the copper mines and outlying farms, to the great quarry under the Cheesewring. These deserted and ruined mine buildings are like chapels, one after another, where now only choirs of birds sing, long lines of 'sacred' places beside the overgrown railway track. This is the dead landscape of early industrialism. It lends a poignancy to the terror of the moor and the deep granite quarries where the famous hard blue granite was cut and transported out of Cornwall.

The early days of copper were rather like a minor gold rush. For years prospectors had been working here in the Caradon area, without much success, since the topography and rock formations gave it the air of a likely place for copper and tin. In 1837, however, the Clymo and Killow brothers discovered a rich main lode. The next year they sold 130 tons of ores and the district was 'made'. Miners poured in and, by 1850, Caradon and the valley below the Cheesewring was one of the richest mining grounds in Cornwall, with over twenty mines working.

Above the giant's shovelful of the quarry, ledged and terraced, a great gap in nature, stands the monumental stone shaping of the Cheesewring which must have been a landmark for the early miners and railway men. These grey blue stones, so similar in colouring but a thousand times larger, to those found on the shore at Crackington Haven, for example, stand impossibly upon one another. A finger placed on the right spot and the monument would collapse. No one has yet found that spot in the stones. Here they stand forever, gathering sun in summer, in moorland exposure of wind and weather which have moulded them into their curious shapes, while sloe bushes and thorn and blackberry creep up towards them from the open moor. They are like some fantastic Turk's cap. And not only the massive Cheesewring itself, a gateway to the moor beyond, but other smaller cheesewrings dot the heights above the quarry where the dome of an endless sky holds the clouds high over the moor to Brown Willy, and the quagmires of East Moor.

When I am up here I cannot help thinking of the eccentric stonecutter, Daniel Gumb. He was a lover of mathematics, completely uneducated and self-taught, who decided to abandon his cottage in one of the hamlets and come here, near the Cheesewing, to live in a kind of rock cave which he enlarged to hold his family. He made a 'quoit' of this recess by propping up a great wide slab of stone for a roof. He made a slit for a bedroom into which he could roll himself sideways. It must have been remarkably uncomfortable. Nevertheless, scratching the date of his new home on the rock outside, he moved his family up here. At least this is the tale that Wilkie Collins heard in 1850, although whether the Cornish were having him on, or whether he did actually see the date on the stone is not proved. I am told, indeed, that the date is still there on the stone but, though I have searched for it, I have never found it.

> Henceforth [he writes] nothing moved, nothing depressed him. The storms of winter rushed over his unsheltered dwelling, but failed to dislodge him. He taught his family to brave solitude and cold in the cavern in the rocks as he braved them. In a cell that he had scooped out for his wife (the roof of which is now fallen in) some of his children died, and others were born. They point out the rock where he used to sit on calm summer evenings, absorbed over his tattered copy of Euclid. A geometrical 'puzzle' traced by his hand still appears on the stone. When he died, what became of his family, no one can tell.

If there had been any trace of poor Daniel after all these years one feels that it would have been removed by 'tourists'. But I, for one, shall still go on searching for anything this strange mathematician left whenever I come up to the Cheesewring.

From this point you can see all Cornwall, and much of Devon, as if you were swinging in a fairground cradle. The English Channel to the south at Looe; north west the Atlantic and the fearful rocks at Beeny Head and Crackington Haven; eastward into the closed circuit of Dartmoor and, perhaps, Exmoor. At hand, is Sharpitor where neolithic man built huts and where seventeenth century man turned an Iron Age village into dwellings. Now sheep curl into the fallen stone circle to hide from the weather. Here, too, can be seen the whole floor of Twelve Men's Moor, where men have tin-streamed from medieval times, and so called because of the twelve tenants of Launceston Priory who owned Bodmin Moor in the thirteenth century.

Go northward into the moor, beyond the quarries and the reach of the old railways, along Withey Bank towards these hut circles. There is a deserted farm with a bull house where in the quiet moorland, in the gorse and heather, his bellow still echoes. The massive, pointless blocks of moorstone which formed his home give back the pitiful sound.

Who lived here beyond the reach of our present style of living? Who baked the bread and salted the pig or lamb? They could not have left their outlying farms often, unless they came down on their ponies into the village for candles or, by the Caradon railway, to

Liskeard on market days. For their eyes must have been northward into the hard-won fields of the moor, to the purple of the corncockle and the flight of the wheatear.

And homeward coming, past the terrible gap of the quarries and the moon-toppling Cheesewring, the age of the moor was in their legs and tearing at their minds and shadowed in their lanterns, where night was ancient before ancient men lived and died where the stones speak. Only when the moon streamed into the hollow grasses of winter, or reflected off the summer hawkweed, would there be any safety from the ghosts of these people who lived shut up in this fortress-walled farmhouse.

Now old shreds of newspaper fall from the bitter plaster, now their cooking place is straw-strewn and the floor a midden. Then, all the way back from the pub at St Cleer under Caradon Hill, the voice of the stoned bull would have reached them, rocking the flat shapes of the Cheesewring, its pleading for release pathetic and unheard in their hard minds.

Gone, too, is the single line railway which ran from the long sands of Perranporth to Chacewater and so to Redruth and the great mining area of Cornwall. I stood on the deserted platform of St Agnes station, the line ripped up, the glass in the windows smashed and thought back to a kind of L.P. Hartley past, when mothers and nannies brought their children on their way back to school at the end of a long summer holiday. The platform was stacked with tuck-boxes and trunks; even the tall green machines still gave Nestles chocolate for a penny, that curiously lovely-tasting railway chocolate.

How easy it is to imagine the platform peopled with holiday-makers waiting for a bus to take them into St Agnes, down to the 'seaside' at Porthtowan, or to the harbour at Portreath where a branch of the Hayle railway opened on December 23rd, 1837. It was constructed mainly to deal with ore and coal shipped into the harbour. In 1846 sometimes as many as twenty boats were being worked in what today looks like an exceedingly difficult harbour to enter. The railway closed down in 1930.

Now all you can do is to walk a little way up the line to the corner to see the gorse taking over, and to imagine you hear the old steam engine's whistle coming down from the north. Or to go off to St Agnes and lose yourself in an even deeper past, the mining past of this whole area.

Everywhere are the ruins of old engine houses, tall, imposing, magnificent. The most romantic is the Blue Hill mine in Trevallas Coombe, running into the sea north of St Agnes, which closed down in 1897. You can no longer come here in the summer for the whole coombe is used by hippies as a camping ground. But in late autumn it is deserted, the ruined ivy-clad engine houses stand alone, the gaunt chimneys signposts to a past populated by the miners who worked below ground and the Bal Maidens who worked above.

These women were the most romantic of all, great numbers of whom were employed on the surface of Cornish mines. 'The work of *spalling*, or breaking up the larger rocks, was performed by the women with long-handled hammers, standing out of doors.' They worked in cramped positions, in draughty sheds which ran with water when it rained. They came over the hills down to the mine in their attractive cardboard 'bonnets', over which they flung a white cotton cloth which came down to their shoulders. They wore, also, a kind of bodice called a Garboldi which they tucked into their skirts and a pinafore to walk back and forth to work. They came down the valley like nuns to convent Mass. Like nuns they were tied into their discipline for life, to work at dawn, and home and away at dusk, the moaning of the sea their only homily. 'Never again,' says Hamilton Jenkin, in his book *The Cornish Miner*, 'will the sound of them going by singing at six o'clock in the summer mornings be heard in the mining areas.'

Now the air down the long bracken lanes from the top of the coombe to the bottom is quiet. Once this whole valley echoed to the miners' voices as they came over the crest of the valley from their cottages in St Agnes down to the extensive township of the mine, and echoed again in the summer night when they went home by moonlight, or in winter, by candle-lit lantern. Bells would be clanging in the dressing sheds to announce a change of shift. The floor of the valley, at the surface, was covered in wooden sheds. The

Caradon old railway track and Sharptor *(Charles Woolf)*

Golytha Falls, Draynes Common *(Ray Bishop)*

The Cheesewring

(*Richard Ho*

activity would have been enormous.

Today all that is left are the massive, sad, engine houses and among the blue spoil heaps, traces of the iron stamp which crushed the ore. It was driven by water coming down the man-made leats from the valley side. In these cathedral-like engine houses rode the great iron beam engine which drained water from the mine, raising it, not to the surface but to adits underground which allowed the water to drain into the valley and so into the sea. The cliffs, here towering to great heights, are riddled with such openings, like immense rabbit burrows; the land behind the deep cliffs at St Agnes is a museum of old engine houses and mine stacks right into Camborne where the chimneys stand like nine-pins. Here are the remains of West Wheel Grenville, with its twin stacks, most lovely ruin of all, or along the valley inland from Porthtowan, where copper was mined, stands the ivy-covered house of Wheal Ellen leading, by sea-mist and tall hill, to the square and round ruin of the United Hills mine.

These unbreakable buildings, from East Grenville, near Troon, through the graceful ruin at South Condurrow at Camborne, to those, like the Phoenix United mines, near the Cheesewring, are as much the historic past of Cornwall as any ruined castle, disused railway line, or closed-down Methodist chapel. Their stark beauty fits the shorn landscapes over which they tower, sad reminders of a hard past.

Before the railway between Lydford and Wadebridge was torn up you could have gone almost to the foot of Brentor, which you can see from Cornwall on its high hill on the edge of Dartmoor. These great rocks, standing sheer above the moor and the sea, have an affinity not only with them but with God. A church or a holy place is nearly always at the top of such mounts as Brentor. In a sense it must always have been a pilgrimage to climb up to them, even if one were too exhausted to pray immediately on arrival. Even if the question of prayer does not enter into the climb at all, they are still places which uplift the spirit.

Brentor has on its summit the church of St Michael of the Rocks. In 1625 Tristram Risdon called it, 'a church, full bleak and weather beaten, all alone, as if it were forsaken.' This October afternoon it shone with soft autumnal sunshine, as I climbed up the steep slope to the summit amongst the cattle and the blackberry bushes still hanging with fruit.

Robert Giffard, about 1130, is said to have built the first church here on what is thought to be part of a volcanic cone. The whole building is surrounded by the usual legends of how a church came to be built here at all. Possibly none of them is true, not even the story that the church was put up by a wealthy merchant who, in the middle of a great storm at sea, thinking he was about to be drowned, vowed that if he escaped he would built a church to St Michael on the first land he saw. Baring-Gould, in his story of *Margery of Quether*, 1884, retells the legend of the Devil throwing down the day's work (as is told, also, of St Breock, near Wadebridge and many other churches.)

> While the church was being built, every night the devil removed as many stones as had been set on the foundations during the day. But the Archangel was too much for him. He waited behind Cox Tor, and one night threw a great rock across and hit the Evil One between the horns, and gave him such a headache that he desisted from interference henceforth.

These small shrines, St Michael's is only thirty seven feet long and fourteen feet six inches wide, have a cell-like atmosphere about them, as if they were the wombs of religion, as if those who worshipped here, in the past and today, were a small select band of souls already half in touch with heaven. Indeed, this church must often have been clouded in the mists of Dartmoor and to enter it then might well have been like going into a mystical haven.

Yet it could hardly have seemed like heaven to those church robbers who, in January 1951, stole six hundredweight of lead from the roof. Was it the same robber who came back in 1964, and stole a seventeenth century 'beef-eater' flagon and a Victorian paten by Spackman?

I lay on the flat top of an altar tomb, out in the sun, to the north of the church and watched a late-hatched red admiral butterfly flitting about the few gravestones like a tiny flag, with almost the whole of the West Country laid out below me, the 225 square miles of Dartmoor to the east, Plymouth Sound and Whitesand Bay to the south, Exmoor to the north and Cornwall to the west. Lying on my back in the warm sun it was possible to imagine the world revolving. Possible to close my eyes, to turn on one side on the warm, hard stone, and think of the Overseers of 1758 who rendered their Accounts for 'The Burying of Jean Fuge' here:

Paid the Parson	1. 0
Paid for the Couffine	8. 0
Paid for Syder	5. 2
Paid for a Pint Brandy	10
Paid for Sope, Candles	4
Paid the Shrouder	3. 6
Paid for making Grave	2. 0
Paid for Liquer at ye Servey of Jean fuge good	3.10[1]

It occurred to me, when I got up to go down the hill again, that two shillings was a small sum to pay a gravedigger to hack his way into this almost earthless graveyard. How, even in 1966, the date of the last burial here, did they get a coffin up this high hill?

As I slipped going down hill from the churchyard gate (as had the last bride to be married here after her wedding) I came face to face with a bull. I did not, this afternoon, need the Archangel to throw a great rock and give the beast a headache, though separate me from it by five hundred years and I should have been convinced that I was looking at the Evil One. The great horns on its head would have been enough for that. Today this bull looked amiable and somehow rather dotty. I reached out and touched the thick brass ring in his nose.

'Bull,' I said, 'I love the feel of you. You are a bull which hasn't been made to suffer. You are a divine bull.'

He made not the slightest protest at my touch, at my fingering the curls of hair between his horns. He flicked flies from his wet nose and went on eating the brambles.

1 Pamphlet. The Church of St Michael, Brentor. Charles K. Burton & Gerald L. Matthews.

St Michael, at Brentor, could shout across Cornwall, if he had a mind to, to St Michael on his high hill at Roche, near St Austell, or to his other mounted church, seaward from Penzance, at St Michael's Mount. Roche Rock has the ruins of a chapel and hermitage, built in 1409, on the top of rocks one hundred feet high, lofting it over the ironmonger's shop and small pub of the village, reflecting the china clay hills at St Austell and the wideness of Goss Moor. An old gnarled grey granite rock for an old gnarled hermit.

St Michael's Mount has to be seen, in sunlight, from the town of Marazion, when light flashes from the glass of the church on the top. Now is the Archangel sharpening his bright sword and you can believe in the host of heaven. The strand which joins the island to the mainland is bright with shells and seaweeds, with Oarweed and Bladder wrack, or the red seaweed from which women used once to make lipstick and rouge. And small cowrie shells, and the piddock shell which is phosphorescent at night, giving forth a pale blueish-white light, and the limpet and purple mussels, those small strong shells with their effective armour. When the tide is full over the strand and the Island is isolated, then is the time for the anemones to open their colours from pink through yellows and whites to a pinkish brown, the Beadlet, the Strawberry, the Daisy, the Dahlia and the Snake Locks anemone, poisoning their prey before pulling it into a central mouth.

The bells are ringing from the lost churches and towers of drowned Lyonesse, just as they ring at Dunwich, in Suffolk, or at Bosham, in Sussex, ringing in a drowned fairyland of Saints and Knights in armour, ringing of love and death and a permanency that is lost. Here, at St Michael's Mount, is the 'dark jewel' which D.H. Lawrence saw some time in 1916 when he, too was living in Cornwall. I saw it first in 1948;

> Brazen the slabs
> Brazen the bold, shearing, seaborne slabs,
> Over a greyskirt bay.
> Ten thousand tumbrils of spawning brass
> Plates on uptiered plates of shields
> Above, reared-up; below handsbreath
> The sparkling closets of a seagreen sea,

Starfished and coral-fed.

Ten thousand scimitars flashing
Skyward to birdcloud.
Over the strand swinging
Over birdhaunting swinging.
Underfoot, shellbright,
All gross and bitter weeds
Upwind and downwind ringing
Beneath seashelly bastions of brass
   The lilywhite
And shells of lilywhite.

All that line from Launceston to Wadebridge is ripped up and gone, the arches of its bridges looking faintly ridiculous. Where, at Tresmeer, my great-uncle came in his trap to ride to Exeter or Plymouth, the station master's cottage is now an ordinary country cottage with no authority before the naked railway track, railless and flower strewn, a long lover's walk into the next village, into Delabole, into Camelford, into Wadebridge. And there, too, the line to Padstow beside the river Camel, one of the loveliest in England, is no more than a track under attack from nature, a valley of bright weeds, lost under scarlet pimpernel and burdock.

The London South Western railway's North Cornwall line reached Wadebridge on the 1st June, 1895. The final section, to Padstow, was opened on the 27th March, 1899. Seventy years later it was closed and torn up, the iron bridge beyond Camel quarries now dangerous and falling, the lobster pots in Padstow's goods yards sunk under a car park.

With the waters of the estuary swinging into Wadebridge the scene is like an early Chirico, under the turning wings of gulls and the green hills opposite. The creeks are deserted and from any of them one might expect the figure of a man to emerge from a hidden boat and stand looking out over the water, a figure which does not see you, or have anything to do with you or your time.

The shunting yards which once served the railway wharves at Wadebridge are blazing with a reddish light caused by intensely hot sun off rusting corrugated iron. Many of the stone buildings are roofed and half-sided with the iron sheets. Even in the shadows created by the buildings themselves the light is brown and still. Indeed stillness is the predominating quality of this off-side part of the town. A cat could hardly slink from one doorway to another without being observed, so quiet is it at midday. This quality of stillness is even reflected off new sacks of grain being unloaded from tall warehouses into lorries and carts. An occasional disturbance is caused by the horde of pigeons which roost high up in an angle of one of the buildings. About once an hour, with great fluttering of wings, the birds fly out, circle the warehouses and return. No one takes the least notice of them.

Yet, if you look again, it is obvious that the stillness of the quarter radiates from the open centre of the square which is crossed by several tracks of rusting, disused railway lines. About this square, surfaced with pot-holed asphalt, dark blue in colour, are ancient workshops, depositories and smithies. And although much modern work is carried out within these buildings, they give the appearance of being at least a hundred years old. In fact, the buildings themselves are far older, many of them having been in use in medieval times. Only the corrugated iron which covers them is comparatively recent.

Not so long ago if you stayed here for long you would have seen a covered goods wagon come silently from the main line, through a lane of such old warehouses, across the open square, to the buffers overlooking the river at the wharf's edge. It came silently, ghost-like, riding tall and sedate, probably full of sacks of fertilizer, until it gently hit the buffers of the last line of similar trucks in the siding.

All this is gone; but through this square, in the afternoon, the horse riders come. They are in their own familiar setting as they pass into the alleyways which lead to the river and towpaths. In a sense they are the last of those horse teams which drew the farm waggons here, fifty years ago, only their bodies are sleeker and they pull no weight. Now they are proud-high-stepping under their mistresses who ride them into the stillness of water.

At the end of this square the noise of farm machinery is generally to be heard. Stacked into yards below the warehouses are gleaming new farm instruments of raucous colours, dung-spreaders, hay-tedders, their circular teeth like huge spiders. Now and then a dignified combine harvester lords it over the humbler instruments and machines, waiting for someone to come and take it away.

These machines give a wonderful air of modernity to otherwise old fashioned surroundings. They are embodied with a life of their own which speaks of wide skies, ripe fields of corn and oats, rains of November and spring wheat. A multitude of gulls, come in on the tide, nearly always circle them, attracted by their bright colours. A pair of swans fly just above the water. Their white bodies, pinked by the sun, tear the bridge in half as they splinter through the main arch to the mud flats beyond.

11. Land of the Virgins

Brychan was a Welsh prince, about 500 A.D. distinguished by his Christian faith and worthiness of life, who gave his wife Gladys a hard time. It was not enough that shortly after his wedding he deserted her and went off to Ireland. There was nothing remarkable in going overseas at that time. But he went because he feared that if he stayed he might beget some offspring of her which would 'hinder him from freely serving the Lord.' Gladys might well have asked why he married her in the first place? And it was going to take her twenty four years to find out. For, at the end of that time, Brychan returned to Wales, found Gladys still living, still in love with him and ready to take up married life. No longer 'feared of not serving the Lord' he bedded her to such good effect that they raised a family of twenty four sons and daughters, one for each year he had been away!

Not only did he beget such a large progeny but, as soon as they were grown up, he despatched the lot to colonise Cornwall, first no doubt, impressing them with the length of his own virginity and bidding them to follow his example. This they effectively did, since we never hear of any of them marrying. Some of the daughters became the virgin saints whose churches and shrines encircle that part of Cornwall, the north, in which I live.

Endelient, Menfrede, Tedda, Maben, Adwena and Juliana who had two shrines, one at St Juliot, near Boscastle, the other at Lanteglos-by-Camelford. Six beautiful and stout-hearted girls of whom their father who, as far as I can make out, never visited them, must have been proud. They had the good sense to live close together and could exchange visits. It seems, however, that

Endelient was the eldest. It must have been a sad day for the others when she died, except that it assured one thing. A church is still standing which bears her name and enshrines her tomb.

Nicholas Roscarrock, the famous hagiologist, who was born at the manor of Roscarrock in the parish, the ruined granite chapel of which stands amongst other granite outbuildings, was obviously very fond of Endelient, for he not only wrote her life (which was not, except for one instance, all that interesting) but also a tender hymn to her in which he calls her 'sister deare.' After saying that he himself was born in her parish (1549?) and confirmed in her church, he adds his wish:

> To emitate in part thy vertues rare,
> Thy faith, Hope, Charite, thy humble mynde,
> Thy chastness, meekness, and thy dyet spare,
> And that which in this world is hard to finde,
> The love which thow to enemye didst showe,
> Reviving him who sought thy overthrowe.[1]

She lived, he tells us, in a part of the parish called Trenteny, where a chapel stood in his time. She existed entirely on the milk of a cow which, one day, strayed on to the land of the lord of Trenteny. This enraged him to such an extent that he killed the cow out of hand. However he forgot one thing. Endelient had for godfather a very powerful man, some go as far as to say that it was King Arthur himself, who came to her rescue and slew the cow-killer. At once Endelient who, naturally, heard of the event very quickly, out of the kindness of her heart, revived him. Alas, we hear nothing of the cow being restored to life. One must assume that the lord of Trenteny replaced it with one of his own in thankfulness for her mercy.

Roscarrock goes on:

> And when she perceived the day of her death drew nigh, she intreated her friends after her death, to lay her dead body on a sled and to bury her there where certain young Stots Bullocks or Calves of a year old should of their own accord draw her, which being done they brought her to a place which

---

1 See the *Children of Brychan in Cornwall*, Rev. Gilbert Doble, Lee, 1930

at that time was a miry waste ground, and a great quagmire on the top of a hill, where in time after there was a Church builded and dedicated to her, bearing her name, which since proved a fine firm and fruitful part of ground, where her feast was accustomed to be yearly remembered the 29th April.

The fine fifteenth century tomb of Catacluese stone which is now used as an altar in the south aisle of the church, is said to be hers and is reputed to have been defaced under Henry VIII.

Nor is it fanciful to imagine Endelient leaving her poor hermitage, after seeing to her cow, coming down the long lane leading to Port Quin, one afternoon in spring when the hedge bottoms were full of wild garlic and celandine, to welcome Ilick who, though not related and who was to live in Port Isaac not far away, was about her own age. Ilick had set out from Ireland on a hurdle. We know that she arrived safely since she had a chapel built to her memory near a holy well, in the parish, which is known to have been served by a priest as far back as 1382.

Roscarrock liked her as well and had a rather alarming story to tell of her.

> The inhabitants there used to say by Tradition that she came miraculously out of Ireland on a Horrow or Hurdell and that she lived there in the time of St Endelient, which by guess we may think to be about the year 550. And the path wherein they used to walk to pass one to the other is noted at this daye by the inhabitants to be greener than any other part, especially after Tillage. There was a tree over her well which those that attempted to cut down had ever harm, so as they gave over to cut it. Till one more bold than the rest did cut it down, who hurting himself was noted to die shortly after. This happened in our time.

But on that day, when Endelient welcomed Ilick at Port Quin, one thing, at least, would have been the same, the little harbour and the sloping fields of the valley down which still runs the stream, bordered by red and white valerian and yellow archangel, from which Endelient and Ilick must have drunk. Though, of course, none of the cottages would have been here. Nowadays they have all been restored about the massive fish cellars which no longer deal in fish.

Nothing can restore the remains of the old fishermen's cottages halfway up the hill towards the path which Endelient and Ilick took when meeting each other and which 'remained greener than any other.' They are now deep under ivy. Here, at the end of the last century, lived the men who are said all to have been drowned one night of terrible storm in the only boat the hamlet owned. So that no one was left but the women and children and they went away. The hamlet was deserted.

Possibly this is true though Norden, the Cornish historian, tells the same story of the place in about 1545. Perhaps it is the kind of legend which once attracted to a place never dies, as are the legends and stories of the six virgins. At all events when I first saw Port Quin, on a January day in 1934, it was certainly deserted. No one was in the lanes; I walked past the falling-down cottages and met the sole inhabitant, a pig, rootling in the stream where it runs into the sea. I was told then, when I got back to St Minver where I was staying, that I could buy the entire hamlet for five hundred pounds. How much I would have liked that!

Who is to say that Endelient and her friend Ilick did not fish from the same rocks below Kellan Head where the young man stands tonight and brings in a fine bass? She may have lived only on cow's milk but Ilick, after her hazardous journey, would have needed something more substantial and, once the gossip was over, she would have been very hungry. In summer evenings might they not have walked along Reedy Cliff, high above the sea, where the small meterological hut now stands overlooking Port Isaac bay, to watch the sun set? There could not have been all that number of people who needed healing that they did not have a little spare time. And, further, so early are they, they must have been imbued with an animistic sense of nature and probably possessed of powers of clairvoyance. Their 'cures' must have relied heavily upon plants, the gathering of which would have meant much walking. The only wonder to me is that no-one has ever said that they met her ghost here and about the church.

I was in the church late on such a summer night with a friend, Meg. All the light we had was the moon through the clear glass windows and the hanging light before the Sacrament. Endelient could well have been there with us since there was, too, a lamp burning over her shrine, that wonderfully carved stone altar which has always been attributed to the Master of St Endellion, whoever he was. And in the graveyard outside, with the farm animals blowing into the dewy grass, the bindweed and the ladies lace and the slow summer sea banging away in the cove at Port Quin:

> Was there nothing we wanted
> Here, when the clock struck,
> But to be flitting like two ghosts
> In the hollow vault
> Of this wind-shorne church?
>
> Would you not have thought
> That those Elements
> Behind the candle-lit curtain
> Would have warmed us?
>
> In the cold outside, scanning
> The funeral slabs for a tombstone
> Which didn't exist (though
> I said it did), and so for
> Cottage-watchers creating
> A spinning of hobgoblins,
> We were cold.
>
> It rests there on a northern shore,
> With its aumbry and its candlelit interior.
> Day and night it doesn't change.
> Only we do that.

Port Isaac was young when Ilick lived there. But now it is drowned with age and damp. In its centre deep, down the narrow lanes, it is foundering in fish heads and men who gaze always seaward. They must have tumbled into their beds in the side-by-side cottages waiting for the call for the lifeboat, when the wind raged outside. And then, blind with sleep, with everyone in the village awake, gone up to help pull the lifeboat down the crooked street to the harbour, with the power of the rollers ahead of them, the whales of waves their fate to be launched into. You can see, in the huddled wall of the main street, the hollows cut by the boat's gunwhales as it was heaved below and out into the waters, with the shells rattling up its side from the foreshore, swinging in the dark sea, and behind it and the men in it were the tower of St Endellion church, the sites of old mansions and older Stones, tumuli and quarries.

Adwena chose a more inland parish for her hermitage. I always feel that she must have been the loneliest of all the sisters. It is true that she had Juliana at Lanteglos-by-Camelford. But she herself was stuck up on the edge of the moors and, only in summer, would the other sisters have cared to go into such a bleak wilderness. Such a journey, in winter, might even have been dangerous, since this part of Cornwall was more wooded then and there would have been wolves, even bears.

Adwena's experience of God would not have been soft like her sister's. She would have known the hardness of moorstone and lived on the reliance of wild animals. Her paths were sketched with the carcases of dead beasts and the birds which came to feed on them. Her heaven a sketch of granite; her happiness in solitude and open spaces. Her God was the wind in high places. His voice spoke in the funnels of moorland, in the sharp dry grasses, in the veridian glow of bogs. She would have half seen his beard in the bog cotton for she looked north to the tors of Brown Willy and Roughtor. Just as to the neolithic people who lived here before her, God spoke to her from their heights sometimes in terror, sometimes in peace. What would she have made of the ruins of neolithic huts on the hill's slopes when she stood looking down at them, the homes of people who were nearer to her than to us? She would not have gone near them at night. For all her Christian upbringing, their spirits were still, at this time, too dark, too frightening to be faced in anything but full daylight, their magic still too powerful, a dark veil at the back of her mind which Christianity was too young yet to destroy completely.

Even today to walk in the valley behind Roughtor, with Brown Willy and Garrow before you, can be an alarming experience. None of the sisters would have risked it, their Christian souls being too frail and new-born to combat this magic which is still potent today.

Adwena's church, marking her shrine, is away over the fields, lonely, deserted, a stone upthrust of tower which can take you by surprise. But loved by the villagers who have recently restored the building. Here are laid, down the centuries, the skeletons of Advent, beneath the funeral slabs surrounding the church, communing with themselves as dusk begins to fall. Why should they not? There is no one else to talk to as the meadow is filled with the yellow light of buttercups and the daisies close. What might they think of an occasional visitor? They scuttle back beneath their slate shells and whisper to one another, 'As we are, so shalt thou be.' Their church lies sadly in the meadows, a place where you feel you, too, have come to your end.

If, however, Adwena needed company she could have come down the hill from her hermitage and so along the river walk (as we do today) into the settlement which is now Camelford, though there would have been no sewage works to pass at the end of the valley. The river Camel is still young here, rising a few miles away on Hendraburnick Down. In Adwena's time the woods which line the walk were denser and thicker. Here she might have met her sister from Lanteglos, Juliana, whose shrine is in deeper woods and hollows than any of them. Or her sister Mabyn from another inland parish, or Tedda from the present-day parish of St Teath. They would have brushed each other's hair by the side of the stream and drunk a cup of milk which Endelient had brought over with her. They would have chatted about their home in Ireland and wept with homesickness.

The woods of Helland would have been more extensive than they are today when Tedda went there from the village, St Teath, named after her to gather bluebells and primroses and wood anemones to take to her sister Endelient, or Mabyn at another inland hermitage, or even to Menfrede at present day St Minver. Canon Doble, in his *Children of Brychan* says that nothing is known of Tedda. Roscarrock merely says that her feast day is 1st May and that a small collegiate church existed at St Teath in the Middle Ages.

I think that, being so self-effacing, Tedda would have understood completely Anne Jefferies and what happened to her, though she would have disapproved strongly of the magical quality of Anne's experience. Anne was born in St Teath, in 1626, the daughter of a labourer. Until she was nineteen she lived a perfectly ordinary life and went as a servent to Moses Pitt in his big house in St Teath. Actually she was, at first, nursemaid to Moses. But as he grew up and Anne remained on as servant, he became interested in her experiences and wrote about them. Moses later became a prison reformer in London.

For some unknown reason, since Anne was reputed to be a 'bold' girl, she took an enormous interest in fairies. Of course she was uneducated and innocent and, perhaps, a little simple. On the other hand, since she was looking after the boy Moses, who was later called to given evidence about her miraculous cures, was it not possible that she was only trying to amuse her charge. She actually it was said, went about the fields and hedgerows (as might any other village girl of that time) looking under fern leaves and into the bells of hollyhocks searching for fairies.

I remember, when I was a very small boy, my nurse telling me almost exactly the same kind of story, that fairies inhabited the flowers. I walked through the Kent fields 'obsessed' with the 'little people' in much the same way as I believe Anne to have been. So that when she began her mysterious cures the only way she could explain them was to refer them to the fairies who, she claimed, came to her one afternoon when she was resting in a garden arbour. For the time it was, doubtless, a reasonable explanation. At least until the Church heard of it.

That afternoon, she said, she heard tiny, mocking laughter and presently, saw standing before her a miniature man dressed in green with a red feather in his cap. More followed, dropping out of the rosebushes and trees. One of them passed his fingers over her eyes. She became momentarily blinded and was whirled away to a fairyland of trees with exotic fruits and wonderful flowers. In short to a paradise where there was no looking after children, no housework, no illness. The odd thing was, she declared, that the inhabitants of this paradise were no longer small but of normal proportions. When she was eventually returned to the garden in St Teath she woke up in the same position as when she was suddenly rendered blind.

Most of this can, of course, be explained as being either a dream or some kind of fit. Indeed, Moses Pitt writing about her later said that she was in a state of delirium for the entire winter and that, when she recovered, she was a shambling, witless creature. When the summer came again she recovered. Had such a thing happened to a country girl today she would have been whisked away to some psychiatrist and submitted to various inhuman cures. The entire innocence of the story (which is not unlike the stories attached to the Virgin Saints) would have been lost.

Anne, herself, of course, believed her 'visitations' to be a form of magic. More was to follow which is not so easily explained. She found she had acquired the power of healing. Probably she discovered the homeopathic value of wild flowers. People came from all over Cornwall, even from London, to be cured by her, just as other people came to be cured by the power of holy wells. Her reputation came about from the fact that when Moses's mother fell, in the garden, and injured herself Anne cured her immediately.

Anne would never allow anyone to pay her money for her cures, and an even more magical property began to manifest itself. She never bought any medicines and she needed no ordinary food. She declared that she was being fed by the 'fairies'. This continued from harvest time to the following Christmas Day. Moses Pitt, who was not very old at the time, later said that he thought she was existing on field mushrooms and bread made from harvest gleanings. He questioned her, asking what fairy food tasted like. Anne gave him a piece of 'their' bread. He ate it and said it was the tastiest he had ever eaten.

Naturally Anne made enemies. The most powerful was Jan Tregeagle, a noted J.P. and steward to Lord Robartes of Lanhydrock House, near Bodmin. Tregeagle had an evil reputation. He had Anne arrested and thrown into Bodmin Gaol, where she refused all food of any kind. After a number of weeks Tregeagle, thinking that she must be getting food from somewhere, removed her to his own house at Trevorder, near Wadebridge. Yet the same thing happened. Closely watched on all occasions Anne never showed the least sign of starvation. Tregeagle was forced to release her on condition that she did not return to the Pitt household. Anne finally gave up all 'correspondence' with magic or the fairies because the Church forbade her to continue. She went into service in Padstow and married William Warren. It is not known when she died.

The 'magic' of fairies and her curative powers is the explanation of Anne Jefferies from a rustic, village, point of view. Her fellow villagers would have understood completely and venerated her. This was the danger. For Tregeagle was not an uneducated man. He was rich and owned a number of houses other than Trevorder one of which, in 1964, became my own home, Treneague, not far from Trevorder and divided from it by a wood called Squirrel's Hunt. Tregeagle was, as I've said, the steward to Lord Robartes, the leading Parliamentarian of the county in this period of Civil War. And when Anne went about St Teath praying, 'very much and bids people keepe ye old form of prayer; she says the King shall shortly enjoy his own, and be revenged on his enemyes,' she was unlikely to recommend herself to the forces of Cromwell who were busy destroying the home of the Carminows in the same parish. It seems to me inevitable that she should have been imprisoned and starved if only to keep her from propagating such reactionary ideas.

When she was released, well and strong, the country people naturally attributed her health to the 'fairies' she had spoken of after her fit in the orchard. And this side of her story, in its associations with very ancient magic, is the most interesting.

It has similarities with the story of the Green Children. Only in reverse. They, two children, emerged from an unknown land into a field in the village of Woolpit, in East Anglia, where men were working in a harvest field. Their skin was light green and no one could understand a word they said. They were wearing dresses of a material not known in that part of the world. When, at last, they were able to explain themselves and their native land, they told the villagers that everyone in that land was green in colour. The sun never shone there but the air was illumined with a soft sunset-like light. They explained their arrival in Woolpit by saying that, one day they were following their green sheep and came on a huge cavern. They went into it and were seduced by the sweet sound of bells ringing. So they went on and came out in the Woolpit wheat field and were stunned by the sound of voices. Turning to flee they were unable to find the entrance to the cavern by which they had arrived and were caught.

Perhaps they had come from the very fairyland which Anne is supposed to have visited, the bells, the lovely, soft colours, the sweet sound of music seems to point that way. And although the boy died a little after his arrival, the girl settled down, gradually lost her green colour and, like Anne, married. Like Anne again she never referred to the land from which she had come.

St Teath is a hill village, sheltering under the brow of Delabole. You come down the hedged lanes and past the site of the old mine at Treburgett which was working as early as 1838. The chimney and engine house were blown up in 1920. Now nothing remains on the surface but sloe and blackberry bushes and traces of foundations where stonechats nest. Below are still the shafts and adits, Grinder's Shaft, Footway Shaft, Massey's and Engine Shaft. From 1871 and for the following ten years the mine was thriving, producing 2180 tons of lead ore, 9530 ozs of silver, 44 tons of zinc ore, 120 tons of pyrite and 62 tons of iron ore.

Down the lanes — or across the meadows — past Quarry Park from which the stone was taken to build my present home in 1899, are the remains of the Carminow's mansion at Tregannick (now a farm) which was destroyed, as I've said, in Anne Jefferies time, in the Civil War. The Carminows traced their descent from King Arthur and, no doubt, early members of the family knew Endelient, if Arthur *was* her godfather. Their motto was 'Cala Rag Whetlow' which means, 'A Straw for a Talebearer.'

I was digging in my garden a few weeks after we moved in. It had not, this particular patch, been cultivated for over sixty years, a huge shed being erected over it in 1914. I dug up a Commonwealth cannon ball which must date back to this time. One of those, presumably, which was not fired at Tregannick. It is very heavy and gives one some idea what it must have been like to have been hit by such a missile.

Over the rolling landscape, with Helsbury Castle on the horizon at Michaelstow, as you come down into the Allen valley, is the top of the church tower in the centre of St Teath village which has the

Carminow arms on the pulpit. When you reach the valley of the river Allen, which Rowlandson painted a great deal in the late eighteenth century, you are on one of the loveliest roads in Cornwall, that from Camelford to Wadebridge which was little known before it became, some five years ago, a Holiday Route. It is sheltered on one side by Foxhole woods, leading to Tower Woods, both of which are carpets of bluebells in early summer, and on the other side by the rancid watermeadows running from Knight's Mill, until they open out into the flat sweet level of farmland.

On your right hand, over the wooded hill, the deserted railway runs through Trelill tunnel above which stands one of the loveliest small Methodist Chapels in Cornwall. A turning to the left takes you to Tedda's sister, Mabyn's hermitage, who died (says Rosscarrock) in 550. Another turning off this long valley road brings you to yet another sister's parish, that of Menfrede, at St Minver, where as I have explained, I first became aware of nature properly when I fed the calf with milk. Menfrede was the most spirited of the sisters, the one who stood no nonsense. Roscarrock tells us how he himself remembered a chapel dedicated to her, at Tredresick, which was 'less than two miles from the place where her sister Endelient lived. And there is also a well of her name.'

It was here that the Devil came to molest her. Menfrede was combing her hair beside the well at the time and was in no mood to argue theology or anything else with the 'Ghostlie Adversarie'. Instead she threw her comb at him and he fled. A rather cowardly Devil, who was frightened of fierce women and chose the wrong sister to pester, for the best he could do was to leave a note behind him at a place called Topalundy, beside 'a deepe strange Hoale' which he made himself as an escape route from the enraged Saint. No one has said what was in the note. The 'Devil' sounds all too human to me, a local out to seduce the girl. At all events the hole is still there. You pass it as you walk from Port Quin to Lundy Bay. Here, at high tides, the sea roars in. The noise can hardly be, today, the voice of a Devil disappointed as long ago as 550 A.D.!

If Tedda had wanted to she and her sisters could have taken a picnic out of the village north west, either to the rock-strewn Tregardock beach to which, even today, few people come, or taken a stroll round the almost medieval hamlet of Treligga, though the Methodist chapel (now a private dwelling house) would not have been there, even if the rough, unmade-up lanes through the hamlet would. For Treligga is that oddity today, a hamlet which looks the same as it did in the Middle Ages, the farms, just off the 'main' street, with middens at the door, pigs wandering past the houses, gardens giving straight on to the grassland, almost treeless here on the northern shore. If it were suddenly deserted it would, in a few years, become another, a more modern, Chysauster.

They could have gone on past Trebarwith Strand and its great caves to the harbour at Boscastle and so by deep meadows and woods to visit Julitta who, although her chief shrine was at Lanteglos-by-Camelford, had extended her influence northwards up the coast. Being so much the most active, the most explorer-minded of them all, she might not have approved of their wandering about visiting. They ought rather to be more ardent in spreading the Gospel further into Cornwall.

And it was to Julitta's church, beginning as a chapel in 1238, that Thomas Hardy came as architect for the restoration, in March 1870, and met his first wife Emma.

That the church needed to be restored is obvious from Emma's description of it. She was the rector's sister-in-law, living with him and his wife in the rectory. She played the harmonium for services and must have known the building intimately and the 'tower which went on cracking year to year.' The carved bench ends were falling apart with rot, ivy trailed from the roof which was full of bird's nests.

Thomas Hardy was twenty-nine when he first came to Cornwall. That day he dressed by candlelight in the cottage at Bockhampton, in Dorset, where he was born. It was still dark when he set out. He went by train from Dorchester to Launceston. Here he hired a trap for the last sixteen miles to St Juliot, where he arrived between six and seven in the evening. Emma was also twenty-nine.

She received him, as the rector was ill in bed with gout and Helen, Emma's sister, was looking after him. Hardy was wearing, she tells us, 'a rather shabby overcoat', his voice was soft and his beard yellowish. In spite of this Emma records that she felt him to be no stranger to her, for she had already seen him in a dream and 'was immediately arrested by his familiar appearance'.[1]

The next day Hardy began the work of measuring the half-ruined church, and notes for *A Pair of Blue Eyes* were going down on the blue scrap paper he always carried. For him the double romance of Cornwall, which he always called Lyonesse, and Emma Gifford, had begun.

By the gate into the church you can still see pieces of the stonework which Hardy rejected from the restoration, the piscina he threw out and the odd bits of window stone. I have sat on the gate into the churchyard, in hard weather, and heard the sea booming in the Beeny caverns and away on the stoney beach of the Strangles, and thought of these two courting, in these still lonely lanes, one hundred years ago.

> I rode my pretty mare and he walked by my side and I showed him some (more) of the neighbourhood — the cliffs, along the roads, and through the scattered hamlets, sometimes gazing down at the solemn small shores (below) where the seals lived, coming out of great caverns occasionally. We sketched and talked of books; often we walked down the beautiful (Valency) valley to Boscastle harbour where we had to jump over stones and climb a low wall by rough steps, (or) get through by narrow pathways to come out on the great wide spaces suddenly, with a pearling little brook going the same way, into which we once lost a tiny picnic-tumbler, and there it is to this day no doubt, between two small boulders.[1]

Emma Gifford was born in Plymouth on 24th November 1840. In her book *Some Recollections* she does not slur over the fact that her father suffered from depression and drunken bouts. As she grew older she, too, 'became obsessed by the difference between her social status and that of her husband, making painful references to it in public.'

But now, in 1870, everything was different. It is those two lovers one remembers when you take this walk along the Valency valley from the village of Boscastle, for they must often have come this way. Emma would be wearing 'a soft deep dark coloured brown

---

1 *Some Recollections* by Emma Hardy. Edited by Evelyn Hardy and Robert Gittings. O.U.P. 1961
1 *Some Recollections*. Emma Hardy

habit' and 'a brown felt hat turned up at the sides.' Her mare, called Fanny, was brown, too. Hardy, as they came down the long path and the secret meadows beneath the cliffs and beside the stream would have walked ahead holding the bridle.

If they were coming from St Juliot itself they would have passed the old farm cottage by the lane and come to the turning and the bridge over the Valency brook which leads upwards, through the woods, to Minster church. Emma would have dismounted. The climb upwards reminds you of something from a Scott novel, so steep is it between the rowan trees and the spindleberry. Brown with the autumn bracken and the red parson-in-the-pulpit; free of tourists; exactly as it was, remote and lonely in Hardy's time, winding high up above the river and coming out beside a barn, the path dropping over a stile to the church.

The graveyard is sloping down through a cutting in the woods, with tombs which must have been here when they came and tied up Fanny by the gate and watched, as I did, the fox run down the valley and into that parkland which takes you back to Boscastle.

This is the church of St Merteriana, Virgin, who is also the patroness of Tintagel, though no relation to Brychan's Virgins. When Hardy and Emma visited it it had been recently restored, in 1869. He would have come to compare the restoration with what he was doing at St Juliot. The church itself, set in its exquisitely beautiful and remote glen has lost all the interest it must have had when it was a pre-Conquest monastery. Being an alien — it had been given by William de Bottreaux, with the manor of Polefant, to the monks of SS Sergius and Bacchus at Angers, in 1190 — it was confiscated by the Crown during the Hundred Year's War.

Though in 1386 the church and monastic buildings were in ruin, by 1407 it must have been restored to some kind of order, for the Norman church consisted only of a nave and chancel. This was, in the fifteenth century, enlarged with an aisle and tower. And from this tower (with memories of the monastery below) is a fine view over the cliffs to the sea. Did Hardy and Emma climb to the top and look towards Emma's home, the rectory at St Juliot, or out towards their favourite spot, Beeny Cliff? At least Hardy wrote a poem on that cliff which begins:

O the opal and the sapphire of that wandering western sea,
And the woman riding high above with bright hair flapping free —
The woman whom I loved so, and who loyally loved me.

Minster is the mother church of Boscastle. And though the village is crowded by tourists in summer, in winter it becomes much as it must have been when Bottreaux Castle was the home of the great family of Bottreaux and when the church, before the Reformation, was a scene of pilgrimage to the shrine of St Merteriana.

So the long Cornish summers passed for the sisters between healing and praying, between combating their Devils and endless bright prayer. In a world of nature they were half conscious of earlier religions, the desires of magic, and not a little frightened of their own naturalistic powers. So much so that they would have avoided Rocky Valley where, even today, are the cabalistic designs of neolithic man's religion, two mazes cut out of the rock face beside the stream falling to the sea. They were there when the sisters were living. Though they could have known nothing about the legend of the Minotaur, instinctively they would have regarded these traces as magical and part of a religion they had come, if not to destroy, at least to absorb.

By all their acts they sought to prove that the mission on which Brychan, their father, had sent them was a mission of love. And when winter came they huddled within their huts which cannot have been so different from the neolithic huts on the moors, or on the sandhills at Harlyn Bay, and drew themselves into the warmth of animals, sheep and cows. They became part of the need of nature to survive, waiting for the sun to return in spring.

12. Slate

At St Neot, near Liskeard, are famous slate quarries. They are a series of labyrinths (now open to the public) going back, in their working, much longer than the written records of eighty years ago. These quarries are chambers running into the hillside some three hundred feet, parallel to each other, divided by pillars of unwrought stone. From these caves were mined the famous 'St Neot's Blues,' the dark slates which were shifted to Fowey by packhorse trains.

Perhaps at the same time as the first man dug slate at St Neot, another first man put in his pick at an outcrop of slate to the north of the county. Anyway, over four hundred years have gone by since that first slate was dug and split. The result, today, is that the most celebrated slate quarry in Cornwall (if not actually in the world) is some five hundred feet deep and over a mile round the perimeter. The rocks of north Cornwall were formed by the breakdown of older rocks into very small particles by weathering. The sediment which resulted from this breaking-down found its way to the sea through small inland streams where it came to rest as mud on the sea floor. Enormous pressures and heat (such as that from the Bodmin moor granite) recrystallised the particles in the mud into various new minerals, the most important for Delabole slate being seracite, which being a plate-like mineral imparts to slate its characteristic cleavage.

Delabole Slate quarries have been famous for well over a hundred years, as witness an entry in Murray's *Handbook for Devon and Cornwall*. It is dated 1859; after directing the traveller how to get to Delabole it goes on:

The quarries present one of the most astonishing and animated scenes imaginable. The traveller suddenly beholds three enormous pits, which, excavated by the uninterrupted labour of centuries, are encompassed by dark blue hills of rubbish, continually on the increase, and slowly encroaching upon the domain of the farmer. The scene is enlivened by a throng of men, busily engaged in various noisy employments, while waggons and horses are everywhere in rapid motion, and steam-engines are lifting with a harsh sound their ponderous arms, and raising loaded trucks from the depths of the pit, or masses of slate of several tons weight, which are seen slowly ascending *guide-chains* to stages which overhang the quarries ... About one thousand men are employed in these works, who raise on an average one hundred and twenty tons of slate per day, which, manufactured on the spot into roofing slates, cisterns and other articles, are exported to various parts of the United Kingdom, and to France, Belgium, the West Indies and America ... If the stranger should be desirous of comparing the produce from the different quarries, all within the one quarry, he can ascertain the quality by the *sound* when the stone is struck, which should be clear and sonorous; by the *colour*, since the light blue is firm and close, the blackish blue of a loose texture and apt to imbibe water; and lastly by the *feel*, a good stone being hard and rough to the touch, and a bad one smooth and oily. The best slate from any quarry is called the *bottom-stone*, and at Delabole is found at and below a depth of twenty four fath, from the surface.

When I was a boy we came along the railway from Launceston (where we had changed from London) past the hamlet of Tresmeer where my great-uncle had been vicar. At Delabole, three stations further on, we could look down into this tremendous pit of the quarries as the train passed. Some of the quarry faces were practically sheer. Men had to be lowered on ropes to work the slate from them. Blasting used to take place at specific times of day and, after the blast, the smoke and falling rubble and stone. It seemed to us, then, fresh from London, a romantic place. It is still that today.

In those days (since the sea-coast was, for the most part, more exciting and what we had come for) I never went into the quarries. The most I did was to walk to the bottom edge through Helland Wood. Then, by a lane, to the actual edge where to look over was to peer down into a Jules Verne world. The men working the quarry bottom were like midgets, those appearing, here and there, in the mouths of the slate galleries all the way up the face, gradually grew larger and larger. The ledges of the slate were like barren gardens, watered by falling streams which, striking slate, filled with air with colours of the slate itself.

Before the first world war some five hundred men and boys worked here, either in the actual mining, the loading of the slate blocks into trucks to be hauled to the surface up an incline by steel ropes, or in the sawing and slate-splitting sheds. In those days (now, alas, gone, though there is a new application of 'fine' slate for etching and the tourist trade) the slate of the most perfect quality was used for headstones and wall plaques. It had to be free from any flaw. The result is obvious in every churchyard in Cornwall, with their memorial verses like the one in Tintagel, of April 8th, 1702:

> The body that here buried lies
> By lightning felt Death's sacrifice,
> To Him Elijah's fate was given,
> He rode in flames of fire to Heaven.

When the sawing and splitting was done, the slate went to the dressing machines which squared it into various sizes according to measure, Duchies or Duchess, 24" x 12"; Counties or Countess, 20" x 10" and so on, such as Ladies, Queens, Rags and Imperials. The small slates called Scantle, were cut by hand, using a horse and zex. The horse was a block of wood with a travel iron and the zex a heavy knife. The rustic red colouring of some of the slate is due to iron-bearing metals in that part of the quarry from which it is taken. All the homes I have ever had in Cornwall have been roofed with this wonderful grey-blue Delabole slate. It gives one a deep sense of security.

In the seventeenth century and later, the slate was taken by waggon to Port Gaverne, north of Port Isaac. Women loaded it on to ships. Then, with the arrival of the railway, sidings were built right into the quarries. Now even that has gone and the little slate that is bought and used for roofing (owing to the expense of quarrying and the availability of newer, more unattractive roofing materials) is carried away by lorry as is, also, the material called *Delafil*, manufactured here, a finely ground slate powder used as a 'filler' for other industrial products and for roofing felt. Lorries full of the powder rattle past my present home daily.

To walk through Helland Wood from the mill pond at Newhall and to come to the lip of the quarries at night, over the ripped-up railways lines, is an eerie experience. The street lights of the village of Delabole cast a faint glow over the edge and there is an endless tiny noise of water gently falling, of earth and stones moving below. The pit itself is a vast area of blackness in which one can just make out the several white roads in the slate at the bottom.

As with all quarries there have been tragedies at Delabole. In 1843 a huge slab of rock fell on six men and threw them into an old working full of water where they were crushed and drowned. In 1845, ground from the edge of Clock Tower meadow fell two hundred and fifty feet upon men working at that depth and killed four of them.

On April 21st, 1869, women with their children came to the quarry with food for their husbands. Almost as soon as they arrived the whole of the pappot head, including six landing places, fell into the quarry pit. It carried men, women and children and ten thousand tons of rock down in a terrible landslide. Even today the quarry is not without its dangers.

Few people, I imagine, read Eden Phillpotts today. In 1915 he published his novel *Old Delabole* which is now a rare book. It is both a lengthy love story in the fashion of the time and a description of the slate mines and village of Delabole, with attractive landscapes at Treligga, the nearby village, which has hardly changed for over a hundred years, above the rocky beach of Tregardock:

> For this is Delabole, [he wrote] a hamlet created by one industry, whose men and boys to the number of five hundred work in the slate quarries as their fathers have done and their children's children will do. Since Tudor times the slate of Delabole has come to market, for men worked here before Shakespeare wrote.

He was being optimistic for, today, only ninety men work at the quarries and Delabole is as much a village of holiday cottages and people retired from the Midlands as it is a quarry 'town'. Yet he gives brilliant and still valid pictures of what the quarries were like in the days he was writing about which must have been about 1900:

> The immensity of the quarries might well be marked from below. Over the green pool at the bottom of the pit there passed a trestle-bridge, and around it the space that appeared shrunk to nothing from above, spread out in some acres of apparent confusion and chaos. A village might have stood here ... At this season much water was finding its way into the quarries and the pool often rose a foot in a night. Many a rill spouted against the purple and olive sides of the slate, and from rifts and cracks in the quarry walls came threads of water.
> When the low sun burned into the depths, it set a rainbow there. Then the faces of the rock were transformed and their wetness shone orange-tawny, gold and crimson.

Today, from the back rooms of my home, in St Teath, I can look out at the great spoil heaps of the quarries which contain, so Mr Brian Setchell, the manager, told me, something like seventy five million tons of rubbish deposited here over the centuries. Between my house and that colossal pile are farms and the lovely Helland wood, one of the few secret and private 'worlds' in Cornwall.

Through the farmyard at Newhall Mill, in which lived one of Phillpott's 'heroes', Wesley Blake, you cross a meadow full of scrub bushes and little ponds and wild flowers, cattle and geese and chickens from the farm, with a few cats sleeping peacefully under sheds, and enter a long walk with stone walls covered in moss. This path takes you gently upward to the villages of Pengelly and Higher Pengelly, parts of Delabole itself. You are drawn through the wood inevitably by the sight of the spoil heaps getting nearer and nearer, and by the ghosts of old Cornishmen who used this path to come and go to work in the quarry.

Now no walk is lovelier. The trees hang touching overhead; wood sorrel and bluebells are at your feet. To the right the woods fall away to the valley and its little stream, the early Allen river below. But for the fact that the Mill is now the studio of the artist Henry Isaacs, little has changed here from what Eden Phillpotts saw:

> Here spread a wide combe that opened westerly between the hills. Within it, under the lea of the land, trees grew to maturity, woods throve and sank to deep dingles by a streamlet. Beech and oak, spruce and fir flourished from the larches, at every breath of the winter wind, flew the dead needles like a cloud of gold dust. St Teath's squat tower rose at the bottom of the valley among the last autumn brightness of the trees.

It was down this sylvan path that the coffin-bearers used to come before there was a church at Delabole. The people, then, were buried in St Teath churchyard which contains one of the oldest of Delabole slate tombstones on record, dated 1580.

They came down this long woodland path, in solemn procession, past the entrance to Helland farm (the new drive is higher up, nearer the village of Pengelly) stopping, here and there, to lay the coffin down or to change bearers, to the lane into the village of Trewalder and so up the longer lane and past what is now my house, but was then meadows, into St Teath. They would have stopped for a drink of water from one of the village's three wells which was situated beside my house but which has now been filled in.

They carried the coffin on poles as they do today and sang songs and hymns on the journey, so that the expression 'seeing him home' when the Cornish bury a man, became very real and prolonged as they walked sedately through nature beneath the trees and through knee-high bracken. It was the last green journey for the dead, in summer accompanied by butterflies and the songs of birds. It was, as much as anything, a funeral poem written in fallen leaves or in spring flowers. To the children who followed in the train of the coffin it was a never-to-be-forgotten journey.

Today the passage-ways below the main path which led to the farm at Delinuth are grown over where the land falls to the Allen, coming down through the long valley to Knight's Mill and the rush of the main holiday route road. Yet the trees, the wild flowers, the birds and bumble bees remain interlaced with wild honeysuckle and free from noxious sprays, here just below the upthrust of the slate quarries.

Of course much is changed at Delabole since Eden Phillpotts wrote his novel. But it still remains an Old Testament landscape in which you expect to see a white-bearded Prophet fulminating against the wickedness of today, or a Job opening his boils with a sliver of slate. It is still a colossal hole in nature, indeed one of the largest open-cast quarries in the country. Looking down into this hole one does not believe it, because it is hidden so well from the surrounding countryside. One is shocked at the size of this huge opening, as one was shocked by the size of bombcraters in the last war which, on a massive scale, it resembles even to the willow-herb growing within it. It is big enough to hold an entire village or small town. It is the immense hollow tooth of Cornwall.

I stood with Mr Setchell looking down to the water at the bottom. He explained to me how, in the old days, all this open space we were looking at would have been covered in aerial tramlines and that the whole pit would have been a hive of activity. The quarry seems to be driven down a valley. Originally, there were five quarries called Load Work, Lease Work, Grove, Delabole, and Clark's Hole or Ash Tree because of the ash tree which grew from the slate at that spot.

In the pit bottom were huge moraines of recent falls. The fall on the west side is of brown rock and is unusable as slate. This fall occured naturally in 1967. The fall to the east would have happened naturally in the course of time. But for safety's sake it was thought right to precipitate a fall by diverting a stream into fissures in the rock. 'At 4.15 p.m. on 2nd January, 1973, the attempt commenced and at 8.30 p.m. an estimated 245,000 tons of rock fell away from the face — the largest manmade rock fall in the British Isles this century.'[1]

I asked Mr Setchell if Wesley had ever preached here — it is exactly the right spot for him to have done so — but he said no, only Clark, a compatriot of Wesley's had ever preached here and this was the reason for the naming of one of the faces as 'Clarks'! Here, beside an outcrop of rock is the actual hitching post that Clark tied his horse to before preaching to the quarriers. His voice must have rocked off the far walls to the west of the quarry and gone racing out into North Cornwall on the fierce winds that blow at Delabole as he gave back to the miners the spiritual sustenance which they had lacked for so long. And then he would have gone back to Cornish tea in some cottage in the village of Delabole, until it was time for him to move on in the endless circuits these early Wesleyans undertook, in all weathers and often with very

1 Quoted from *Old Delabole Slate Quarry*, Pamphlet by Frederick Ross', Delaviews Ltd

little food inside them, to rescue the rough and sometimes brutal, because neglected, Cornish miners.

Delabole is an amphitheatre compared to which Gwennap Pit is a saucer to a deep soup bowl. It is a pit round which a man's voice could echo till the end of time and where the Word preached would not be easily forgotten. Perhaps this aspect of the slate mines is what reminds me so foribly of the Old Testament. In a thunderstorm up here one thinks not so much of the rain as of the clouds opening and the Old Testament God appearing, upon a sulphurish light, in the centre of the pit.

All these old 'faces' or workings were amalgamated in 1840. I stood and looked over from the platform on the surface where visitors are welcomed. How few ever understand the essence of this hardness, the living vitality of the slate, the numinous quality of the light here? Below now only two men were working at the enormous moraine of the recent fall, a wart of slate on the open palm of the quarry. What a lifetime to pick over such a massive heap!

One man was operating an hydraulic hammer and chisel; the other a dump truck which, when filled, would presently come up one of the three or four white roads that lead from the depths of this moraine to the surface. They quarry five tons of useable slate to every ninety five tons of waste.

Today the sun was shining powerfully down into the quarry, lightening up the patches of green scrub on the 'old' sides and the fantastic crop of scarlet pimpernel which grows here on the quarry shelves and elsewhere. Red slate was winking in the sun. High up on the deserted mine cliffs and terraces jackdaws were nesting and herring gulls flying, regular coronets of birds, free on their unreachable ledges beyond the now deserted railway. They have had buzzards, kestrels and ravens nesting here which is not surprising, for it is a fine place for these birds with the lowlands so available for hunting. They drop down from their perches in the slate upon their prey going in the hay meadows and cool waters of the stream. The terraces are riddled with fox earths.

Now I could see the outline of the railway along which I came when I was a boy on holiday and thought of all the old men who had worked here and, on special days, put on their best clothes and went off to Launceston or to Padstow. I thought of the enormous amount of sweat and toil in those days when men relied so greatly on their muscles and the strength of their bodies (and the strength of horses). I thought, too, of the women and children who had come to hear Clark preach on hell and the Devil, and sometimes on Love and Heaven, high up here on the opening of the quarries. I thought of the hard hands of those workers, with the feel of the slate in them, a poem of slate in their expert minds and the songs of the endless wire ropes which brought their labour to the surface.

We came away from the edge, from the slatescape of red and green and white, back into the 'workings', powdered with white dust past the ruins of a tall chimney, built in 1928, past walls of old sheds where forty or fifty men might have worked, to a stone house with four enormous winches and drums, now lying idle. Each drum has a fifty horse power motor attached to it which operated the 'railway' up and down a long incline to the pit bottom. The rails are still there; the little wooden trucks, now of no use, are still on the rails, forlorn, desolate, the scarlet pimpernel growing about their iron wheels. Rusty waggons and other machinery lay about and gave colour to the grey walls and the grey slate chippings on which we were walking.

I stood at the top of the incline and asked Mr Setchell if there had ever been a house actually inside the quarry as there is in Eden Phillpotts's novel.

'Yes,' he said, 'just below where we're standing, but it went ages ago. We pump pit water from the bottom to an adit below here, too, by the wooden bridge there, at the rate of sixty gallons a minute. The southern end is covered by rubble, but we know where it is.'

We went now to the crushing sheds where the slate not used for splitting and sawing, undergoes its first pulverisation. Powder already filled the air and my throat, and the sun had a haze circle about it. The crushed slate passes up conveyor belts into the enormous industrial shed where it is further broken down, parcelled into paper bags and taken to the railway. Or else loaded into aluminium-coloured containers and driven to the rail-head at Wadebridge. This is the powder which is used either for roofing felt or for filling and extending paints and protective coatings.

Roche Rock showing the ruins of the old chapel

(*Richard Hawken*)

The Hurlers *(Richard Ha...)*

Mazes in Rocky Valley, cut in the rock face by neolithic man *(Charles V...)*

The noise in this 'powder' shed was colossal; it is like an enormous factory in itself, full of massive hoppers and cylinders giving on to an even greater cylinder, outside, where the powder is stored. Here is the life-blood, the heart of the present-day activities of the slate mines. Through the mist created by the floating powder I could just see Delabole village and the church. This was modern Delabole at work.

What I had really come to see, however, was the splitting of the slate, the work for which the quarry had been famous for centuries. Before we went into the wide, long shed we stood on the edge of the spoil heap and looked back at a Cornwall unchanged for hundreds of years. Brown Willy, Roughtor and Garrow Tor were across the valley in which tiny cows and sheep were grazing below. Men had begun to cut the hay in the handkerchief fields bordered with the last of the hawthorn blossom which has been particularly fine this year filling every lane with its perfume.

Two hundred and fifty feet below and about two miles away were the back windows of my home and St Teath church. A cuckoo was calling in Helland Wood, and the tops of the trees looked like a lawn laid beside the little Allen stream. When we turned to go into the shed the cuckoo was flying over the valley. It was June and it had already, I could hear, changed its tune. I followed it as far as the trees about the village of Trewalder and then it was gone. It is the first time I have ever been *above* this bird. It was the last time I should see so unspoilt a landscape. Tall electricity pylons are already being erected along it.

Beside the splitting shed were growing, in a corner of old slate walls (new walls are invariably of china clay concrete blocks), purple orchids, hawkweed, thistles and sloe bushes. Jackdaws were still swooping into the quarry behind us as I watched a man perform one of the oldest crafts in England. I had, in the past watched men splitting flints in the sheds behind the pub at Brandon in the Brecklands, in Suffolk, a craft as old as this.

But this was different. The flint-splitter holds the whole flint in his hand and hits it exactly in the right place with a small hammer. Here, at Delabole, the man sits on a stool in his own wide alcove in the long shed, with a leather protector up his left leg and thigh against which he leans the slate. With the ancient tools of chisel and bettle (a small wooden mallet) he taps the slate along one edge, turns it about and taps down the long edge in the same way, inserts the chisel in the small cracks thus made and, with the gentlest of pushes, the slate is separated into two halves. These may then be split again. Such skill is fascinating for the layman to watch, for the slate has to be hit in exactly the right place for it to split evenly.

At one time ninety men used to work in this shed. Now, alas, only six are left to carry on the craft and to deliver the split slate to the man working a guillotine which shapes the ends and edges of the slate by means of a huge knife whirling in a cage large and sharp enough to take the head off a 'Countess' or a 'Duchess' slate without breaking any other part of it. Beyond them, now, in the same shed, are huge saws which cut the blocks of slate, weighing over a ton or more, into manageable widths. They work slowly, with water constantly played upon them. In a further shed what they called the 'architectural' slate, for polished work, is cut and split. Some of this is very fine.

Once more in the yard, beyond the reach of the powder dust, is the platform, over three hundred feet long, where the finished slates for roofing, are laid before being carried away. Today there are very few occupying this vast level shelf where, in years gone by, endless alexandrines of slate reposed.

I came away a little sad at the depletion in the traditional craftmanship of the quarries, but aware that this quarry, and the men who still work here, is still very much part of the colossal strength of Cornwall. The hard knife-edges of the slate have much in common with the rock sea-coast and, although it has to be fetched from the bowels of the earth, it looks natural and beautiful and superbly reliable when it is finished and ready for use. I thought of how Eden Phillpotts had seen it and how, basically, it has not changed very much. It is one of the permanencies of Cornwall.

Here, too, growing things have found a foothold, and bird-borne, air-borne, water-borne seeds have germinated in the high crags and lonely workings. Saplings of ash, beech and willow make shift to grow, and the rust of deserted tramways or obsolete machinery is hidden under ferns and grasses and wild blossoms. To the east, where falling waters sheet a great red rock-surface, wakens the monkey-flower to fling a flash of gold amid the blues and greys. In summer the sea mists find it, fill it, conceal the whole wonder of it, and muffle the din of the workers at the bottom. Evening fills the quarry with wine-purple that mounts to the brim as night falls upon it; dawn chases the sides with silver and sunrise often floods it with red-gold.[1]

1 *Old Delabole*, Eden Phillpotts. Heinemann 1915

13. Some Clergy

Warleggan is a lost parish on the edge of Bodmin Moor. Above it is the deep pool of water at Maidenwell which is part of the Royal Navy's training and holiday home. Here the moor is silent but for the birds and the occasional voices of cattle. Warleggan itself is set between Cardinham, with its steep wooded valleys and its castle, an earthwork fortress, and St Neot on its own river.

Warleggan, too, has its stream called either the Warleggan or the Bedalder, coming down off the moor from its two head-streams which flow round the oasis of Temple. But when the Bedalder leaves the moor it passes through the deep glen below Warleggan church and joins its tributary the Dewy coming down from Castle Dewy. The Bedalder has run past tumuli on Carburrow Tor, through the woods of Higher Cabilla, and goes on to join the river Fowey below Haltroad Downs.

Panter's Bridge, here in the Warleggan glen dates from the fifteenth century, its two pointed arches having double rings of thin slate and a roadway of eight and a half feet across. This bridge is one of the prettiest in Cornwall. The river passes Trengoffe, which was a manor house set in an avenue of limes, and comes to the Fowey at a place called Bellasize where there was once a popular shrine to St James with a holy well nearby.

In short, Warleggan is a remote parish set in woodland, more populated a hundred years ago and earlier when Treveddo, upstream, was a manor as well as a tin-streaming location. It is a bird sanctuary amidst a farming community. I have sat on the bridge, below the rectory, and watched a spotted wood-pecker driving his powerful beak into a tree trunk, either to begin his nest or in search of grubs; the lanes are full of magpies, and chaffinches sing all day from the thickets. Night-walking here beside the river is owl-haunted and the fox runs freely until hunted later in the year. Night-jars whirr away the midnight hours.

It is hardly surprising to find that, in the years 1931-1953, the incumbent of the parish was an extraordinary man. He was the Rev Frederick William Densham. Certainly an eccentric, he was unfortunate enough to annoy his parishioners to such an extent that they had nothing to do with him or he with them. In fact, except that Warleggan was his home and presumably he loved it, it seems pointless that he remained here so long, fostering his oddities and meeting no one.

It would have been understandable if, for example, he had been a botanist who spent most of his time on the moors or in the woods looking for specimens of rare plants; understandable if he had been a scholar devoting all his time to Bible exegesis. He was neither. It hardly appears that he ever read books, shut away in his rectory, his garden surrounded by wire netting six feet high and guarded by fierce Alsatian dogs which he half starved. What weird rites did he practise behind the safety of their bared fangs? He should, of course, never have been a parish priest. His life is essentially that of an enclosed monk, afraid of the world; or of a man so overwhelmed by the fact that he was incapable of dealing with ordinary life, that he needed to shut himself into a paradise of his own making. For the rectory garden and glebe is big enough to have formed a small 'world' of its own, over which he exercised complete jurisdiction. Nothing happened here unless he made it happen, even his own servant could not enter the house without first asking permission.

Mr Densham must, in fact, have led a very curious existence, for he was unmarried. Undoubtedly his hermit life behind the walls of his 'fortress' would have given rise to every kind of rumour as to what went on inside. Yet nothing has ever been proved against him except that he did not appear to like his fellow man. In the past I have known odd clergymen, so bound into their own particular world of madness that they declared they actually saw the Virgin Mary in the garden. And one went so far as to mistake a dove in his bedroom for the Holy Ghost. But nothing so mad as this was ever stated to have happened to Mr Densham. He had no visions. At least none he was prepared to surprise the village people with.

In 1938, the then Bishop of Truro, visited the parish because of complaints reaching him from the parishioners. At this investigation nothing was proved against the rector, though the complaints ranged from closing the Sunday School to threatening to sell the organ put in as a War Memorial for the first World War. The Bishop — incidentally Mr Densham had no use for such ecclesiastical authority — found nothing on which he could order the rector's removal. Mr Densham, however, attended the hearing and came away exonerated to shut himself up, once more, in his lonely rooms, or to devise a new 'motto' to paint over the doors of the rectory bedrooms. It was almost as if the Bishop had given authority for his odd way of life. Pilate had washed his hands.

He was one of the last of that period of grossly eccentric churchmen who, conscious of their own small power in a parish, used it merely because it was power. No one can tell if he was a godly man because no one ever saw him at his prayers. Even at service, in the church nearby, there was no congregation and he would often write this fact in the Service Book. There is, in fact, no record that he ever left Warleggan until the day of his death when his body was carried to his funeral, not at Warleggan, but at Liskeard on 29th January, 1953. He was cremated and his ashes scattered in the public garden of remembrance at Plymouth. It was far from being what he wanted, since he left instructions that he be buried in the rectory garden, in the ground which he must have consecrated himself in some queer rite of his own devising.

One sees him, in cassock and surplice, with a Cranmer-cap, which he always wore, on his head (and could therefore be legitimately suspected of being at least half Roman), bringing a bottle of holy water into the garden and sprinkling it on ground at the back of the house and muttering certain prayers over it. Perhaps the heavens opened and a great light burst upon him. Who knows? But such actions, in a remote parish like Warleggan, would have been frowned upon.

Without a doubt he was half a clergyman, half a witch. In the middle ages his dogs would have been taken for his familiars and what little power he had in the thirties, forties and early fifties (which was much less than he imagined) would have been much greater. He would certainly have been burnt at the stake and not in a civilized crematorium. He would have been feared, whereas, in his lifetime he was despised and ignored.

It is, of course, inevitable that people who have visited the rectory, before it became what it is now, a holiday house, say that they have seen Mr Densham's ghost haunting the garden he made in his rectory grounds, or in the glebe beyond, or in the long walk from the house, past the stables, to the church. Warleggan is permeated with his memory and like all such deep country parishes, that memory will last a long time and even be added to.

I have explored the parish, the church and the rectory. I wrote of Mr Densham in my book *Ghosts of the South West*[1] (which gives the full story) and I saw nothing. I have made a television film there about the rector but have never seen his ghost. That it is a place which *could* well be haunted it obvious. The possibility of a shade returning to a place where, in life, it had been so lonely, so closed-in on itself, is obvious, too. Yet, as I finished my essay on this strange man:

> For all his oddity and the pity one feels for him in his everlastingly dark world, one thing Mr Densham did unconsciously create here at Warleggan. Beyond the chimeras which possessed his waking mind, the garden, the overgrown orchard with its gnarled fruit trees and bramble thickets, became a bird sanctuary. However sad his voice may still be, or pathetic his figure, in its torn cassock and shovel hat, haunting the place on which he left such indelible marks, he has about him what hardly any other ghost has, a choir of birdsong from the rooks in early spring swinging in the wind in the tall beech trees, to the chaffinches singing in the camellias and the woodpeckers in the glebe sycamores.

If you walk past Polurrian Cove to Poldhu Cove where, at certain times and tides, the sea 'sings' in a deeply haunting manner, to the towans above Gunwalloe, you can cross the sands to the romantic church built so close to the sea that it is often covered in spray. This church, said to have been built as an oblation in the hope that its parishioners would be kept safe from the sea, has an arcade of

---

1 David & Charles. 1973

granite pillars which 'have a wonderful grey-green look as if they had been for years under water.'[1] Not far away is the sister church of Cury. Here, in 1919, very odd things occurred in connection with the then incumbent, Sandys Wason.

And yet if one looks back into Cornish history similiar 'invasions' have been made upon rector and rectories. At St Keyne, for instance, William Lamb was rector in 1554. He was careless enough to marry in Edward VI's reign. But, during Mary's reign and the return to Roman Catholicism, the Cornish came out against him. Several JPs, gathering a crowd of angry farmers and church people, invaded the rectory at midnight, seized both the rector and his wife from their bed and took them to Duloe. Here they put them in the stocks where they remained for twelve hours. Presumably William was allowed to return to St Keyne when his punishment was over.

Father Leighton Sandys Wason was not so lucky at Cury. In 1919, on Thursday, 2nd October, he was forcibly ejected from the vicarage by men who insulted him in every possible way.

Who was this curious priest and what had he done so to enrage the Cornish people who, it must not be forgotten, did exactly the same thing to D.H. Lawrence, at Zennor, on the north coast, in 1916? In Lawrence's case it was the fact that a man, married to a German, who appeared to be doing nothing in the middle of the Great War, chose to come and live at Zennor where, of all idiocy, he was supposed to be able to signal to passing German ships and submarines. He was thought, then, to be a German spy. Furthermore, he made no bones about his dislike of the Cornish. In Wason's case it was the fact that he 'used Popish practices' in his churches and was thought, by a section of his parishioners, to be the Devil himself.

Father Sandys Wason called himself, to the day of his death, the Perpetual Curate of Cury-with-Gunwalloe. When, on that day in early October 1919, he was forcibly turned out of Cury he took refuge at St Hilary, with Bernard Walke whose church was later to suffer the appalling vandalism of extreme protestantism. In Bernard Walke Wason had a like-minded friend, both were

1 *Cornwall*, A Shell Guide. John Betjeman. Faber

advocates of the Catholic revival. Indeed, at this time the then Bishop of Truro had held a public visitation at St Hilary and condemned many of Walke's Catholic practices.

But Wason had been deprived of his living, for the same reason, by a Court which he rightly held to have no spiritual authority. He considered himself to be the lawful parish priest and resisted all attempts to remove him. Bernard Walke, one of the best and holiest of men, writes:

> The living had been declared vacant, but the Bishop was unwilling to proceed further since an action for contempt of court would involve an indefinite term of imprisonment. But the farmers around Cury were of a different mind. If the Bishop would not proceed against him they would deal with him themselves. 'We'll have 'en out,' they said, 'like as we draw a badger.'

Walke was daily expecting an attack to be made on Cury vicarage where Wason had transformed the house 'into a castle' and was living with his 'garrison' of Geoffrey Biddulph, his cousin, Ralph Nelson, his gardener, Ralph's wife Emma and their little girl, Stella. The attack was not long delayed. Walke was giving a luncheon party at St Hilary, when one of his guests remarked 'There seems to be a car-load of people coming to visit you.' Bernard Walke describes the scene.

> Looking out I saw Farther Wason climbing out of the car. He came into the room dressed in his cassock and biretta, followed by his housekeeper Emma, who carried a roll of toilet paper which she waved in the air as she shouted excitedly. 'The brutes have thrown us out and we have nowhere to go but St Hilary'. Why out of all the wreckage she should have chosen to save a roll of toilet paper, I do not know. Father Wason, with a face ashen white, walked slowly towards the mantelpiece. When I said, 'Come and sit down, Wason, and tell us what has happened,' he answered, 'I have the Holy Oils and must go to the church and place them in the aumbry.'

When he returned he settled down to play a game of chess with one of the guests and refused to show any interest in anything else. All this Bernard Walke related in his book *Twenty Years at St Hilary*.

Very little is known of Wason's early life beyond the fact that he was born on December 31st, 1867, was at Westminster School from 1881 to 1884 and Christchurch, Oxford, in 1889. By the time he arrived at Oxford he had lost his father and mother and had begun to weave legends about himself. Compton Mackenzie, who knew him well when he was at Cury and just after, says in his preface to *Palafox*, Wason's one published novel, 'that he was reputed to have married a widow with six children. This must have seemed extravagant behaviour even to a freshman, but being Wason no doubt he carried off the ridiculous legend with as much dignity as, in later years, he carried off episcopal visitations and archdiaconal admonishments.' Compton Mackenzie goes on:

> My own friendship with him began when as a boy of thirteen I saw him driving past the gate of our cottage in Hampshire on his way to take up a temporary post at an ecclesiastical foundation in the neighbourhood. I had the good sense, I am glad to remember now, to recognise him instantly as what nowadays we should call 'the goods', and I lost no time in getting acquainted with him, and thence onwards for many many years his friendship has been a delight. My wife and I lived with him at the vicarage in Cornwall, from which he was — well really 'dethroned' is the only word I can use, and a delicious mad year it was, including as it did the writing of most of my first novel, *The Passionate Elopement*, to the accompaniment of endless absurdities in the nonesense world that Wason knew so well how to create about him.

All his life Wason gathered odd legends about him as, for example, the story of how, one wild All Soul's Day, he threw a wreath of 'immortelles' into the sea at Gunwalloe as a tribute to drowned sailors and then waded out, in his cope and with his dog, to recover it. Or the story of how, when passing the stalls in the gangway of a West End theatre, he genuflected. When told that he was not at Mass, he replied 'Everything is Mass to me.'

Or the even more delightful story, told by Bernard Walke, of the day when he and his wife, Annie Walke, were invited by Faith and Compton Mackenzie, to lunch to celebrate the publication of his novel *Carnival*. Martin Secker, the publisher, was there and while they were drinking champagne they suddenly decided that it was right to ask Father Wason to lunch as well. They at once sent off a telegram and the reply came back, 'Have gone to bed to think out the best way to get to you. Sandys Wason.'

Bernard Walke goes on. 'He arrived eventually in a cab from Gwinear Road, very tired and very cross that we had not waited dinner for him.'

'You ought to try and think, Monty,' he said, 'I told you I had gone to bed. It was hardly necessary to say that I might be late.'

'That's all very well, Wason,' Monty said, 'But what we want you to explain is why you went to bed if you intended coming here to dinner?'

'When I have had some wine — and you had better open another bottle of champagne,' he continued, 'I will explain to you how much easier it is to think out the kind of problem I was faced with when you are in bed.'

It was on such simple faith (going to bed to solve a problem; 'Everything is Mass to me') that Wason based his life, for he early lost any sense of wordly reality. He was wrapped up in the Catholic religion and despised the Anglo-Catholics as well as most bishops; he was an original writer who was hardly able to complete a sentence or paragraph without working it over, sometimes for six months or more; and a priest who, although in the forefront of the Catholic revival in Cornwall in the twenties, should never have come, as a parish priest, to Cornwall in the hope that he might be a success. In this he was very like Mr Densham of Warleggan. Neither he nor Bernard Walke were strong enough men to be leaders. Walke was, also, physically sick with tuberculosis. But such men should not be forgotten.

As Frank Baker writes in *The Cornish Review*

> It is odd to remember that when Father Wason said Mass in the Latin tongue in Cury Church, he came up against the same stubborn Cornish resistance to the innovation which, in Queen Elizabeth's reign, had refused to accept the Service of Holy Communion in the English language then, of course, a foreign tongue to the Cornish. 'Give us back the Latin we understand,' they cried, 'and the Mass our fathers loved. We will have none of your new-fangled stuff.' Yet, in 1919, the Cornish were crying angrily, 'Give us back Morning prayer in English, Hymns Ancient and Modern, and the simple Communion Service our fathers loved.'

Of course, between the men of Elizabeth's time and that of Wason, John Wesley had 'reconverted' the Cornish. Wesley, too, in his own time was disowned by the Establishment as a rebel.

Wason was obviously a gentle man who relied entirely on the God he served. When driven from Cury, as we have seen, he said 'I am on the road. I have no employment.' And, in one sense, he never did have any employment. Frank Baker goes on:

> But it is not alone of Wason as rebel priest of the Church of England that I

like to write. He was many other things and it would be quite impossible to imagine this strange, most loveable and timeless personality in any other capacity. Towards the end of his life, sitting by the fire in his room in the East India Dock Road, with a biretta sliding forwards over his white skull, his fingers fumbling in the pages of his breviary, his typewritten sheets of prose and poetry sliding round his chair and the floor and sometimes serving to light his cigarette — there, where the lorries thundered up to the docks and the walls were grimed with the smoke and dust of East London — Wason was still the priest, still Perpetual Curate of Cury-with-Gunwalloe.

When he left Cury he became a wanderer, never staying very long in any place. He 'settled' at one time in a council house in Newport, Monmouthshire; at another he ran a bookshop in London which failed because he never left his game of chess to attend to customers. In a sense he lived in a kind of fairyland which he put on paper in his novel *Palafox* which describes the adventures of a young man who owns 'a small, convex, metal disc' which has the power of reading other people's thoughts. A rather horrifying idea, like the dream of a child. But then Wason was a child, 'a child of God' he would have said, who read what he wrote to anyone, not caring if it were good or bad. 'One perfect line,' he would say, 'I only want to write one perfect line.'

There is a kind of perfection in such a life, child-like as it may seem to us, which relies entirely upon God to provide, which takes no notice of time, work, money. A kind of purity beyond every-day things which allowed him to spend years, for example, in perfecting his small collection of religious verse, or when another novel he was writing was, by mistake, put into the rubbish bin at his home in Newport, to advertise for boy scouts to search the paper dump. Bernard Walke gives a last picture of him in London:

> He had bought an old-established church publishing firm, Cope and Fenwick, and rented premises in Old Burlington Street, where, in addition to liturgies he also sold 'pieties'. It was probably the name 'Cope and Fenwick' that first attracted him. 'Most distinguished' he said, 'and bound to bring customers.' He had very few customers, however, and those who did venture into the shop were never encouraged to buy anything. 'What do you want?' he would say, looking up from his breviary, 'Nothing here. All rubbish.' And return to his office.

For all his oddity Wason has not lacked a degree of posthumous fame. John Betjeman calls him 'the greatest living master of nonsense-verse.'

In the prevailing climate of religious opinion in Cornwall at this time, it was inevitable that the attack on Father Wason would be repeated on Bernard Walke at St Hilary. The parish is still remote and lonely; it must have been more so at that time except for the fact of the success of the St Hilary Christmas play, broadcast for many years, which assured that the church and its vicar were universally known.

Walke tells us how, like Lawrence, during the War, the local people who didn't know him really well, suspected him of being a German spy. He was being driven out in a barouche-landau, visiting when the man on the box turned to him, shook his whip at him and shouted, 'You call yourself a parson, but you're nothing but a German spy. Half your pay do come from the Pope and the other half from the Kaiser. You ought to hang from one of your tallest trees. And that's what you will do one night.'

So the attack on St Hilary could not have been unexpected. Unlike Wason, however, Bernard Walke was able to return to his vicarage and church after it was over. He gives a vivid picture of what happened that 10th August, 1932. The headlines in a London paper read:

> CROWBAR RAID ON A CHURCH
> THE KENSITITES AT ST HILARY
> ORNAMENTS SMASHED AND CARRIED OFF
> VICAR A PRISONER

> The beautiful reredos at the back of the Altar, designed by Ernest Proctor ARA, was destroyed, and the canopy torn down. Two tabernacles were removed, the Venetian bracket supporting the image of St Joseph was dug out of the wall and the images of St Anne and Our Lady removed. The fifteenth century font was smashed and the plinth at the foot of the memorial to Canon Rogers, a former vicar of Penzance, was broken.

'I have not yet escaped' Bernard Walke writes:

> from the scenes I witnessed that day and possibly never shall; whenever I enter an old country church and see the signs of destruction wrought there in the sixteenth century, I can hear the sound of hammering and the crash of falling images. The men working this havoc have in my imagination the same faces as those who invaded St Hilary that morning in August. The old church quite peaceful when I entered, is filled with phantoms I have conjured up. I see them tearing down the figure of Christ upon the Rood and casting out the Mother from the House of her Son. Often, in leaving, my eyes will rest on the broken face of a once-smiling cherub, a witness to all that happened there, and I am glad to escape.

He was able to rescue the Tabernacle containing the Holy Sacrament, for it was obvious to the invaders that he and others were prepared to defend it at all costs. When he came out of the church, carrying the Tabernacle, he found, 'a number of people who live close by. As I came from the little doorway of the Lady Chapel carrying the Holy Sacrament, I found them all on their knees lining the pathway through the churchyard, with lighted candles in their hands. I had passed from the noise of tumult, of passion, to a quiet world of faith.'

Later the same day, when the destroyers had gone, the Holy Sacrament was borne back to the church:

> All along the roadway to church were rows of people with bowed heads; as the procession passed slowly by they sang the hymn of St Thomas:
>
> Bow we then in adoration
> This great Sacrament revere
>
> words in which the summit of man's faith is reached. Never had I so realised the God-given quality of faith as on that night when, together with this company of people, I entered the dismantled church.

The following week people from the village came to restore the ravaged church; other images were substituted for those taken away and the church was filled with flowers. 'Everything was as it had been; but the cycle of peace which we had enjoyed for the past ten years had come to an end.'

It was, indeed, the end. St Hilary was now a tourist attraction, it was no longer hidden from the world in its circle of trees:

> Its name appeared in newspaper head-lines; a sign-post was set up on the highroad pointing a finger to the Church-town; crowds came to visit the church and at times invaded our garden. The place had lost its old air of peace.

Though St Hilary is once again a peaceful place hidden behind the romantic coves of Prussia and Bessy's Cove, renowned for smuggling, it has lost a 'glory' which it had when Bernard Walke was alive, when the church was hung with paintings by members of the St Ives group, such as Harold Knight, Dod Proctor and Annie Walke herself. One day was alone sufficient to finish that glory, the day when two protestant bigots from St Minver, a Miss King and a Mr Poynter Adams, hired their thugs to break in and smash up the church. It has remained a barren building ever since.

14. Baron Munchausen and the Great Dolcoath Mine

It is hardly to be expected that the book which delighted us when we were children, *The Travels of Baron Munchausen*[1], since it deals with the often ludicrous and highly unlikely adventures of a German Baron, would have any connection with Cornwall, least of all with the great Cornish copper and tin mine, Dolcoath.

Camborne, and the area round Carn Brea was, in 1782, flourishing. In all directions there were heaps of stones and sand, ranges of buildings, tall chimneys (still there, though ruined) and gigantic machinery. This was the chief mining area of Cornwall, and Dolcoath was the deepest and was to become the richest mine in the world. Borlaze, writing, in 1746, spoke of Dolcoath as 'a very considerable mine' and Price, thirty five years later, said it was nearly one hundred fathoms deep. At this time copper alone was being mined. When, in 1787, Dolcoath was stopped because of the huge output of the Parys copper mine in Anglesea which reduced the price, Dolcoath had reached the depth of one hundred and thirty two fathoms and had yielded a million and a quarter's worth of copper.

Dolcoath lay idle until 1800 when it was re-opened for the mining of copper and continued until 1832 when the copper seams were exhausted. And, indeed, the mine would have been abandoned entirely if Captain Charles Thomas, who as a boy of twelve had been working at Dolcoath for some years, had not had the inspiration of following down the copper deposits. He argued

---

1 There is no record of a 1st edition. The 2nd, in the British Museum, was published anonymously. *Baron Munchausen's Narrative of his Marvellous travels and Campaigns in Russia, humbly dedicated and recommended to Country Gentlemen*, Oxford. M. Smith 1786

that rich tin ground would be found below. For some years he could persuade no one to back his theories of deep-mining. But when, in 1844, the then manager, William Petherick, died, Thomas was appointed in his place.

He, at once, had the twenty five fathoms of water, which had been at the bottom of the mine since 1836, pumped out. He persuaded Lady Bassett, of Tehidy, who was the largest shareholder and her fellow 'Adventurers,' to spend over three thousand pounds on sinking deeper and, in 1853, the first dividends were paid from the massively rich lodes he found below the copper. In 1867 Thomas's health failed, owing to serious disease contracted when he was underground agent. He died a year later, 'respected by thousands of mining men and beloved by the Methodists of Camborne, with whom he had laboured practically all his life.'

Dolcoath was not only, then, the chief tin mine in the county but it was thought to be inexhaustible. But in the 1890's the decline began. A series of falls in abandoned workings as well as serious fires started the rot. Although it was immensely valuable during the First World War, it was forced to close in the slump of the Twenties. It was then 3,300 feet deep, and had yielded over ten million pounds value of ore.

The story of the author Rudolph Erick Raspe, who was a scholar, an opportunist, a minor rogue and his own worst enemy who, escaping from a prison at Klausthal in the Harz Mountains, first came to London and, then in 1782, to the Dolcoath mine, to be Assay Master to the Cornish Metal Company, set up by Matthew Boulton, the Birmingham ironmaster, is almost as fantastic as one of the Baron's, which he invented.

The edition which I was given when a boy is considerably knocked about by use. It has Doré's illustrations which added to the grimness of the Baron's adventures when looked at by the light of my nursery fire. Here I would sit while my nurse read the 'Adventures' to me. I remember going to bed excited and often afraid. Truth to tell I was, then, so young, that I believed it all which is, perhaps, the right thing to have done at that age.

Naturally the Baron went to the moon two hundred years before such a journey became a fact. His first visit was while he was a

The Slate Quarries at Delabole

(*Delaviews Ltd*)

Mr Sandercock, a slate splitter at Delabole

(Delaviews)

prisoner of the Sultan of Turkey and was put to looking after the royal apiary. He goes on:

> One evening I missed a bee, and soon observed that two bears had fallen upon her to tear her to pieces for the honey she carried. I had nothing like an offensive weapon in my hands but the silver hatchet, which is the badge of the Sultan's gardeners and farmers. I threw it at the robbers, with an intention to frighten them away, and set the poor bee at liberty; but, by an unlucky turn of my arm, it flew upwards, and continued rising until it reached the moon.

To a small boy there was nothing at all unusual in this. Or, in how the Baron himself went after it and reached the moon. In fact the way to do so was obvious to anyone brought up on Jack and the Beanstalk.

> I recollected that Turkey beans grow very quick, (the Baron is never at a loss for a solution). I planted one immediately; it grew and actually fastened itself to one of the moon's horns. I had no more to do but to climb up it into the moon, where I safely arrived, and had a troublesome piece of business before I could find my silver hatchet, in a place where everything has the brightness of silver. At last, however, I found it in a heap of chaff and chopped straw.

It was at this point in the story that my nurse always stopped. With all my faith in the Baron I knew, of course, that he would arrive safely back on earth. But how, that was the point? My nurse liked to tantalise me. 'I was now returning,' wrote the Baron, 'but, alas! the heat of the sun had dried up my bean, it was totally useless for my descent.'

The answer, I knew, was simplicity itself. The Baron fell to work and soon twisted up a rope of the chopped straw which he fastened to one of the moon's horns and slid down to the end of it. But it was nothing like long enough to reach the earth. One again the solution was obvious. All he had to do was to cut the length, down which he had slid from the moon, and fasten it to the end below him.

> This repeated splicing and tying of the rope did not improve its quality or bring me down to the Sultan's farms. I was four or five miles from the earth, at least, when it broke. I fell to the ground with such amazing violence that I found myself stunned, and in a hole about nine fathoms deep, made by the weight of my body falling from so great a height. I recovered (of course!) but knew not how to get out again. However, necessity is a good counsellor. I dug a sort of flight of stairs with my finger nails and easily accomplished it.

I could hardly wait until my nurse got to the Baron's second moon visit. It was some time, however, because the story comes nearly at the end of the book. It was no more delightful for that. After all he had not seen much on that first visit.

The Baron sets out with a friend in a ship to look for a nation of people such as Gulliver pretends to have found in Brobdingnag. After eighteen days travel the ship is driven upwards to the height of one thousand leagues by a hurricane. Eventually, with a fair wind, they come to harbour.

> I need hardly tell you that the glittering island on which we had landed was the moon. We saw there beings of gigantic stature riding on griffins, each of which had three heads. To give you an idea of the size of these birds, I must tell you that from the tip of one wing to the tip of the other is a distance six times as long as the longest of our walking sticks. The inhabitants of the moon use these birds, instead of horses, for riding and driving.

At the time of his arrival the King of the Moon was at war with the King of the Sun, but the Baron refused a commission in the army, preferring to explore. He found that everything was of extraordinary size, a house fly being as large as a sheep. Then again.

> The arms used by the army are sticks of horseradish, which they handle as we do javelins, and which kill all who are struck by them. When the season for horseradish is over, they use stalks of asparagus. Enormous mushrooms serve them for shields.

He found, too, a number of interesting things such as that the inhabitants, when they grow old do not die they melt away and disappear in smoke; they carry their heads under their right arm and leave them at home when they go on a journey, 'for they can ask its advice no matter how far off.' When they want information, they merely send their heads into the streets to find out. He found that the inhabitants of the moon grow on trees, like nuts.

> When these are ripe they are carefully gathered and preserved as long as is thought desirable. When it is wished to get at the kernel the nuts are thrown into a cauldron of boiling water. After some hours the shells peel off, and out comes a living creature.

As for their eyes they can take them out and put them in again as they wish:

> and when they hold them in their hands, they can see as well as if they had them in their heads. Should they chance to lose or break one they can hire or buy a new one. You see people selling eyes at the corners of the streets. They keep a very great variety, for fashion frequently changes — sometimes blue eyes are worn, sometimes black.

So enchanted was I, as a small boy, with these stories that it came as a great shock (like the shock of being told that Father Christmas never existed) when I was told that the Baron was known as the 'Greatest Liar on Earth.' Who, then, was the author of these fascinating lies? One thing was certain he must have read the 'Voyages of Sir John Mandeville' — and improved on them. It was not until many years later that I learned his name. It was Rudolph Erick Raspe. It was even longer before I knew that Raspe had once lived in Cornwall.

The book itself first appeared in London in 1785. It consisted of forty-nine small octavo pages. The *Critical Review* for December said of it, 'the marvellous has never been carried to a more whimsical and ludicrous extent.' Edition quickly followed edition with stories added by other hands and mainly of some political significance. But it was established, in 1824, that the author of the original (who got only a few shillings for his manuscript) was Rudolph Erick Raspe who was in England in 1780 and, undoubtedly, knew the real Baron Munchausen.

Furthermore we know from Horace Walpole that Raspe was a brilliant linguist. Writing to his friend Mason, in 1780, Walpole says 'Raspe writes English much above ill and speaks it as readily as French.' So well did Raspe know the languages that, in 1871, he translated Lessing's *Nathan the Wise* and Zachariae's *Tibby in Elysium*. When, in Germany, he was on the run from the police — the 'adventure' which brought him to London and later to Cornwall — he is described as 'long-faced man, with small eyes, crooked nose, red hair under a stumpy periwig and a jerky gait.' He usually wore a scarlet dress embroidered with gold, but sometimes dressed in black, blue or grey clothes.

Raspe was born in Hanover, in 1737, the son of an accountant in the department of mines and forests. His mother, Luisa Catherine von Einem, was of higher social standing than her husband. Raspe, when he left school studied at Gottingen and Leipsic Universities. While he was an undergraduate he became interested in the silver, lead and copper mines of the Harz mountains. On holiday he even went down them exploring. In 1760, after graduation, he was appointed as one of the clerks in the University of Hanover on the strength of his knowledge of natural history and antiquities which was, in fact, to lead to his downfall.

As well as being a philosopher and antiquary, he was a courtier. He wrote a bad poem on the birthday of Queen and Electress Charlotte called the 'Forsaken Peasant Girl,' which pleased her. He began to translate Leibniz's philosophical works and published an allegorical poem on the age of chivalry called 'Hermin and Gunhilde' which had some success. Infused with enthusiasm for the early Romantic movement, he translated (and believed in) the poems of Ossian. With this behind him he went on to translate *Percy's Reliques of Ancient Poetry* which earned him the appointment of Professor at the Collegeium Carolinum in Cassell, and keeper of the Landgrave of Heese's rich and curious collection of antique gems and medals which had never been properly catalogued. Yet it was this appointment which, because of his massive debts, led to his downfall. In the spring of 1774, the Landgrave let him out of his sight for the first time and ordered him to Italy to collect more articles of *vertu*.

Now his debts were beginning to come home to him. As soon as he returned from Italy he began illicitly selling valuable coins from the Landgrave's collection. This he did by asking for permission to go to Berlin. He was fully prepared for a final get-away. He took the coins with him — sent the key of the cabinets back to the authorities — and then disappeared. He proved to be quite useless as a thief and was caught when he had got no further than Klausthal in the Harz mountains.

It was, in a way, fitting that he should be caught at Klausthal because, as a boy, he met the miners of the district and learned how, in a cave beneath Hammersteinklipper, not far from Klausthal, Barbarossa still lived among his knights ready to be resurrected when the honour of Germany demanded it. A legend which must have enchanted the romantic boy as much as the possible resurrection of King Arthur in England enchants romantic boys today.

Apparently, though a bad runaway thief, he had no difficulty in escaping his prison. The episode is worthy of Munchausen. Dining with his gaoler, von Weltheim, Raspe tells him the whole story of his debts and embezzlement which he called his 'folly', and no doubt painting himself as a romantic hero, even going so far as to tell his host that, as soon as his debts were paid, he intended buying back the gems and returning them to the Landgrave. This story so affects von Weltheim that he rises from the table, goes to the french window and saying 'he must do his duty' leaves the room. Raspe has a clear escape. No sooner has von Weltheim left the room and is walking in the garden than Raspe follows, scales the garden wall and is off.

He went first to Holland, probably to Amsterdam, and then to England never to return to the Continent or the wife, Elizabeth Langens, whom he had married in Cassel in 1771. Elizabeth — nicknamed Babet, — was twenty, pretty and high-spirited. But, after Raspe's escape from Klausthal they never saw each other again.

Once in London, having sold the antique medals and coins he had stolen from the Landgrave, Raspe returned to authorship and the company of scholars. Horace Walpole (who probably knew about his arrest and escape, since he knew most of the gossip of the time) wrote to Mason again. 'There is a Dutch *scavant* (apparently Raspe was passing himself off as a Dutchman) come over who is author of several pieces so learned that I do not even know their titles (they were actually a book about German volcanoes and the mineralogical travels of Faber in Italy and Hungary); but he has made a discovery in my way which you may be sure I believe, for it proves what I expected and hinted at in my *Anecdotes of Painting*, that the use of oil colours was known long before Van Dyck.'

Raspe had discovered a manuscript of Theophilus, a German monk of the fourth century, who gave receipts for preparing colours and had thereby convicted Vasari of error. He certainly found a patron in Walpole who ended his letter to Mason, 'Raspe is poor and I shall try and get subscriptions to enable him to print his work which is sensible, clear and unpretending.' In fact Walpole used his good services to have the book, *An Essay on the Origin of Oil Painting*, published in 1781. Raspe was made a Fellow of the Royal Society in 1769 for his papers on the bones and teeth of elephants and other animals found in North America and 'various boreal regions of the world.' When I read this I was, at once, thrown back to my young days, as I have described, to Mr Worsfold and the day or two I spent with him on the mudflats at Swalecliff and his putting into my hands a mammoth's tooth. The difference was that Mr Worsford had not been a petty crook like Raspe. Indeed, within a few days of his last letter Walpole was again writing to Mason, 'Poor Raspe is arrested by his *tailor*. I have sent him a little money and he hopes to recover his liberty, but I question whether he will be able to struggle on here.'

Although Walpole does not mention it, by now the reputation he had gained in Europe was catching up with him. He was struck off the Rolls of the Royal Society, 'since on authentic information... he stands charged with divers frauds and breaches of trust... the President and Council being duly informed of the infamy of his character... do therefore recommend that the said Rudolphus Erick Raspe be forthwith Ejected.'

He could no longer stay in London. So, because of his mining knowledge, he made for Cornwall. It was far enough from the capital for his reputation to take a long time to catch up with him. A further reason was that he had made the acquaintance of Matthew Boulton who, with Watt, had begun to introduce new pumping engines into Cornish mines. Raspe, with his knowledge of minerals and how to prospect for them, would be invaluable in finding new sources of wealth.

Boulton now set up his organisation, with headquarters, at Cosgarne House, near Chacewater. And here Raspe was employed an Assay Master to the new firm, the Cornish Metal Company, whose chief shareholder was Sir Francis Basset of Tehidy. He was also the owner of Dolcoath mine and the wealthiest of all Cornish mine owners. Raspe was on good terms with Sir Francis; he had been down many of the principal mines and, in his own opinion, was about to become a person of some importance. Not least, for his better fortunes, he was well regarded by the miners themselves. He was now lodging in Redruth, with a man called Phillips, a Quaker and a firm believer in Boulton and his mine reforms.

It was while working here, at Dolcoath, that he wrote the original pamphlet, *Baron Munchausen's Narrative of his Marvellous Travels and Campaigns in Russia*. It was published, in London, in 1785.

But why Munchausen? When Raspe was living in Gottingen, a man then of some fame, he was often a visitor at the house of Hieronynimus Karl Friedrick von Munchausen, in Bodenwerder. Hieronynimus was born at Bodenwerder on May 11th, 1720, and served as a page in the service of Prince Anton Ulrich of Brunswick. He entered the Russian service in the Brunswick Regiment and served two hard campaigns against the Turks. In 1750 the Empress Elizabeth promoted him Captain, but, ten years later, he retired to Bodenwerder and devoted himself to hunting and the company of his paragon of a huntsman, Rosemeyer. He kept open house and was a fine and amusing raconteur.

> He told his stories with imperturbable *sang froid*, in a dry manner and with perfect naturalness. He spoke as a man of the world, without circumlocution; his adventures were numerous and perhaps singular, but only such as might have been expected to happen to a man of so much experience. A smile never traversed his face as he related the least credible of his tales which the less intimate of his acquaintance began in time to think he meant to be taken seriously. 'Munchausen Stories' became a by-word among a host of appreciative friends. Among these was Raspe who, years afterwards, when he was starving in London (sic), bethought himself of the incomparable Baron. He half remembered some of his sporting stories and supplemented these by gleanings from his own commonplace book. The result is a curious medley, which testifies clearly to learning and wit, and also to the turning over of musty old books of *facetiae* written in execrable Latin.[1]

But the sequel is not as amusing,

> The unscrupulous manner in which Raspe affixed Munchausen's own name to the completed *jeu d'esprit* is, ethically speaking, the least pardonable of his crimes; for the genial old Baron found himself the victim of an unmerciful caricature and without a rag of concealment. It is consequently not surprising to hear that he became soured and reticent before his death at Bodenwerder in 1797.[2]

Raspe stayed only three years with the Dolcoath mine, though when he left he was still Assayer to Boulton's Cornish Tin Company. All his life he had swung from one enthusiasm to another, though the cataloguing of medals and gems was an

---

[1] Thomas Seccombe. His Introduction to Lawrence & Bullen's edition of *Munchausen*. London 1895
[2] As above.

abiding pleasure. He was still respected as a scholar and a man who wanted to bring 'Art' to the millions. It is probable that he met the Scot, James Tassie, at Clowance, Sir John St Aubyn's house, in Cornwall. At all events, on his visit to London in 1784 he went to Tassie's workshop. When Boulton and Basset closed the Entral Assay office Raspe, out of work again came to London permanently (as he thought) and lodged at 19 Porter Street, Newport Market, not far from Tassie's shop.

Tassie and an amateur chemist Dr Quin, of Dublin, had discovered a process which would lead eventually to the present day mass production methods. It was a paste which could be used for direct modelling or taking impressions. Tassie asked Raspe to catalogue his collection of 'Pastes and Impressions from Ancient and Modern Gems'. Two quarto volumes, with Raspe's elaborate introduction, appeared at Edinburgh on April 16th, 1790.

It was his friendship with Tassie, however, which sent him prospecting, once again, to Scotland for two years 1787-89. He came at the invitation of Sir John Ulbstern who was anxious to exploit the supposed mineral wealth of his barren Highland properties. A curious (and quite untrue) story got about that large quantities of a bright material were brought down, from Skinnet Moor, to Thurso Castle, home of Sir John, as bait to lure him into putting up large sums of money for further exploration. It goes on to declare that the bait was taken and, the moment mining operations were to begin, Raspe disappeared with the money. It was as well that he did, the story goes on, because nothing was ever found in the barren moors. Raspe, they said, up to his old tricks, had imported the promising ore from Cornwall and planted it where it was found.[1]

When nothing was to be found in Scotland Raspe, once again, returned to London, to 3 Aire Street, Piccadilly, in order to see Tassie's Catalogue through the press. He made a long journey to visit Colonel Johnnes at his great house at Hafod, near

---

[1] This story is founded mainly on Sir John's daughter's Catherine's allegations. Though obviously absurd — where did Raspe get the money to import ore? — no reason is given why she should have hated him so much as to put the story about. See, the best book on Raspe *The Prospector*, John Carswell, Cresset Press, 1950. p 229

Aberystwyth. Everyone of note, at this time, visited Johnes to see the results of the improvements of land, his planting of over three million trees in the barren Welsh valleys and his mining activities. Raspe was back in London by January 1793 with 'a bad cough' which the fogs and mists of Wales had done nothing to cure.

In September of the same year he was off again. This time to Dublin and the derelict copper mines of Muchross, near Killarney. Here, in weak health, he succumbed to the epidemic of spotted fever and died. 'He lived there long enough — though it can only have been a few months at the most — to leave behind him a remembrance of his character and a tradition (which still endures) that he is buried in the hillside graveyard of Killeaghy Chapel, among the lakes of Killarney.'

Neither was he forgotten. He and his adventures became part of 'romance'. He was an excellent character on which to base fiction. Apart altogether from his *Munchausen* (which could have made him a fortune), Scott introduced him, in 1816, as the Adept in his novel *The Antiquary*, where he is called Hermann Dousterswivel. He plays the same trick which Catherine Sinclair had accused him of, that of hiding valuable gold and silver as a bait of more to follow, on Sir Arthur Wardour, as he is supposed to have done on Sir John Sinclair. Though Scott does not mention Raspe by name — even in one of his copious notes — he says of Dousterswivel:

> The knavery of the Adept in the following pages may appear forced and improbable; but the reader may rest assured that this part of the narrative is founded on a fact of actual occurrence.

Again, in 1896, Smith Elder published Sabine Baring-Gould's novel *John Herring*. It is one of his early books (he wrote 150) in which he introduces, as his villain, Sampson Trampleasure who plays similar tricks to Raspe on the non-conformists of Cornwall and other people, by 'working' the Ophir gold mine on Bodmin Moor, 'with gold dust' especially planted, thus getting them to invest in a non-existent mine. The book is full of the usual cliches of the period and is now a rarity. But in the middle of the usual 'library book' plot there are excellent pieces of descriptive writing on Cornwall, such as; 'There was still much light entangled in the upper atmosphere. The whole of the north was full of silvery twilight.' Or the description of Welltown, John Herring's family home near Boscastle:

> Welltown was a bleak spot. It stood against a hill, only a little way in from the head of the cliffs. The hill had been quarried for stone of which the house was built, and then the end of the house had been thrust into the hole thus scooped. The hill rose rapidly, and its drip fell over the eaves of the old quarry about the walls of the house. If the hill had been to seaward it would have afforded some shelter. But it was on the inland side, and the house was therefore exposed to the raging blasts, salt with Atlantic spray, that roared over the bare surface of the land. Not a tree could stand against it, not a shrub, except privet and the so-called teaplant. Larches shot up a few feet and lost their leaders, even the ash died at the head, and bore leaves only near the ground. A few beech trees were like broken-backed beggars bent double. Day and night the roar of the ocean that rolled in unbroken swell to Labrador and dashed itself against the ironbound coast in surprise and fury at being arrested; beneath its stormy blows the very mainland quivered.

How many Cornish cottages are exactly like this today! Nor can I resist quoting his seascape from the same novel because it is a scene endlessly repeated today:

> The storm of last night had subsided and the wind had shifted. A thaw had set in and the sun was streaming over the melting snow. The blue sea was strewn with foam streaks. Though the wind had abated, the sea was still churning. The passion of the night could not abate at once; the pulses of the Atlantic were throbbing. The sight was magnificent. The billows that rolled upon the headland at once shattered and sent up columns of foam white as the snow upon the ground.
>
> Earlier the morning sun had painted rainbows in the salt drift, but now the sun hung over the sea, and if he painted them still, did so unseen by those on land. The whole coast was fringed with a deep border of fluttering white lace. The air was salt and the lips of all who faced it became briny.
>
> Out at sea stood the Merchard, an islet of inaccessible black rock, capped with turf. On this no snow rested. The waves besieged the Merchard on all sides, like the rabble of Paris attacking the Bastille; they appeared to explode on touching the rock into volumes of white steam, that rushed up whirling, and swept the crown. The reflection of the sun in the sea was shivered into countless, ever-changing flakes of fire. Over the surface of the water gulls were fluttering in vast numbers — they seemed like sea-foam vivified.

How often I have stood watching just such a sea from the top of Tregardock, or Constantine Bay, or the Dodman? It is hardly too much to say that Raspe, in his spare time, must often have witnessed similar scenes from the headlands of St Agnes. And how often, in his weary wandering, did he look back to his wife, Babet, and his two children and sit, as Brandes, the actor saw him sitting, in 1775, at the time of his purloining of the Landgrave's 'gems':

> But sometimes, when he was in his most cheerful mood, he would fall, quite unexpectedly, into the deepest gloom, and at the sight of his wife's picture (which he carried with him) he often failed to keep back tears.[1]

---

1 Quoted from *The Prospector*, by John Carswell. Cresset Press, 1950

15. Nightwalkers

Cornwall is ideal night-walking country.

These are the dark woods at the centre of Cornwall, untouched for centuries except by those men who came to trim the hazel thickets. Even this is no longer done on a big scale, though a few do come to cut bean sticks. A stream runs the whole length of the wood. In summer they are hazed over with low mist. In winter the holly trees hang with ungathered berries for there are too many even for the birds.

No one ever walks here at night except me because there is, to most people, no reason to do so. Certainly holiday-makers in Cornwall would not venture into the darkness of these copses and thickets up the Forestry Commission road and into the far scrub where the badgers have their setts. I confess that I, too, have been frightened at times. I have waited here, under a full moon, and listened so often that I seem to know every tree and spindle bush, every turn in the small, shallow stream, every tussock and every group of bluebells. And yet, every time, something is different, something is not quite in the same place as I think I remembered it.

Tonight I moved off from the clay road and into the mass of bramble and bracken and decayed tree trunks (for no one ever noted the fall of a tree on this side of the path) where, in autumn, the blackberries are so large and perfect. I threw myself down on a patch of coarse grass and listened to the slight breeze in the tree tops. An owl hooted above me. It was midnight. The whole world of the wood and the fields beyond, over which I had come, were different in this yellow light, drawing the colour from grasses and bushes and even from the water.

In the old days this was poacher's land. They came across the same fields and netted them for rabbits which are practically non-existent today, though they are coming back a little. It is, also, on the outcrops of rock beyond the wood, adder country.

Tonight it was lonely and haunted. I felt that I had no business here in these silent hours, even though I was out at night so often. But, of course, night in the country is far from silent. Small animals were still rustling in the dead anemone beds and shook the tops of nettles as they passed. A fish rose in the stream, its plop like the sound of a drum; dry sticks crackled. I thought someone was approaching. But I have been caught like that before in a wood at night. It was no one. Probably a fox had made a mistake and trodden on the stick and was now either a hundred yards away down the well-worn tracks of the badgers, or frozen at the foot of a bramble bush.

That it was a fox I knew a moment later for I heard the sad cry of a rabbit as it died. So they were getting about again! I moved gently so that I could see the light in the cottage window which I passed at the entrance of the wood. It was still shining. Once a woodsman's cottage, when this was part of a large estate, it had been bought by up-country people, reconstructed and added to, and was now a handsome property having absolutely nothing to do with the countryside around it, empty half the year, a rich holiday cottage. And yet a property saved from falling into complete dereliction, for none of the local people would have done so much for it.

I wondered who was reading so late. This was stupid, of course for what I was really doing was remembering the cottage as it had been in the 'old' days, when Tom lived there. Tom Bunt, surrounded by his patch of cabbages and foxgloves and old kettles lying about and bedsteads in the hedge. All that had been cleaned up now. Some time had passed since the day when I had gone with others of his friends to 'see him home', as they say in Cornwall, in his plot six foot deep in the churchyard up the lane. If he had been alive now there would have been no light in the window, unless he or his wife were ill, for he had to be up early and consequently was in bed at least by ten o'clock. Unless, of course, he was after rabbit or down on the beach after salmon peel. I wondered if he would approve of my roaming the lanes and the woods so late at night. I think it would have amused him, for he would never have believed that I came only to watch the badgers. 'You'm be damned daft,' he would have said.

Now the moon was shining full on the hollow where the badgers lived. I put up my glasses and there she was coming out of the sett shaking herself violently, her blunt striped muzzle suddenly lifted, grinning, towards the moon as if she welcomed it. It was an exciting moment. Never mind how often I see it, the moment a badger emerges from its sett is still one of the most thrilling in all nature. Because they are so shy, so timid, so anxious to avoid any contact with human beings I always feel privileged to be watching them. And, as yet, she was not aware of me so close to her, lying full length in the bracken and grass.

Once the mother was fully out of the burrow (and it was usually the male which emerged first, perhaps he was already off foraging?) her cubs followed. They were nicely grown I saw since the first time I had seen them in late April, though they must have been born in February, perhaps, since this is Cornwall, even earlier. They began the usual play, rushing round the bushes after each other, uttering yelping squeals of delight, while mother sat admiringly by.

I was wrong about the old man being away hunting, however, for a few moments later he appeared. I knew him by the thickness of his neck and the fact that his head was broader than the sow's. He began, at once, to scratch on a nearby oak tree, sharpening his claws and cleaning them. I was relieved to see that no one had interfered with the family since I was here last for, of course, badgers had been here in these woods probably for hundreds of years and many of the local farmers must have known about them. At least none of them had gone in for that offensive 'sport' they called badger baiting.

I was not to see them for long tonight. Whatever it was that frightened them (they might have caught my scent, one has to be so careful about this) the boar, looking straight at me, suddenly turned with a grunt, which must have been heard through the wood and up the hill behind, and disappeared, followed swiftly by the cubs and the sow. It looked to me as if the boar was a bit of a coward. By all accounts he should have allowed his family to go ahead of him.

When they were gone everything was very quiet. I got up. The animals would not emerge again for some time. I noticed, too, that the light in the cottage had gone out. It was useless to remain and, in any case, I could come again the next night and the night after if I wanted to, the badgers would not go away and the cubs would probably go on living with their parents until the autumn.

I found another way home. Though the wood was deep and secret where the badgers lived, there were other parts of its just as closed-in and unvisited. I went by the path to the black hole of the quarry and the ruined cottage. It was so ruined, in fact, that no one would ever think it worth while buying and rebuilding. It was past recall. It was reputed to have been a smithy, but I was never able to find any evidence of this though, from the oldest maps, it was apparent that more cottages had been here, near the stream, at one time about fifty years ago.

The moonlight made the cliff of the quarry (from which, of course, this ruined cottage and any others about had been built) much steeper than it really was in the daytime. In fact, this is one of the odd things about night-walking, everything looks twice its real size. I suppose this is due to the soft shadows cast by the moon. The shape of the roots of holly and sycamore trees where odd, too, bulging outwards as if gasping for air and, in certain of the thickets, the leaves were very clearly defined. Most colour of the daylight had gone, of course, from the blackberry flowers. The redness of campion looked a pale yellow. At this time of night I began to wonder which was the 'real' world.

I disturbed a sleeping blackbird which fled in alarm, and all the time I was walking the owl went on hooting at regular intervals. The only pity was that no nightingale was singing for they do not get as far as Cornwall, finding enough food in Devon, one supposes.

Standing at the entrance of the small quarry, on a large lump of discarded stone grown over with ivy and moss, I thought that this was the exact setting for a ghost to appear. None ever had, not while I had been walking these woods, but I was aware of time standing still. This was as much due to the cloudless sky as anything, and I did not fear ghosts anyway. Not even if the old tramp who lived in these quarries during the last war and had disappeared in 1946, should appear. It was assumed that he was dead, but where he died no one knew. He had always seemed to me very like the badgers. He would disappear in the same manner or, at least, if disturbed, stand so still that, in his old clothes, he was indistinguishable from the trees and the deep undergrowth. For much of the time he lived on berries and mushrooms and pots of tea he brewed on a fire here in a right angle of the quarry, under an overhang of roots and stone. It was, if you liked that kind of life, not uncomfortable.

He was known locally as 'Chippy of the Woods' and I don't really know whether he died or not. He was there one night when I went through the woods because I dropped a small screw of tea (a little of my own ration) into his waiting hand. I never saw him again. Perhaps he had found a better home and gone off to it. Yet he was as much a creature of the woods as the badgers, and as great a poacher as any fox.

I think, on the whole, he lived well and knew so much that he did not need human companionship, he had built some kind of relationship with the animals which would be incomprehensible to most of us. Alas, such characters are fast dying out. Yet, after all, it was not an unreasonable way of life in a world gone mad with materialism. He had everything necessary. Even if my few neighbours and myself had not given him a little tea and sugar every now and then, he had rabbits and pheasant to poach, apples from a cottage garden a mile away and the stream to wash in and fill his kettle. Only once he asked me for anything. Salt. How odd it was, I thought that we should screw a little from our rations to give him and yet had not thought of salt.

Since he, too, mostly moved at night, he had no need of towns or a conveyance of any kind. I suppose the police knew about him, but they never troubled him. It would have been hopeless, anyway. A creature of the woods, with few words, he would have escaped from any police station and returned. What history did he have? Alas, he never told me. In fact, I'm not sure that he didn't despise me and the others, and all human beings who did not live like he did.

Tonight I missed him, though he had been gone from the quarry for over fifteen years. I peered into the blackness of his old home and shone my torch about, but there was nothing. Why should there be? It was so long ago that I could hardly remember what he looked like. The owl hooted again, a kind of laughter, I thought, as I came away over the fields, across the lane where the wild leeks were growing on top of the stone hedge and so, by a wicket gate, into my own garden.

I shone my torch on the vegetables which seemed almost as mysterious as the flowers in the beds nearer the house. My light picked out the onion beds. How many people ever walk in their gardens as late (or as early) as this, I wondered, looking down on the white globes, twice as large in the torchlight. They seemed to be moving, coming towards me. That was nonsense, of course. They were resting, white and immense, on the dark earth like the tops of minarets and, above them, hung rows of tomatoes tied to canes, their green plants (now quite colourless) hanging with unripe fruit. A light breeze was turning the long seed whips of last season's spinach. They gave, with the onions, an oriental aspect to the garden. Each side of the path cabbage lettuces rose from the earth, ready to eat, full and abundant. Slugs were going in their rows and caterpillars were devouring the tough outer leaves where rot had not set in. They lay like carpets of soft green on the soil, small pools in the torchlight spilled over from seed packets I had bought in early spring.

Some of the lettuce had, in fact, already gone to seed, had put out great tongues full of seed, ripe and mature and full to bursting. The earth would presently, like the woodlands, be clouded with seed for birds. Leeks were hanging their grey-green leaves like stilettos and there was a scent of sweet peas, wafted on the night air, from the long row at the top of the garden. Birds of paradise might have flitted in the blooms.

A white moth darted into the torchlight and then three larger moths. A thin, wraith-like, moth was going up and down a row of runner beans and the spikes of garlic were fingers reaching to the stars. An apple fell to the ground with an enormous crash in the stillness. Chrysanthemum flowers, much too early for my liking, but an American variety, were like the faces of forgotten children, and bats were squeaking in the eaves of the old farm shed on the next property. Darkness itself, as the moon sank, was painting the green darker and light was being withdrawn from moon daisies and the figwort which had sprung up between the rows of seedling wallflower.

I lay beside the delphiniums in the bed I had made beside the stone wall which I knew to be at least three hundred years old, and looked up at the moon. It was riding at a furious pace down the sky and over the farm buildings next door as if it were in a hurry to drown itself in the sea ten miles away. I could feel the world turning and knew that buildings, barns, cottages, whole towns were digging in their claws still to remain fixed upright to the earth.

The owl hooted again and, perhaps, I thought, my badgers are out of their sett again, going down their well-defined paths in search of food, in search of mice, earthworms, voles, frogs, snails or wasps. Perhaps if I lay long enough old brock would come into my garden and steal a few lettuce. At least there was enough for both of us. He could eat the slugs as well!

The long line of State forest stretches into Launceston, bordering the road from Camelford, split by fire breaks and the clusters of witches brooms and other beating-out instruments on long poles. These are placed at strategic points in every State forest to guard against fire, once having started, spreading. I have never seen anyone using them and here, of course, the road would prove an effective fire-break if the wind were northerly.

In these forests the quiet is final, intense, growing from the soil beneath the trees. It is a black quiet with the spikes of the firs going up into the moonlight. This land is planted in mathematical formations of endless sameness. These woodlands are the modern architecture of forestry and totally unlike the remains of older beech forests about the side roads from Washaway, near Bodmin, for example, or about the great house at Lanhydrock. Yet the Cornish forests are nothing compared with those of Wales or East Anglia which give to the landscape a feeling of Siberia.

I came through this fir forest, after midnight, and drove into Launceston. I love walking about towns at night when everyone is in bed. Tonight I wanted to see Launceston under moonlight because I was writing a story about a child who lived here and had a ghostly experience in which she met Cuthbert Mayne, the Catholic martyr, and George Fox, who suffered for their religious beliefs in the town gaol not far from the Castle.[1]

Now I was standing in front of the church of St Mary Magdalene, attached to the fourteenth century elvan tower with its Georgian clock-face, which was built in 1511-24, out of moorland, granite. I wondered if Sir Henry Trecarrel, who paid for the building after he lost his wife and only son for whom he was building the mansion of Trecarrel, in Lezant village nearby, had ever stood here, in the dark like I was, with the full moon blazing down, and contemplated his creation. In his sorrow Sir Henry gave all his money to this curiously-carved, granite church which looks like an Indian temple wreathed in intaglio. It is incongruous within the setting of this Cornish town.

I walked the deserted streets to gaze in at the Castle on its high mound. No one could help thinking of Cuthbert Mayne imprisoned here in this now rather dirty and neglected gaol beside the Castle gate and near Eagle House. Cuthbert was, later, hanged, drawn and quartered here in the town, his hacked body sent, in pieces, about Cornwall. One part of him was to be spitted on the bridge at Wadebridge, which I pass every day.

'All towns of this age,' I said to myself, 'are full of blood. You can't escape it.'

The church must have looked very fine and new on that day, 29th November, 1577, when Cuthbert Mayne died, the first martyr of the Jesuit 'underground' school at Douai. The General of the Order (I wondered if he had ever been in Launceston, had ever seen the place where his pupil suffered?), the man who persuaded Mayne, and so many others, that his duty was in England ministering to forbidden Catholics, was a formidable Jesuit, a Fellow of Balliol

---

1 Published, later, under the title of '*The Model*' in a collection *Spectre 1*, edited by Richard Davis, Abelard-Schuman. 1973

College, Robert Persons. It is impossible not to think of him as a kind of Head of M15 today, utterly ruthless and regardless of the hideous tortures and death he was sending his men to. Religion was so much the politics of Mary's and Elizabeth's day.

His idea was, of course, that the English Jesuits, with himself very much in command, were to recapture an erring nation for the Papacy. He was under the delusion of all strong-willed, bigoted men, that there is one path and one alone to Heaven, that there could be no genuine religion or religious feeling without persecution of some kind. England was divided, as he and his followers saw it, into Catholics and heretics, the latter doomed to Hell unless they repented and became Catholic. To him, and to them, there were no shades other than black or white and, although his coming to England himself showed the way to others, it is a singular fact that he was never taken, while those he sent after him were.

So Cuthbert Mayne and his friend, John Paine, arrived by the underground line from Douai, accompanied, though they did not suspect it, by Walsingham's spies. John went to Essex. Cuthbert came first to London, to Sir John Arundell's town house in Clerkenwell and, later, to his other house in the valley of Lanherne, in Cornwall, where he lay hidden. The authorities (who knew where he was) were giving him plenty of rope with the object, of course, of catching others in the net when it finally closed. As, indeed, happened.

For, in Lanherne, people began to talk. Cuthbert had to move to Golden, Francis Tregian's house near Truro. Here there was a priest's hole into which he could escape if there were any danger. This 'hole' had only one entrance, from a trap door in the side of the great kitchen fireplace. When the sheriff struck at last, Cuthbert was not in the hiding place but walking in the garden.

'What art thou?' asked the Sheriff.

'A man,' Cuthbert replied.

Unsatisfied, the Sheriff tore open Cuthbert's jacket. I think his slight figure, in the surroundings of a farm, must anyway have given the Sheriff a clue to what Cuthbert was. No doubt, too, his aesthetic features, the very air of holiness and suffering which was about him. The cheerfulness that he was serving God, must have given him away. Such refinement was not, then, a part of ordinary day-to-day life in Cornwall. At all events, Mayne was wearing a crucifix, the symbol of his mission, round his neck. It was enough to cause him to be tried and murdered at Launceston. Francis Tregian was imprisoned, too, and his lands taken from him. As for John Paine he was caught in Essex. He was hanged at Chelmsford.

I could almost sense, as I stood looking at the low hole of a window in the town gaol this night, the naivete of these Catholic saints. They imagined that it was enough to have faith in God to preserve them from the sophisticated system set to catch them. The truth was they welcomed martyrdom as the quickest and most honourable way to Heaven, and rarely took the most elementary precautions not to be discovered. The Catholic impulse, brain-washed into them at Douai, informed every action.

It was an adventure merely to return to England, to carry 'the Faith, to say Mass'. They undertook the discipline of the Jesuits in much the same way as a man became a paratrooper in the last war, or was sent to France to help the Underground Movement. Alas, the Jesuit military training — to say nothing of its political and 'spy' training — was inadequate. These fine men, many of them young, died for an idea they did not properly understand or, at least, if they understood the idea, were unable to relate it to reality. They lived in a kind of cowboy and Indian dream, out of which they never really grew and for which they finally suffered hideously.

It was this air of innocent suffering which I wanted to bring back into my story. I wanted both Cuthbert Mayne and George Fox, their religious differences overcome and resolved, to 'appear' to my heroine, the girl Serena, just here by the gaol, and late at night. It seemed, standing here, at one o'clock in the night, with no sound, a thing which might easily happen.

I knew Philip Madron when I was a boy. He had shown me all sorts of odd places on the coast because that was where he lived and worked. I don't think, actually, he was much older than myself, yet without him I should never have dared to dive through the narrow underwater passage into what he called, then, 'his secret bay'.

There are still any number of such lonely bays reached only in this way in Cornwall; few people know about them because they are so inaccessible.

I can remember that summer's day as if it were yesterday. We were standing beside a narrow pool between two upthrusts of rock at Cligga Head, south of Perranporth. To go down into the water and through into the far cove looked formidable and dangerous. Suppose we were caught and trapped in the under-water tunnel? Below, in the depths of the pool, not even the sun could penetrate. Only in the transparent water the anemones were a dull red, soft jellies on the seaweedy rocks. Bladder-wrack and tangleweed were gently waving their brown hair, filigrees at the end of long whips attached to the mauve rocks. They were moving to some current in the pool. Acorn barnacles were sharp knives to cut the flesh and butterfish and pipefish were swimming with watery eyes in their secret holes.

'Watch me and then follow' Philip said, 'Kick upward when you feel the sand with your fingers. Anyway, the sun will be reflected off the beach on the other side. You can't miss it.'

His body was a thin knife cleaving the water straight down. Then, when the ripples he made dissolved and cleared, he was nowhere to be seen. I was alone. It was a frightening moment. I had no right to his friendship if I now announced myself as a coward. I turned and looked over my shoulder, only a shag sat on the height of rock and did not look at me. The sea, though small and tumbling feebly on the sand, yet reared and blew and called its terror.

I drew in my breath and dived into the watery cavern and felt suddenly the smooth walls of the pool. The wet rocks were moving under my hands and my mouth bit salt. I opened my eyes towards the split in the rocks that would take me into the far cove and heard the blood racing in my temples. Drums were beating in my head. I was alive in the racing blood, my veins distended with the rapid beating. My hands explored the fright of this world of deep, still black water; my mind the fact that, now, I was committed and had no escape upward. The sides of the tunnel closed me in. Tiny fingers of seaweed, disturbed at my presence, caressed my naked limbs, little brown fish scuttled before my eyes. I thought I saw the claws of a lobster waving from its sea home and, then, I felt and saw the yellowness of sand beneath me. I was home.

I reached up my hands above my head and was released from the darkness of the connecting tunnel. I pushed with my feet and rose above the pool's surface on the other side of the headland. I opened my lungs and drew in air and looked at the formidable cove into which I had come.

That had been years ago. Whenever I am in that bay I go and look at the pool and know that, today, I could still dive into it and come into that other cove, though I have never seen anyone else do it. It is possible, of course, that swimmers of today with their snorkels, find it easy enough. Nevertheless, I would not try again. I want that cove — for me at least — left as I remember it, in the same way as I want the badgers left alone in their wood. For, it seemed to me, that day, that I had come into a pristine world.

Centuries ago these jagged rocks were torn from the last of the land, tumbled here, crushing out the sand and small fish, seaweed and anemone in their falling. They were, it seemed, placed here for all time, to nag at winter's seas, to be the nesting place of oystercatchers, terns and fulmars. Here stood the cormorant and shag in winter feather, their eyes piercing the familiar and fearful depths. One end of the cove, I saw, was closed by a massive rock like those at Bedruthan Steps. It was, this cove, a kind of Eden and we naked in it.

It was not for many years after that adventure that I knew that Philip Madron was also a night-walker, though I might have guessed it with all the holiday houses round the bays being empty all winter and so much good foodstuffs left in them. Indeed, it was not — except for a few holidays — until I came to live in Cornwall permanently, that I became friends with him again.

During the summer he made gifts for tourists, polished stones for which he had often to go miles to such places as Crackington Haven, up near Bude, to fetch the blue-grey stones he found so profitable to polish and sell. Really worthless, he sold them at five shillings a time. Even then they were not worth the money. Except for his work, which only meant putting the stones into a revolving cylinder with some emery powder and letting them revolve slowly for a fortnight or so. It gave him plenty of time for other things.

His workshop and small cottage was back of the headland in the wirey marram grass. Stones lay, all summer, on the shelves and tables where they glittered with light like polished bits of beach blown upon by sand, black, crimson and the famous blue-grey veined with white. The sun would hit their surfaces hard blows until the stones seemed to come alive with spears of coloured light. Perhaps this is what appealed to the holiday-makers.

His cottage was often cut off by the sea and always had soft sand in front of it, sand like a soft golden tongue between the cottage and the land which was laid out to a golf links, a green common, chartreuse-coloured, with·a silver stream, under minute stone bridges, running to the sea.

Philip knew it all, far better than I did. In some curious way, though he was much younger, he resembled the old tramp who lived in the quarry back in the woods where the badgers were. He seemed, except for a few oddments, to be self-supporting in much the same way. The oddments were generally beer and whisky which he walked to the pub in the village for. The night, as he became older, was his time. It fascinated him, I believe, in the same way as it did me. He walked for miles because he was compelled to be about when no one else was. I suppose I have the same compulsion.

He knew every inch of the land and the beaches, as he knew the houses in the village about the golf links and away, past the caves of Stinking Cove, to the bastion of Trevose Head. Oh, he knew it all right. Knew it by day. And in the dark by the feel of his hands. He had been into every winter-locked house in the district after tea and sugar and coffee which the owners left over from the summer. The spider's in the colony of empty houses on the other side of the bay knew him when he came at night, with a torch only, knowing the ways in and out, his slim, strong body working in, his expert fingers taking what was there.

No one ever complained, as far as I know. Perhaps from one holiday to another they forgot. What did a pound of sugar matter when you had four weeks of summer in front of you? Certainly not a pound of sugar you had left behind from a former holiday. If they ever questioned a loss they put it down to Philip and were glad to have a scapegoat they need never ask or accuse.

After all, Madron did odd jobs for them all summer. He was always available to them and his wife, Betty, got their houses ready for them against their arrival in late May or early June. And I believe they were afraid of Philip because of what he knew and they did not. And he never talked. He took their money and walked away. He was proper Cornish. They admired his strong figure, his black hair and mysterious eyes. Life in the bay would have been unthinkable without him.

Madron — this is what he really liked to be called, though sometimes he would allow Philip, — knew the holiday crowds, the money in their eyes never taking in the beauty, their fingers, used to tills, never knowing the subtlety of rocks, of seaweeds, of shags and cormorant; their bodies, centrally heated during the winter, afraid of the deep caverns. He had seen, too often, their drowned bodies, white with overheated houses, and the incomprehension of waves in their eyes. And he knew the compulsion of the sea to these up-country people and the ways of the tides. They listened to him where they might have ignored a Life Saver who cautioned them.

Yet he sold them his polished stones strung on gold thread, and the stone animals he made from bits picked up on the beaches from the south, for there was nothing but sand on the beaches of his home. He despised the rich owners of the holiday houses and walked, at sunset when the sun hit the horizon out to sea, from one bay to another like a king amongst them, his rubber boots splashing in and out of the rock pools, his long hands suddenly darting into rocks and pulling out an underwater crab or lobster, for he knew all the crevices of the bay's rocks by the feel of his fingers. His world was small, it is true, but no man knew it better.

He rarely spoke to anyone. The children often shouted out, seeing him pass at the edge of the sea, 'There's Madron, look. He's going over the sand, let's go and join him.'

And everything then seemed safe and proper to them. Even the sun would come blazing up next day and the sea be harmless because Madron was there, walking in the bay. For, to the children whom he loved, he was old with wisdom; to the grown-ups he was young, his stringy limbs like ropes of seaweed, unhurtable, his eyes uncovering their holiday lechery and their greed for the sun. He was part of the scene as were the gulls and the oyster-catchers which moved very little when he passed. Only the holiday-makers never saw the great black-backed gulls which came into the bays in winter, or heard the tall winter seas which changed the shape of the rocks a few millimetres and shifted a million tons of sand from one position to another. Madron did, of course.

I went with him one moonlight night in early November, over the sands to Fistral Bay the other side of Newquay. The white-crested waves rose like moving castles, higher and higher and then broke, levelled into spume, smoothed out and were sucked back again. The night was full of their moaning.

His eyes, for all I was accustomed to the beaches at night, were seeing far more than mine. I knew where we were going, to the great bay house which I will call Castle Keep, though that is not its name. It stands out on a spur of rock and, at high tide, is battered by waves which have no chance to smooth out. Now, as we approached, they grasped the naked rock in their fisted crests and broke into rising columns of water, pencils of splintered light, illumined by the moon which only half emerged from the darkness of overhead cloud. At moments, it would burst through these clouds and point up the towers and mock castellations of the house, like pennons.

In this light, half dark, half golden, the house did look a formidable place. A fitting setting, I thought, for a murder from a play by Webster or Ford. Not a place I should have cared to break into though I knew this was what Philip was going to do.

The night light was mauve, here and there, edged with gold; the skyscape was as angry as the seascape. Neither, it seemed, could be released from the other and both were enveloping the house in their menace. But nothing in the elements could make the least difference to Philip.

Now, in between us and the house, were the green swards of the sea-walk above the sheer cliffs of rock. In between were the clusters of more modern buildings, the holiday bungalows, the public lavatories, the chalets, the cafes now shut down after the holiday season. They looked woebegone and out of place. They had no interest for Philip. Only, tonight, Castle Keep.

The house had once been a fish cellar. The heart of the now immense house could still be seen where, in the days when fishing, mackerel and herring, was of some importance, barrels had been pressed full of dead fish and boats had stood on the little hard above the beach leading to the double doors, now obscured by the sea. Then someone, in the late twenties, had seen the possibilities of the enormously strong building of Cornish granite and set an architect to work.

The result, today, was like a French chateau above a terrace built out from the rock above the beach below. The house, like a fortress, was sharp and forbidding when the moon let us see it properly, absurdly too strong it seemed until you looked again at that sea hovering, endlessly moving, eternally biting and clawing.

There was a long cloister about a modern swimming pool high above the cliff, at the side of the house. Here I waited for him when he left me and disappeared. I knew there was no danger in going into the house through the ways Philip knew (and had known even when he was a boy) but I could not bring myself to follow him. I sat and waited as it got colder and the night darker and when, at last, he came back I did not ask him what he had been doing or what he had found. All I did know was that if he had not returned I should never have found my way back along the beaches to his home or mine.

Philip is gone now. He was drowned trying to save a child in the bay. I miss him as much as I miss the old tramp. But whereas I often go into the woods at night, I don't think I shall ever walk in that bay at night again. The sound of night birds calling is too sad a memory.

Epilogue

Cornwall is a hard land. The mind of a man is incised by the power of sharp rocks and monstrous seas. Winter and night are the times when this power is most manifest. In spite of the beauty of its spring flowers, its stone hedgerows and its summer-crowded beaches, Cornwall is still a land of terrifying loneliness. Such tracks as Bodmin Moor and Zennor, 'the hillside of rocks and magpies and foxes' where D.H. Lawrence lived for a while, cannot be approached with anything but a hardly disguised terror.

It is a land of legends, submerged only in summer under the feet of holiday makers who rarely dare to enter the interior. Legends with their memories of barbaric rituals, still potent, if one is not careful, to cripple the creative spirit, but which if properly approached can widen a man's horizons. A land of elements and elementals from which poets like Walter de la Mare fled, not feeling safe until he was over the Tamar going east. Finally, scientists confirm the fact that the granite of Cornwall has a high radio-activity.

To reach Cornwall at all you have passed through the soft lands of Devon, Dorset and Somerset. You might say you arrive minus three skins. For Cornwall is a magical country. I came, when a boy, to stay at a lonely farmhouse on the great headland of Pentire and was seduced by Tennyson and Arnold into the romance of the far south-west, into the Arthur legend and the mysteries of Glastonbury, the Vale of Avalon, Tintagel Castle, Loe and Dozmary Pools and the great earth mounds up and down the county (remains of Arthur's castles?), and the neolithic storehouse, now called King Arthur's Hall, on Bodmin Moor. Few, indeed, can be unaffected by the power of the many ancient stone circles to be found in such desolate places, such as Fernacre. Yet these are but the outward remains of something infinitely greater and more subtle.

On Trebarwith Strand, in north Cornwall, in and out of its huge, timeless, caverns, I became aware of the immensity of nature beyond the smallness of suburbia where I was born. The sea here, enclosed upon itself by painful rocks and tall cliffs, opened my mind to the implacability of nature. I grew mentally in the sea's indifference to human beings and the things used by human beings, bottles, old shoes, rusty knives, orange boxes, plastics which land up on every tide. I came to know the feel of a calf's tongue sucking milk, and to peer into the eyes of dead fishes or oiled-up sea birds for whom no pity is ever adequate. This was a largeness beyond myself which all human beings need to discover and which some never do discover.

Turner, the painter, Dickens and Wilkie Collins had been here before me, tramping the long cliff-path which surrounds Cornwall. Today the bays into which this cliff-path leads are 'ruined' for half the year by tourist development, caravan sites, ice-cream vans and bingo halls, the hundred and one adjuncts of the tourist trade by which Cornwall and a great deal of the south-west lives. The essential Cornwall is no longer here on the coast, at least not in summer.

In winter and spring it is different. The roads and lanes are comparatively traffic-free, the long beaches deserted but for black-backed gulls and oyster-catchers, the moors (never very populated even in summer) open themselves to the receptive spirit. As I have said in writing about Bodmin Moor:

> you will not like them, these shorn places unless your mind is attuned to the brilliance of loneliness and the hardness of nature. You will be broken down before them.

Yet this breaking-down is an essential circumstance of growth before the survival (if you do survive) of being built up again 'under their fierce healing powers of myth and beauty.'

INDEX
to Cornish place-names

Advent, 48
Allen River, 146, 147, 157, 161
Altarnun, 29, 30, 97, 99, 104

Badagry, 21
Bedruthan, 34, 199
Beeny Head, 126
Bellasize, 164
Bessy's Cove, 174
Bodellick, 59
Bodmin, 62, 86, 88, 93, 95, 100, 101, 102, 112, 113, 144, 194
Bodmin Moor, 10, 11, 32, 50, 52, 62, 76, 89, 92, 96, 98, 123, 126, 164, 204, 205
Bolventor, 91
Booby's Bay, 36, 107, 108
Boscastle, 26, 54, 97, 136, 148, 149, 150, 151, 185
Brentor, 129, 132
Brown Willy, 91, 94, 95, 96, 97, 125, 141
Browngelly Downs, 91
Bude, 26, 101, 109, 199
Bugle, 11, 88

Cambeak, 33
Camel, River, 10, 31, 43, 59, 60, 118, 133, 142
Camelford, 48, 51, 99, 102, 133, 142, 147, 194
Cape Cornwall, 34, 77
Caradon, 62, 90, 121, 124, 125
Cardingham Moor, 59, 99, 101, 164
Carlyon Bay, 97
Carnanton, 58
Carn Brea, 84, 175
Camborne, 41, 84, 129, 175, 176
Carn Eung, 78
Castle-an-Dinas, 88, 115
Cawsand Bay, 28
Chacewater, 86, 127, 182
Cheesewring, the, 90, 101, 121, 124, 125, 127, 129
Church Cove, 40
Chysauster, 96, 115, 148
Cober, River, 62
Colan, 9, 15, 17, 58, 107
Constantine Bay, 107, 112, 186

Coverack, 40
Crackington Haven, 33, 97, 98, 125, 126, 199
Crane Islands, 84
Crowdy Marsh, 100
Cury, 168, 170, 171

Davidstow, 32, 100
Daymer Bay, 43, 46, 58
De Lank river, 89, 97
Delabole, 133, 146, 153, 155, 156, 157, 158, 159, 161
Delineth, 157
Deweymeads, 92
Dewy, River, 164
Dolceath, 175, 176, 182
Dodman, The, 26, 186
Doney's Shop, 100
Downderry, 27, 29
Dozmary Pool, 61, 64, 76, 91, 92, 102, 204

Edmonton, 59
East Moor, 125

Fal, River, 40
Falmouth, 19, 22, 36, 99
Fernacre, 205
Fistral Bay, 201
Flushing, 19
Forrabury, 54
Fowey, River, 10, 61, 62, 91, 123, 152, 164
Fox Cove, 34, 75
Fraddon, 88

Garrow Tor, 96, 97, 102, 141
Gilhouse, 93
Glynn Valley, 111
Goonhilly Downs, 46, 57
Godolphin, 82
Godrevy, 42, 83, 84
Goss Moor, 9, 12, 88
Greenway Beach, 58
Gulval, 104, 115
Gunwalloe, 31, 40, 167, 168, 170
Gurnard's Head, 34, 78
Gweek, 40
Gwennap, 85, 86
Gwinear Road, 170

Harlyn Bay, 46, 47, 96, 151

Hayle, 31, 41, 78
Hayle, River, 83
Helford River, 39, 40, 41
Helston, 20, 41, 62, 63, 65
Hendraburnick down, 142
Higher Cabilla, 164
Higher Pengelly, 156
Higher Town, 52
Housel, 40

Inny, River, 29, 109

Kenwyn, 23, 24, 25
Kilkhampton, 59
Kilmar Tor, 32
Kynance Cove, 40, 41, 42

Lambrenny, 100
Lamorick, 17
Lamorna Cove, 31
Land's End, 26, 75, 77, 116
Laneast, 30, 106
Lanherne, 196
Lanhydrock, 101, 112, 194
Lanivet, 17, 88
Lanteglos-by-Camelford, 136, 141, 142, 148
Launceston, 46, 49, 95, 98, 99, 100, 102, 126, 133, 148, 153, 160, 194, 195, 197
Lew Trenchard, 46
Liskeard, 90, 95, 105, 121, 123, 152, 166
Lizard, the, 31, 34, 36, 39, 40, 41, 42, 81, 82, 116
Loe Pool, 62, 63, 64, 65, 92, 204
Looe, 75, 126
Lostwithiel, 111
Lower Halwyn, 59
Lowermoor, 100
Lundy Bay, 147
Lundy Island, 33
Luxulyan Valley, 11
Lydford, 129
Lynher, River, 26, 27, 93
Lyonesse, 54, 75, 76, 77, 83, 132, 149

Maidenwell, 59, 164
Marazion, 132
Menacuddle, 13, 14
Menridden, 93
Mevagissey, 75

Michaelstow, 116, 146
Mitchell, 88
Morwenstow, 54
Mother Ivey's Bay, 108
Mount Pleasant, 96
Mount's Bay, 36, 81, 83
Mousehole, 36, 81
Mullion, 35, 42, 73
Mylor, 19, 20

Nanpean, 11
Newhall, 155
Newland, 47
Newquay, 15, 16, 38, 46, 55, 75, 106, 202

Padstow, 26, 31, 34, 40, 43, 46, 47, 58, 59, 98, 107, 112, 118, 133, 160
Pawton, 43, 44
Pengelly, 156, 157
Penlee Point, 79
Penpont Water, 29, 30, 98
Penryn, River, 19
Pentire Head, 31, 38, 39, 44, 45, 46, 98, 204
Penzance, 76, 78, 79, 80, 81, 82, 87, 96, 104, 107, 115, 132, 173
Pepper Cove, 75
Perranarworthal, 20
Perranporth, 26, 86, 127, 198
Pityme, 43
Plymouth, 28, 51, 54, 100, 131, 133, 149
Poldhu, 35, 240, 72, 73, 167
Polurrian Cove, 167
Polzeath, 31, 44, 45, 46, 47, 58
Pordenack Point, 77
Portarlington, 99
Port Eliot, 27
Port Gaverne, 154
Port Isaac, 26, 138, 139, 140, 154
Port Quin, 45, 138, 139, 140, 147
Porth, 34
Porthtowan, 48, 127, 129
Portreath, 84, 127
Portwinkle, 29
Poundstock, 53
Prussia Cove, 174

Railway Terrace, 121
Rame Head, 28

208   *The Stone Peninsula*

Redruth, 84, 104, 127, 182
Roche, 11, 88, 132
Rock, 46, 47
Rocky Valley, 151
Roughtor, 51, 94, 95, 96, 99, 141
Roseland, 20

St. Agnes, 26, 74, 87, 101, 127, 128, 129
St. Austell, 9, 11, 12, 14, 48, 88, 97, 132
St. Blazey, 11
St. Breock Downs, 55, 58, 130
St. Breward, 95, 99
St. Cleer, 90, 127
St. Columb Minar, 105, 106
St. Dennis, 11, 88
St. Endellion, 43, 47
St. Enedoc, 45
St. German's, 27
St. Hilary, 168, 169, 173
St. Issey, 118
St. Ives, 26, 31, 34, 83, 174
St. Juliot, 41, 97, 136, 148, 150
St. Kea, 20
St. Keyne, 105, 168
St. Mawgan, 9, 18, 106
St. Merryn, 107
St. Michael's Mount, 26, 78, 115, 132
St. Minver, 43, 44, 47, 48, 116, 139, 142, 147, 174
St. Neots, 121, 152, 164
St. Stephen, 11
St. Teath, 142, 143, 145, 146, 156, 157, 161
Saltash, 29
Samphire Island
Sancreed, 78
Sandy Bay, 38
Scilly Islands, 75, 76, 79, 97, 115
Seaton, 29
Seaton, River, 27
Sennen Cove, 76
Siblyback, 61
Slaughter Bridge, 59
Smallacombe Downs, 91
South Condurrow, 129
South Petherwin, 10
Stinking Cove, 34, 200
Stithians, 20, 25
Stannon Downs, 100
Strangles, The, 32, 98, 102

Summercourt, 88

Tamar, River, 69, 71, 204
Tehidy, 84, 177, 182
Temple, 92, 93
Tintagel, 32, 96, 118, 154, 204
Trebarwith Strand, 31, 33, 148, 205
Treburgett, 146
Tregardock, 31, 147, 155, 186
Treglasta, 100
Treligga, 148, 155
Treloy, 105
Tremar, 121
Trenant, 123
Tresillian, 22
Tresillian, River, 20
Tresmeer, 99, 100, 133, 152
Treteny, 137
Trevallas Coombe, 128
Trevethy, 91, 124
Trevillian's Gate, 100
Trevone, 38
Trevorder, 144, 145
Trevorrick, 118
Trevose Head, 33, 34, 37, 47, 107, 108, 200
Trewalder, 157, 161
Trewint, 29
Treyarnon Bay, 36, 37
Troon, 129
Truro, 19, 20, 21, 22, 23, 25, 26, 27, 41, 86, 99, 196
Two Bridges, 29
Two Waters Foot, 62

Wadebridge, 31, 43, 55, 59, 102, 120, 129, 130, 133, 144, 147, 160
Warleygan, 54, 98, 164, 165, 166, 167, 171
Washaway, 194
West Indies, 21
West Moor, 29
White Moor, 10
Whitesand Bay, 28, 131
Wilsey Down Forest, 100
Withey Brook, 62, 93
Woolgarden, 100

Zelah, 87, 88
Zennor, 58, 75, 119, 168, 204